Inside Divorce

Edmond Addeo
and Robert Burger

Inside DIVORCE
Is it what you **really** want?

HQ
814
A4

CHILTON BOOK COMPANY Radnor, Pennsylvania

LIBRARY OF CONGRESS CATALOGING IN PUBLICATION DATA

Addeo, Edmond G   1936-
  Inside divorce.

  Includes index.
  1. Divorce. 2. Divorce—United States. 3. Support (Domestic
relations)—United States. I. Burger, Robert E., joint author. II. Title
HQ814.A4   301.42'84   75-6994
ISBN 0-8019-5919-5

FOREWORD
by Melvin Belli

There's a freshening breeze about the world that has blown a good many of our old and revered customs and cultural patterns to the seven seas, perhaps forevermore. Sometimes I wonder if it is "orderly growth," or an abrupt revolution in our thinking and way of life.

Whatever it is, it has pervaded every bit of our doing and living, nationally and internationally. Inflation, which really means our economy is out of gear, is an international problem, but it's galloped its merry way, everything getting "more expensive" even as we try to cope with it. Science has "grown" from the steam engine to the moon shot. Medicine has developed from a sepsis and anesthesia through wonder drugs. Instruments of destruction in war have grown so horribly that they have made war impossible—if any of us still want to live on this planet.

But the change that probably affects all of us the most is the new relationship between "him" and "her." I suppose the basic way of studying this is studying divorce, because that's concerned with what is our most fundamental and basic relationship: man and woman, marriage.

Today half of all the marriages in the United States will end in divorce. And divorce is more prevalent, worldwide, even in countries which heretofore would not countenance divorce, than ever before.

If we could solve the marriage/divorce problem, I suppose there'd be enough happiness and knowledge left over to resolve the big problems of economy, war and peace, politics, science and medicine. Marriage/divorce isn't a cultural segment to be isolated and treated alone any more than a doctor treats a feverish limb without considering the rest of the body.

A book could not attempt to answer the question "Should I get a divorce?" without touching the basic problems of what brought the questioner to his question. So really to consider the whole domestic relations issue one has to consider many of the cultural problems of modern society, even economic.

The fervor of Women's Lib is something new. What part does its philosophy play in disrupting the sanctity of marriage, in creating jealousy between the spouses? Pornography and obscenity, sexual liberality, the pill, the new sex education—how do they contribute to a less than secure marriage, and do they promote a divorce, or make partners more knowledgeable about their relationship, sexual and otherwise, before entering it?

There was an era never really appropriately named, but which we can recognize as the "hippie era," which probably derided the institution of marriage, more than any other spontaneous social movement. But a great deal of soul-searching came out of that barely-past era and a great deal of respect between the sexes developed, or is developing.

What's next after the "hippie era"? More of all of us, certainly minority groups, are going on to higher education and seeking jobs and professional attainments, but more women than ever before are in the forefront of these ranks. This movement is bound to have an effect on marriage in the first place and divorce in the second. It may very well be that more earnest and knowledgeable marriage partners will make for longer marriages and the divorce rate could drop.

The legislatures of most states have finally recognized the magnitude of the divorce problem and the trauma imposed not only upon the spouses, but more brutally, and undeservedly upon the children. So they have made divorce more of a social rather than a legal institution. They have cut the role of the lawyer, as well as his fees, and shortened the length of time actually required to get a divorce.

Whether the new liberality and the new laws will mean more divorces, I'm not so sure. I think the new intelligence, partially attained through the new liberality, might make for more permanent unions. But whatever, for those troubled many who think "divorce" is the only solution, there should be the realization that the relationship, the union and the separation of man and woman in divorce is as complex a problem as the compounding of any of our most modern pharmaceutical nostroms. The authors of this book are aware of this and treat divorce as a variegated thing.

Melvin Belli
San Francisco, 1975

ACKNOWLEDGMENTS

No survey of the scope and depth as the one conducted in preparation of this book can be completed without the help of dozens upon dozens of interested persons willing to give of their time and talents. Whether paid for their assistance or merely contributing their individual efforts gratis out of enthusiasm to see the material published, the persons directly or indirectly cooperating in our research not only are too numerous to list here, but also cannot be adequately thanked other than by the knowledge that their effects may have consoled or guided some distraught person contemplating or experiencing a divorce. However, these come immediately to mind: Ted Downey, consultant on divorce and post-divorce, Omaha, Nebraska; Don Chamberlain, of San Francisco's radio station KNEW and his "California Girls"; Barbara Chase, editor of *Single Parent* magazine, Washington, D.C.; the many chapter presidents of Parents Without Partners, Inc.; the M.O.M.M.A. organization in Los Angeles; Richard F. Doyle, president of Men's Rights Assn. of St. Paul, Minnesota; George Doppler, director of United States Divorce Reform, Inc.; Eugene and Marion Austin of the Missouri Council on Family Law; the person we have called "Penny, 34, Texas travel agent" et al.; Anthony Gil, president of Fathers United for Equal Rights, Inc.; innumerable lawyers, counselors and psychologists; all our respondents and contributors; and Jovita, who wrote hundreds of individual letters as well as licked the stamps and addressed the envelopes, who collated, filed and indexed our research results and typed, proofread and otherwise helped prepare the final manuscript.

CONTENTS

INTRODUCTION

Revolutionary changes have occurred in the divorce laws of most
states in the last few years, changes that have made divorce more
accessible as a solution to marital problems. Divorce now can be
cheaper, quicker and less painful than ever before. Partly for these
reasons, divorce is also more popular—yet at the same time the
*decision to divorce now demands more responsibility from all
married couples.*

This book was written to give married couples the benefit of
the most up-to-date information possible *before* they find themselves in the divorce court. In a very real sense, therefore, this is a
book about marriage rather than about divorce. We have used two
major sources to give married couples an inside look at the divorce decision. First, we have summarized the newspaper stories,
magazine articles, legislation, court opinions, and other serious
analyses pertaining to the marriage/divorce question which have
flooded the country in the last few years. Second, we have gone to
the divorced themselves to find out what they did, how they did
it, and whether they would do it again or do it differently. This
in-depth survey is the most comprehensive person-to-person
study ever undertaken on the causes and the aftermath of American divorce.

If the question of divorce has ever crossed your mind, you

can't afford to ignore the realities of divorce, American-style, in the 1970's. If you want to know what to expect, you can't afford to rely on the opinions of a few friends, on the advice of relatives, or even on the counsel of one or two "experts." In *Inside Divorce* we have tried to let the facts, and the divorced, speak for themselves. On a question as vital as your own marital happiness, you be the expert.

E.G.A.
R.E.B.
New Year's Day, 1975

PART ONE

What's the Score?

In our marriage and divorce habits, as in every other area of human behavior, we tend to do what we're expected to do. More than we'd like to admit, we follow the crowd. We're concerned with our "roles." We fulfill not only our own prophecies but those of economists, statisticians, sociologists, and advice-to-the-lovelorn columnists. And so it's important to examine the evidence about marriage and divorce rates, not as an academic exercise, but as a first line of defense against basing our behavior on faulty information.

What is the "guy next door" actually doing? Has he ever attended an orgy? How much wife-swapping is going on in the neighborhood? Are all my high school friends divorced or thinking about it? If I am still married after twenty years, am I some kind of a freak? Am I a victim of a "closed" marriage, while all around me my liberated friends are having an explosion of self-awareness and sexual variety? Should my college-age daughter "live together" with her boyfriend as a suitable alternative to an early marriage? Is the young generation proving that you can have all the sexual gratification you want without necessarily ruining your chances for a responsible marriage? In general, am I missing out?

The credo of the individualist or the idealist, of course, is that we need not do something just because everybody else is doing it. Because the divorce rate is increasing, we need not conclude that monogamy is a lost cause. For the individualist, ethics is not so much a matter of what people are doing as what they *should* be doing, not so much a description as a prescription. Yet in practice we are individualists perhaps 10% of the time, and part of the herd for the rest. In striving to avoid conformity, at the same time we can at least be aware of *what* we are conforming to. There is really no contradiction between the pragmatist and the idealist on this point: both must start from the facts.

The single most-quoted fact about marriage and divorce in modern America is that for every three marriages there is at least one divorce. Simple though it may seem, however, this statistic —the ratio of marriages to divorces—is widely misinterpreted and misused. Newspaper reports, magazine articles, and radio and television documentaries seem almost perverse in their distortion of what this statistic means. What *is* the divorce rate?

In "Divorce: Is It The New National Pastime?" (*Town & Country*, June 1973), Mary Bralove states that in 1900 "one in 13 marriages ended in divorce." Dr. Lucille Duberman, in *Marriage and Its Alternatives* (Praeger Publishers, 1974), says that in 1900 "one in every eight marriages ended in divorce." Who is right? Both. But the one-in-thirteen figure should be carefully rephrased. In 1900, there were 13 marriages entered into for every divorce granted. But of those marriages which were *terminated* in 1900, one out of 8 was terminated in a divorce. What the two figures show, taken together, is that marriage was on the upswing at the turn of the century due to an increasing population and a lowering of the marriage age.

To bring the same type of statistic up to date, in 1973 there were three new marriages for every divorce decree, but of every four terminations only one was due to divorce. Dr. Duberman expresses this latter fact in a more natural way: "Today, approximately one in four [marriages] ends in divorce." One might easily be misled by this formulation to think that the odds of a 1974 newlywed of eventually being divorced is one in four. But the quoted ratio applies only to events that occurred in the given year. Actually, if present trends continue, the chances of a current marriage ending in the death of one of the partners is likely to be not much better than 50-50.

Using current information, moreover, the same fact can be stated quite ominously or quite optimistically, depending on one's point of view. A defender of monogamy can rightly point out that three out of four marriages currently adhere to the religious ideal "till death do us part." The other side of the coin is Dr. Duberman's "one in four ends in divorce."

When it serves their purposes, popular writers can make the figures appear to jump. In a syndicated column entitled "Upsurge In Divorces" in early 1973, Sylvia Porter began with the dire warning, "More than 1,500,000 of you will be divorced and another 1,500,000 will take the first steps toward divorce in 1973." This tends to sound like 3,000,000 divorces in one year, or perhaps 1.5 million this year and an equal number next year. But the figure refers to divorced *people,* not divorces. So it is twice as high as the reader tends to expect. Also, if a rising trend were indeed indicated, why should the number of divorces to be *filed* remain the same? Porter compounds the exaggeration by adding, "This is almost four times the incidence of divorces of only ten years ago." First off, "incidence" is a rate and not a total; one would have to compare the number of marriages to the population in the same year to establish an accurate figure. If her implication is that in 1963 the number of divorces was less than 200,000 (4 x 200,000 = 800,000 divorces = 1,600,000 divorced people), she's wrong, badly. The fact is that there were 610,000 divorces in 1946, and the ratio of divorces to marriages remained relatively stable for the next two decades.

Even wilder is the claim of the March/April 1974 issue of *Marriage & Divorce* that "it is a fact of life today that at least two out of five of all American marriages will end in divorce." Is this a prediction of what the "termination" figure will be some years hence, or is it a simple confusion with the ratio of divorces to marriages in any given year, perhaps projecting for 1974? This figure is suspect enough, but now comes the further revelation that "two million will receive their final divorce decrees" in 1974, and "2.3 million will file for divorce." Sylvia Porter and *Marriage & Divorce* agree in using "people" instead of "divorces" each year, but their figures are apart by 500,000 for 1974. The magazine tends to exaggerate in the opposite direction when it comes to projecting the number of *marriages* in 1974. They guess 1.9 million, even though the figures for 1971 were 2.1 million and for 1972 and 1973 exceeded 2.3 million. Using their low figure for marriage and their high figure for divorce, the ratio of people divorced to people married in 1974 should have been 2.3 to 3.8, or about 3 to 5. Compare this with the 1 to 3 ratio of 1971 and 1 to 13 ratio of 1900, and it begins to look as if people will soon be leaving the institution of marriage as often as they enter it.

As if this hocus-pocus with statistics were not enough, there are a myriad of qualifications which can inflate or deflate the figures. We can refer only to "first-time brides"—in which case the 2.3 million figure for 1973 reduces to 1.8 million. Or we can restrict the figures to "urban areas." Thus a story originating from the Institute of Soviet-American Relations in Moscow in 1973 began, "Three out of four marriages in Russia's largest cities are ending in divorce." The headline in the newspapers did not mention the "largest cities" qualification. Later in the story, a figure from the U.S.S.R. 1970 census is quoted—and doubted: "26.8% of marriages ended in divorce," which, as we have pointed out above, really means that 26.8% of terminations in a given year were due to divorce. This figure, incidentally, was somewhat higher at the time than a comparable figure for the U.S. What should we make of Dr. Duberman's statement, then, that "next to Egypt, the United States has the highest divorce rate in the world . . . ?" The divorce rate in Sweden, as well, has long been higher than that of the U.S.

And when the divorced are analyzed by social status, race, and income, worse confusions enter. Sylvia Porter asks, "Who are the most divorce-prone?" Her answer: women between 27 and 32; non-whites; city-dwellers; the poor; the less-educated. And she insists in reinforcing these new myths: "The smaller your family income and the lower your educational level, the greater the likelihood that you will get divorced—contrary though this may be to popular belief." Popular belief happens to be right. At the lowest occupational and educational level, below semi-skilled, both divorce and desertion *rates* (not total numbers) are less than at all other levels except "professionals" and "proprietors." Indeed, one of the strongest arguments for divorce reform over the past few years has been the hardship which the poor and the poorly educated suffer by not having the money and the know-how to cope with the entanglements of divorce. ~~~~~

On the delicate question of white versus non-white, the raw figures again are superficial. It is true, as Sylvia Porter reports, that for every 1,000 non-white married couples there are 78 divorced people, compared to 45 divorced individuals for every 1,000 white married couples. Yet when these figures are broken down by social class, the ratios tell a different story. The non-white are more numerous in the *economic categories* which account for almost 80% of all divorces. Thus race may be entirely accidental to the condition of being "divorce-prone"—and indeed every study of the causes for divorce has pointed to economic factors first and only incidentally to racial factors.

We could go on and on. We've come to expect a news story or a magazine piece on divorce to begin with something like, "With two out of five marriages currently destined for divorce. . . ." We are conditioned to hear the worst about the American family. We have seen how statistics on race and intelligence have been argued and reargued for years without either side seeming to see the point of view of the other. What can be said, therefore, with any kind of assurance about the "way things are" in American marriage?

First of all, in the plethora of rates and percentages and statistics it's best to focus on the *total body of married people* rather than on the annual events in marriage and divorce. The Department of Sociology at the University of Southern California was apparently the first to use this measure. There are currently about 80 million married people (40 million couples) in the United States. Of that group, how many persons will decide to "split" in any given year? Currently, about 2.4 million, according to the most pessimistic estimates. This is 3% of all those who *could* divorce. It is not a sensational figure—quite a bit less than the unemployment rate. So our first statement of the condition of American marriage is that it is *superficially* 97% satisfactory in any given year.

Second, even though this 3% dissolution figure sounds comforting, isn't it more important to consider what it bodes as a trend? Of course. It is important to try to understand what is happening in Southern California, where dissolutions now outnumber marriages in any year. But trends are affected by many demographic events. In point of fact, the "dissolution rate" of 1946 has yet to be surpassed. There are more *divorces* now (the record was broken in 1972). And there are fewer new marriages now per population. But in 1946 there were more divorces as a percentage of the married population than ever before or since. The Second World War obviously caused this unhappy circumstance (on a smaller scale, 39 of the 420 married American prisoners of war returning from Vietnam in 1973 were divorced within six months of their return). Our second statement of the condition of American marriage is, therefore, that no *single* statistic can point to the success or failure of the institution.

To give a few curious examples: the engagement period of a prospective married couple is currently about 11 months. Long engagements mean better marriage preparation, right? Yet the ages of the typical bride and bridegroom continue to be lower each year, indicating less deliberate decisions. Even more contradictory, ten years ago, when the divorce rate was far less ominous to social observers, the engagement period was less than six months!

One could also minimize the divorce problem by referring to the statistic that the total number of people involved in a divorce in a given year is less than 1% of the population of the country. This fact is small comfort to the person facing the agony of divorce. A better figure to quote to him or her is that second marriages are less likely to end in divorce than first marriages.

An even more drastic example of unqualified statistics is the use of opinions from groups obviously having a stake in marriage or divorce as an institution. In early 1974, the National Organization for Women held a conference on marriage and divorce in New York City, and released their findings on the viability of marriage. Only two out of 175 conferees thought that the institution of marriage should be continued in its current state. The headline announcing this declaration asked, "Is Marriage the Real Enemy?"

This quandary leads inevitably to our third statement on the status of American marriage: Nothing can be said rationally about marriage without first distinguishing between the legality of the institution and the *function* of the institution. In 1900, when only one couple was daring to file for divorce while 13 others were taking the fateful step, were men and women that different, were sexual roles that much more satisfactory, were families that much more content than they are now? Or did the requirements of the law merely disguise a functional breakdown much as we have today? Have times and morals and aspirations changed so drastically in the last three-quarters of a century that an institution has become outmoded, or is it more realistic to assume that the institution has simply been recognized for what it is: a means to an end, not an end in itself?

We tend not to think of this distinction, between the function and the legality of marriage. Yet it has not only a psychological impact, but a practical one as well. The Internal Revenue Service denied a man a deduction for alimony, in 1973, on the grounds that he later had his marriage annulled. They argued that if there was no marriage, there could be no alimony. Fortunately for common sense, the Tax Court held that, regardless of whether there was a marriage under the law or not, there was a "certain limited vitality" to the union. He got his deduction, just as he and his "wife" received the functional benefits of marriage.

The most important corollary of this distinction is that the "divorce rate" (whatever we take that to be) may not be indicative at all of the success or failure of marriage as an institution. It may only indicate the *legal* success or failure. As we shall see in the course of this book, there can be a great disparity between legal failure and practical failure. To put it bluntly, the statistics are concerned only with what clerks are able to record.

Our fourth statement follows from this corollary. The divorce rate is greatest where all of the social indicators of our times say it *should* be greatest. No one should be surprised to learn that authors, social scientists, and architects "run the highest risk of instability in their marriage, among professionals," as a survey conducted by the University of California Medical School at San Francisco divulged in 1972. Another study might find nuclear physicists, animal trainers, and Latin teachers equally divorce-prone. The fact is that the divorce laws are most open to the *informed* and are likely to be used by the *volatile*. We do not learn much about marriage as an institution by studying these figures; we learn more about certain types of people by studying how they react in varying circumstances, including marriage. Marriage (or divorce) is only one result of social pressures on individuals.

The importance of this distinction is again not theoretical, but highly practical. A good number of young people currently disdain the formality of marriage on the grounds that it somehow "poisons" an otherwise compatible relationship. "Love and marriage don't mix," is the old way of putting it. Yet, either there is a commitment in marriage (and in any union) or there isn't. If a commitment exists, the legal formalities are of small concern to the couple. If there is less than a full commitment, it is obvious that a formal union can be obnoxious to one or both parties. In a later chapter we will examine more completely why this apparently simple distinction continues to be a stumbling block to many young couples. Their point of view, of course, is that the psychological impact of legalities cannot so easily be dismissed.

The final caveat we must make in saying what "the score" is comes back again to the matter of interpreting numbers. No one would give the unemployment figure as the number of people fired compared to the number of people entering the job market. (Yet this is similar to what it means to say "there is one divorce for every three marriages.") No one would give the unemployment figure as the number of people fired compared to the number of people retiring from the job market in a given year. (Yet this is similar to what it means to say "one out of four marriages currently ends in divorce.") We have already suggested that it makes more sense to say how many are getting divorced, or how many are unemployed, compared to how many are married, or how many are employed. As a final suggestion, we think the stability of marriage (or of a job) is best measured by the length of time it is engaged in.

Currently, the median age (or duration) of a marriage is about seven years. That means that about half of all marriages end before seven years, and half after seven years—the famous "seven year itch." Assuming that people are now freer than ever to end un-

happy marriages (and have been for three decades), the dur
of marriages takes on a realistic value. And it is a figure w
will become more honest as the option of divorce becomes l⸗⸗
legalistic and more a matter of practicality. Looking at this figure
over the past few years, we can say that the institution of marriage
has not lost its stability to any extent at all; the median age of
marriages has continued to hover around seven years.

In addition to the median age of marriages, the statistic which
tells us something about the durability of the institution is the
total married population compared with the total who have ever
been divorced. A recent lead article in a national women's
magazine began with this episode:

*When Aaron Beck introduced Phyllis, his wife for 23 years, at a
California party, a lot of his colleagues gulped and reached for
another martini . . . . "They couldn't believe she was my first
wife . . . . they were all on their second or third wives."*

In typical fashion, the article continues, "With the current
national divorce rate at the ratio of one divorce for every three
marriages, couples like the Becks, while not headed for extinc-
tion, are becoming a rare breed."

Exactly how rare a breed is a couple without a divorce in their
past? There are about 15 million Americans who have been
through a divorce, and this figure is increased by roughly two
million a year (some divorces obviously occur among previously
divorced persons). There are about 80 million married men and
women in all of the U.S., and this figure is growing somewhat
faster than the divorce figure. So the odds of a married person
having been previously divorced is less than one in five. To put it
another way, the chances of a couple having either partner divorced would be about two in five, and the odds of, let's say, four
couples at a party *each* having at least one divorced partner would
be 16 out of 625, or about one in 40. If it is any consolation to the
never-divorced couple, it is the previously divorced person who
is the rare breed.

So the statistics on marriage and divorce are less desperate
than the doomsday prophets would have us believe. We are not

grasping at straws, or trying to call a half-empty glass "half-full." (Sometimes there is merit even in this. *Better Homes & Gardens* recently headlined an advertisement, "Seventy-Five Percent of All Divorces End in Marriage.") We do know that all aspects of marriage and sex and divorce are more open to public debate than ever before. *The New York Post* (among other leading metropolitan newspapers) casually runs advertisements for abortion in which the main appeal is price: "$100 any weekday, weekends slightly higher." There *is* a sexual revolution. The mistake is assuming that, once given the freedom to do whatever they want, Americans will choose to take the easiest path, the shortest-term gratification, the quickest way out. The Kinsey Report and the Playboy philosophy and the divorce-mongers are facts of life in the third quarter of this century, the moral legacy of recent times. Yet, after we have taken stock of "what the score is," of all the numbers, we must still weigh the judgment of thoughtful observers of our age, such as W. H. Auden:

Like everything which is not the result of fleeting emotion but of time and will, any marriage, happy or unhappy, is infinitely more interesting and significant than any romance, however passionate.

Legacy II
The Failure to Grow Up

Truffaut's delicate story of a marriage in his film *Bed and Board* stands as a classic depiction of the cycle of young love, conflict, and eventual maturity. In the end, the couple has grown together in a kind of fatalistic realization of the weakness of each; yet it is a happy ending, as if each has come to grips with "the way life is." Most movie plots these days—and a majority of marriages, according to our survey—seem to end at the second stage of the cycle. When the first conflict occurs—which the survey shows is usually infidelity, alcohol or a financial difficulty, closely followed by "emotional immaturity" and failure to grow together—the entire relationship seems to collapse.

The question we examine in this chapter is whether there is a "reason" for divorce, i.e. for the failure of a marriage, other than *the failure of one or both partners to become a full human being.* In our survey, the overwhelming majority—indeed, 85% of the respondents—listed "immaturity when married" as the "reason" for their divorce. "Immaturity" is an umbrella word, encompassing quite a few emotional problems, yet the simple fact is that getting married too young (which we define as "an inexperienced age") is the single most dangerous event in the history of a marriage.

In asking the question, we imply that marriage is not some

accidental appendage on life, but rather the "normal" condition of adulthood, in the same sense that having a father and a mother is the "normal" condition of childhood. A significant number of respondents in the survey replied to Question #3 with some variation of the observation that "it is a couple's world," and that "society is geared to couples, especially married couples."

There is no real comparison to the close relationship between being an adult and being a married person. To say that your marriage failed is entirely different from saying that you failed chemistry, or failed to learn how to ski, or failed to negotiate the driveway in the family car. Marriage is more a state of mind than a tangible B+, or a lift ticket, or bent fender. A happy couple nowadays can be expected to answer the question "Are you married?" with "No, we never bothered to get a license," without shocking anyone. The "legality" of marriage has become abhorrent to confirmed bachelors, "swingles," and liberated women. Our conditioned reflex to marriage, spawned by so many horror stories of divorce and familial hatred over the years, has prepared us to think of legal cohabitation as a doomed existence, a relationship fated to fall apart. But we know that growing up cannot be separated from trying to find a mate.

Various studies which have been made on this apparently vital issue—why marriages fail—drift into two diverse patterns. Ignoring the self-serving bestsellers and commercially-stimulated "studies," we first come to the testimony of marriage and divorce counselors, divorce attorneys, and judges. In general, their firsthand experience points to the "single event" theory—an event either so traumatic in itself as to disrupt a relationship, or simply the straw that breaks the camel's back.

Thus a 35-year-old Chicagoan, father of two: "I thought my life had been ideal. . . . You know, things just went along (school, University of Michigan, a stint in the army, work, marriage to a 'nice' girl to take care of the house and kids). I mean, everything went the way I thought it was supposed to go, even the order of things (first a boy, then a girl). In the meantime, I was getting my 'action' everywhere else but at home. We even tried therapy. Why not? Marriage counselors were fashionable! There were fights, but I didn't think much about it. It all seemed part of the pattern, breaking up and making up, until the last scene. That particular evening, we had a big, extra-loud fight. I don't know even what it was all about, something real dumb, like who should take the kids to school in the morning. Then it happened. . . . I was yelling at the top of my voice, just frustrated to beat hell. I couldn't get through to her. She was so close but she just stared right past me as if I was nothing. I hit her, hard, right in the face. I grabbed my arms in front of me and tried to tear myself apart, but I couldn't take back that smack in the face. There was no way I could tell her I didn't mean it. I would have done anything to erase it from that evening. That was it. She screamed until I got out of the house. I haven't been back since, except to pick up my clothes."

Or take the equally typical case of a 24-year-old mother of two daughters, about a year apart in age, and the youngest still in diapers: "That night when Ken didn't show up for supper I dialed his office number. The switchboard was closed, but the superintendent said, yes, my husband was still upstairs working with Ivy, his secretary. That was the way I found out about the other woman in Ken's life—and the knowledge was a jolt, I assure you. I had introduced Ivy to Ken. Ivy was the receptionist-bookkeeper at a secretarial school I once attended. When Ken opened his office, I urged him to give Ivy a chance because she was unemployed. Ivy is a top-flight secretary, but she is not at all attractive . . . at least I thought. It was dawn before Ken came home. He confessed he had been sleeping with Ivy, but he swore he did not love her. We tried to put this affair in the past, but it was no good. Then my parents got involved. My strict father demanded a separation, and that's where we are now. . . . "

Or the "single event" can be dramatic enough to warrant a newspaper story, as this San Francisco *Chronicle* story describes:

Helen Coons, 43, is unusual in that she knows with a clarity that time will never blur the moment that her marriage with Edward, 46, first fissured and began breaking up. . . . On a February day ten years ago, Edward Coons had just returned from taking a load of trash to the dump with their boys, James and Jeffrey. He brought them in the house and said to give them lunch. Helen started fixing macaroni and cheese. . . . Somehow, little Jeff, then

18 months old, managed to open the screen door and toddle off unnoticed after his father. When Edward started to drive away, Jeff was knocked down and one of the front wheels rolled over his face. . . . Looking back, Helen now realizes that the worst wound in the accident was one which couldn't be seen. The shock and horror of what had happened changed her husband overnight. Edward became silent, brooding. . . . Sometimes, he wouldn't speak for weeks. Helen filed for divorce, after years of virtual separation, and Edward couldn't even answer Helen's argument that she was just making it legal.

A hit in the face, an office infidelity, an injury to a child—did these events shatter the marriage or were they merely the outward signal of a fundamental malaise?

In contrast, the other general pattern of reasons given for divorce is less specific, more broadly sociological. The Family Counseling Association in Birmingham, Alabama gives the general reasons it has encountered for marital breakups: lack of preparation for marriage, a search for personal identity, new roles for men and women, family problems, finances, sexual adjustment, and unrealistic attitudes toward marriage. The most prominent of these we will discuss in succeeding chapters. The critical question, outside of a single traumatic event is this: doesn't it appear that the basic reason for the failure of marriage is the failure to grow up?

Lorene Putsch, executive director of the Birmingham F.C.A. says, "We're astonished at how many young couples are coming in. During the first six months of 1972, the head of the household was in his 20's in 35% of the families we saw."

The Rev. John H. Wiley, Jr., a pastoral counselor in Birmingham, echoes this theme: "The biggest cause of divorce and marital problems is society's inability to prepare young people for marriage. We have not figured out a way to prepare them for this close relationship."

Dr. Mac C. S. Webb, counselor and psychology instructor at Northwest Nazarene College, cites lack of empathy and lack of communication, both aspects of immaturity, as being at the heart of the problem. "Emotional dishonesty is at fault in most marriage failures. Not telling your spouse how you really feel . . . that's emotional dishonesty.''

Putsch adds to this, "Half of the problems we see are the acting out of feelings people aren't able to express . . . and I don't mean words. Communication is a revealing of yourself, of letting the other person know more of yourself. . . .

The young couples you worry about are the ones who marry to escape a bad family situation, or those who marry because they don't feel like a complete person. These are 'lean-to' marriages. These are people who don't have enough security in themselves. They have some feeling that through marriage they can find a completeness in themselves that will give them their own identity."

Martha Weinman Lear, a frequent analyst of family problems in the mass media, agrees: "This is one of the main reasons we fall in love and marry—in hope that our loved one will magically endow us, as though by osmosis, with those qualities we cannot supply for ourselves. . . . It is parasitic, unrealistic, and dumb —really dumb—to expect your marital partner to make you happy (or smart or successful or important or socially acceptable—or whatever it is you want to be). That's your responsibility."

And statistically, there is indeed a relationship between youthful marriage and divorce. Paul C. Glick, in *American Families,* cites figures in the mid 1950's to show that women then marrying between 22 and 24 were three times less likely to be divorced than those marrying before the age of 18.

The common expression for this "immaturity trap" is "What happens when the honeymoon is over?" Judge William Cole, who hears 30 to 40 divorce cases a week in Jefferson County, Alabama, puts it typically: "Sometimes I think these young people think the courtship is going to go on forever. You find this more in the women, and when they get down to the grim realities it really shakes them up—the men too. It doesn't stay all hearts and flowers.''

The high failure rate for youthful marriages is so well documented—regardless of other circumstances—that it is categorically given as one of the major reasons for the current increase in the number of divorces overall. For it has also been well established that Americans are tending to marry at progressively more tender ages. Contrary to the popular mythology, the option of "living together" and the freedom from the threat of unwanted pregnancies and resultant "shotgun" marriages have not caused a decrease in the rate of young marriages. The median age of new marriages has continued to fall year by year. And there is no dispute that a good portion of the increase in the divorce rate comes from the under-21 newlyweds.

There is little that is startling in this. As most observers of marriage trends have pointed out, the younger couple must face at least three critical problems of adulthood *at one time:* establishing a career at the low end of the income scale, having children, and breaking away from parental influence. (This latter point should not be minimized. As Rev. John H. Wiley, Jr. puts it, "More problems are caused by families than we realize. Not in-laws, but natural parents. The couple needs to assert themselves as persons, to develop confidence that they can make the right decisions.")

The alleged villain—or, as we shall see, the scapegoat—in all of this usually turns out to be one or several of the following: (a) the "myth" of romantic love, (b) the destructiveness of sexual monopoly, (c) the impossible ideal of monogamy, (d) the failure of marriage as a useful institution.

The problem in analyzing or understanding the relationship between all of these "causes" for the high divorce rate is that they are on different logical levels, and can operate simultaneously and independently. It is no wonder that the mass media continues to be flooded with article after article on the "real reason" for marriage failure. Few stop to consider that the failure of a marriage is the failure of a person, a multifarious, complex, highly individual person.

A person may "fail," for example, because of:

1. a physical setback
2. a confluence of overwhelming problems
3. an unrealistic view of the world
4. lack of character or talent
5. or even, bad luck

Most of the commonly given reasons for marital failure fall into these basic categories. The more general reason that marriage

is simply too difficult for modern man to handle is just a summa-
tion of all five categories. The most convenient rationalization for
personal failure is that something is wrong with our institutions,
that is, with marriage in its present state.

As a practical matter, a person is in a better position to clear
up in his own mind how his marriage is doing when he realizes
the *different logical levels* of his problems. Financial difficulties
can drive one couple apart and bring another couple closer together. Thus the reason or reasons for failure in one case and
success in the other must basically lie elsewhere. It may truly be a
mistake (and one that is often made, according to marriage counselors) to assume that financial success in the first case could save
the marriage.

The five "scapegoats" mentioned above are on quite a different logical level from the causes commonly given in the courts:
infidelity, alcohol, mental cruelty, and the omnibus "irreconcilable differences." We think it is fair to say that the majority of
young couples really believe they are marrying for love, and only
a small percentage of those couples who eventually break up do
so because they were misled by this "myth."

Romantic love is nevertheless the leading villain in the eyes
of popular psychologists. Despite the fact that "marrying for love"
is more possible in this century than at any other time in history,
the most vocal observers insist that we don't really know what
love is. William J. Lederer and Don D. Jackson, in their book *The
Mirages of Marriage*, flatly claim, "Very few people actually marry
because they're in love. They think they are, but what they usually
take to be love is something else—often a strong sex drive, a fear
of being unloved, or a hunger for approval." This dismal report is
followed by the cheering news that love is not necessary for marriage, anyway. "A working marriage may be achieved if both parties feel they are better off together than they would have been
separately. They may not be ecstatically happy, and they may not
be "in love," but they are not lonely, and they do have areas of
shared contentment." One does not have to be an idealist to feel
that this description of coexistence doesn't say much for human
intelligence and discernment. Lederer and Jackson write as if they
are describing two human beings—of either sex—washed up by
chance on a raft.

David H. Olson repeats this theme in a recent article in the sociological journal, *Family Coordinator:* "People marry for love and married people are in love," is a basic myth too many people bring to marriage.

It has become fashionable to underline the inadequacies of what we used to admire as "romance," especially in feminist literature. Author Veronica Geng is described in a recent issue of *Ms.* as being "especially interested in the wrongheadedness of romantic love."

Whether or not these observers are dead right in their points of view about love, they obviously signal a trend away from the conception of marriage as a "vessel of love," and toward an idea of it as an occasional convenience. Part of our failure to grow up, they are saying, is our inability to be realistic about love.

As if to emphasize the emptiness of the romantic ideal, Lederer and Jackson point out that, according to their surveys, at least 80% of all married people seriously consider divorce at some time during their marriage. In an older study, reported in *Marriage and Family Living* in 1950, Clifford Adams went so far as to say that the "true" divorce rate even then was higher than 70%—by "true" meaning more realistic in describing those who legally live together without any interaction, those who are informally separated, and those who have deserted or been deserted. Martha Weinman Lear echoes this evaluation in a recent magazine article:

There are not any 'new' problems in marriage—just new attitudes toward the same old problems. And the failure rate is probably no higher than it ever was; there is simply a greater readiness to admit failure by getting divorced. I think of my grandparents. . . . Although they never became a divorce statistic, their marriage, by any criterion of human happiness, would have to be called a failure.

Vance Packard, in *The Sexual Wilderness*, added his imprimatur to the charges against marriage: the chances of a marriage remaining even legally intact in the late sixties were only 50-50, he speculated. The accumulation of all this evidence, he and others implied, points to the possibility that the institution itself may be at fault, and not the unwitting participants. The death knell of the institution has been tolled many times, but seldom as gloomily as by Myron Orleans and Florence Wolfson, in "Future of the Family," in *The Futurist* (1970): "Evidence of its collapse is visible in the multitude of unhappy, broken families and miserable people."

As we enter the last quarter of the twentieth century, the problems of divorce we face are older than the problems of romantic love, or changing roles of the sexes, or greater mobility of the population. As Ms. Lear says specifically, "Your marital problems are a lot older than your marriage. They all started when you were a tyke."

In examining the reasons for divorce in the following chapters, it is well to remember this basic legacy: there is no scapegoat if we fail to live up to our abilities as human beings—and one of those is the ability to adjust to, and even change, our institutions.

Legacy III
Sex: Public Enemy Number One?

For many years there was only one ground for divorce which would hold up in most courtrooms of the nation: adultery. The breach of the sexual vows of marriage, in other words, used to be taken as the most serious offense against the institution. For this legacy we need not blame the Puritans, who have suffered far too long as our sexual scapegoats. In every patriarchal society from the Hebrews to the Romans to the Teutonic tribes, a husband could dismiss his wife commonly for either barrenness or adultery. In the Christian era, adultery continued to be the major ground for marital breakup: divorce for the Protestants, separation for the Catholics. It was, ironically, the Puritans who moved matters of marriage and divorce out of the jurisdiction of the ministers and priests and into the hands of civil authorities. And at that moment in history, courts and legislatures for the first time on a broad scale began to define both the requirements for marriage and the prerequisites for divorce.

If the Puritans were guilty of anything, it was opening a Pandora's box of legal and social horrors; they brought the delicate subtleties of the dissolution of a family into the cold courts of law. In the words of Ted Downey, an experienced divorce counselor in Omaha, Nebraska, "If a family dissolution requires delicate surgery, they are currently performing it with a blunt butcher's knife, and giving the patient no postoperative care."

There is no greater indictment of the hypocrisy of American jurisprudence than the divorce settlement situation in America today, and the use to which adultery has been put in such settlements. For probably a century, judge, lawyer, plaintiff, and defendant have been conducting a Punch-and-Judy show in the divorce courts, a sexual scenario that can only be described as comedy in bad taste.

In the classic Fred Astaire-Ginger Rogers spoof, *The Gay Divorcée,* the ludicrous proportions of the adultery requirements were the basis for a plot line that was taken for granted as a fact of life. Hollywood would have us believe that a proper divorce required a retinue of gigolos, house detectives, helpful friends and outraged parents. Strange, but the courts themselves have perpetuated this preposterous fiction.

Why? The cynic would say, along with a vast majority of the respondents in our survey, that the adversary proceedings of divorce cases stand to benefit only the lawyers involved, and in not a few cases, especially in some Pennsylvania counties, the judges themselves. Our study told of outright payoffs to judges and *sub rosa* agreements between opposing lawyers (to *each* adversary's disadvantage). In the states which have proposed "no-fault" divorce laws similar to recent no-fault automobile insurance laws, the loudest cry against reform *and for maintaining the adversary system* has been from the legal profession.

Is it any wonder a significant portion of our respondents (almost 80 percent!) place divorce attorneys in the same category as pimps, panderers and dope pushers?

In the sexual aspects of divorce, however, perhaps the greatest negative pressure has come from a moralistic society—not so much Puritanical as Victorian. Such a society has been powerful enough to try to inflict its sentiments on the drinking habits of the country, and more recently to invade certain areas of "victimless" crimes. Society is saying, and the courts are repeating, "If you deviate from our moral beliefs, you are breaking the law." So we see the quiet but forceful movement of aware young people away from the law, much to the chagrin of their forbears who have inherited the legacy of sex as a public enemy.

The ancient enormity attached to adultery, which is still one of the strongest legacies in marriage, underlines a basic confusion of sex and sexuality. Society looks at sex as an overt act, for evidence of deviation from its standards. And in its absorption with this act, it has become oblivious to the broader relationships between men and women which Freud first hinted at in his studies of childhood sexuality.

Beyond adultery, society has also proscribed other "sex acts" as deviation from its collective moral standards, and even these have created vast anomalies in the Pandora's box of marriage/divorce litigation (e.g., oral sex is still illegal in most states). Our Victorian forbears, though not nearly as straight-laced as popular images would have them, perpetrated a sexual code on succeeding generations which categorized behavior as proper or improper, wholesome or unwholesome, but not sexual or unsexual. For them there was nothing wrong with being "unsexual"—even though clearly for the knowledgeable adult today the worst offense against one's lover is to deny one's sexuality to him or her.

In an important if paradoxical sense, the Victorian morality was sex-oriented with an obsession far exceeding the present ethic. Each succeeding generation has had to try to break out of the confines of this dominant morality, though the Victorians apparently believed they were regulating "immoral" behavior and not confining the natural expression of their humanity. And so, in similar but unparallel outbursts, there were the "flappers," "flaming youth," the post-World War II Kinsey generation, the "beatniks," and finally the hippie communes and "living-together arrangements" and wife-swapping. This is not to say that any or all of these expressions of rebellion have been headed in a sane direction; yet they were and are demonstrations against intrusions into the personal development of human sexuality.

The studies which have documented the increased freedom of men and women (but especially women) in sexual affairs are well known. In the 1930's it was the Terman study, which focused on premarital intercourse. Women in their thirties had no sexual intercourse before marriage in about half of the cases; women over forty could say the same thing in about seven out of eight cases. The Kinsey Report confirmed this, and extended it to other areas of human relationships. Women were, in the 1940's and 1950's, about as virginal at the time of marriage as their sisters in the 1930's, but they no longer confined their premarital experience primarily to fiancés. Burgess and Wallin added comparisons between the sexual activities of men and women, confirming the widespread understanding that men tended to be two or three times as sexually active, outside marriage, as women. Finally, the Masters and Johnson studies, among others, showed how rapidly this generalization is going out of date, even though the pressures of society (if not some innate difference between the sexes) continue to result in a higher incidence of promiscuity among men than women.

An apparent accompaniment to this trend in personal sexual choices is the utter breakdown (or opening up, depending on your point of view) of public standards in publishing and entertainment. Whereas once *Lady Chatterley's Lover* or *Ulysses* had to be smuggled into the country, nowadays material that is pornographic by admission of the publisher is for sale publicly in every major city. Nudity in films and on stage is not new, only more tolerated. Respectability has come to the merchandising of the female form with *Playboy* magazine and its many imitators. Yet morally the worst that can be said about this trend is that it may have gone far beyond its purported goal: to liberate man (and woman) from Victorian morality.

The legacy we have inherited from our most recent past is somewhat more disturbing than a legacy of permissiveness. It is the legacy of what we might call the "let's be reasonable" syndrome.

Being reasonable, we must admit that marriages are not made in heaven. Being reasonable, we must realize that many youngsters are married in the heat of emotion, an emotion that cannot long endure. Being reasonable, we must realize that sex is not unlike eating or drinking or getting dressed. And so we drift to the inevitable conclusion that variety is the spice of sex, as it is the spice of life; or that trying on a mate is something like trying on a pair of shoes—you keep trying until you find ones that fit.

We have come to expect movie stars, prompted by their press agents, to say things like "I can't eat the same food every day," when asked why they have been divorced so often. But to a lesser degree much the same thing is echoed by sociologists, anthropologists, and psychologists in trying to make sense out of the sexual malaise of our society. Margaret Mead sums up the argument well: "Divorce is a solution that is wholly congruent with our belief that people can cut their losses and go on to a better future . . . (Yet) with divorce we also get broken families. . . . It is in this context that we have to see the "arrangement"—living together without marriage—as an attempt on the part of many educated young people to avoid the disasters brought about by unwise choices. . . . This arrangement takes into account the modern realization that sexual compatibility is not a gift from heaven." The line of reasoning is simply that to avoid the perils of divorce it is wise to make sure of sexual compatibility, among other things, before getting married. *It is not divorce that is wrong, but the havoc caused by divorce in our current society, with its unrealistic pressures and sanctions.* Mead insists that the "arrangement" is not a real commitment: "An arrangement gets its validity, its ethical support, from the fact that the two people entering into it are saying, 'This isn't a real marriage.' "

The proposition that sex must be tried on for size, and that experimentation is the way to determine sexual compatibility, sounds reasonable enough. Yet it seems to us to miss the significance of modern insights into the role of sexuality in our lives. It treats sex in the same framework as does Victorian morality; sex is an act, to be promoted, curbed, improved upon or shunned. John F. Cuber and Peggy B. Haroff, in *Sex and the Significant Americans* (Penguin, 1968), present a far more comprehensive view of the sexuality of husband and wife, underlined by the simple fact that "closeness" in the marriages they studied was very often not correlated with intensity or frequency of sexual intercourse. Sexuality involves the entire human psyche, and is as complex as the human being itself. To pretend that a one- or two-year Living Together Arrangement can plumb its depths or can prepare for the myriad changes that occur in the development of human beings as parents, as people in the crisis of middle age, or as grandparents is presumptuous. The literature of Western civilization, on the contrary, suggests either that (1) compatibility can better be predicted by "matchmakers" and by traditional courting, or, less cynically, that (2) compatibility is indeed not a gift from heaven but is the result of hard work *after* marriage.

The argument for "living together" which is presented by Mead is faulty on purely logical grounds as well—although this is not to say that there may not be other good reasons for the "arrangement." Mead assumes that one can test a commitment in a situation that does not involve a commitment; the result is no test at all. The Living Together Arrangement, which we will discuss specifically in a later chapter, is akin to a common mistake in marketing. A magazine publisher sends a letter to a thousand potential subscribers asking, "If this magazine were offered to you, would you subscribe?" The result is that 50% say they would. But when the *actual* offer is made, only 2% send in their money. Was the sample too small? Not at all; it was simply not the same offer. One does not find out what it is like to be committed to someone or to something by pretending that he is *not* committed.

Implicit in Mead's outline of the LTA is the subterfuge that it is only the *legality* of marriage which causes the grief of divorce. Yet there is no necessary reason why the breakup of an arrangement is any less traumatic than the dissolution of a marriage. Whether or not two people think they are committed, the act of living together is the bond which fashions all of the attachments that hurt in a separation. There is nothing essential to an LTA which excludes children, much less shared experiences, mutual comfort, and recognition on the part of others as being "together." These are the things which devastate the emotions in a divorce, wanted or unwanted. It is true that the legal stamp (or stigmata, some would have it) which marriage bears has the additional effect of requiring financial disentanglement. Yet alimony and child support are hardly considerations at the beginning of a "relationship."

However, while it may be true that some social psychologists are finding that an LTA termination can cause just as many—and just as serious—emotional traumas as the dissolution of a legal marriage, our research had shown that the *chances* of such traumas are far less among childless LTA couples than legally married ones. There is no question that an LTA couple mutually wishing to split, and having no children, can more easily divide property and finances equitably and in a mutually agreeable manner than a couple who are tearing each other's throats out at the behest of greedy and oftentimes unscrupulous lawyers and judges. Whether late 1970's America likes it or not, the continuing trouble with divorce lies in the courts, not in the law or in the married persons themselves.

The "let's be reasonable" syndrome is also apparent in much professional analysis of adultery and "playing around." There is no question that extramarital affairs are quite common, if not increasing. Albert Ellis, in Extra-Marital Relations (Prentice-Hall, 1966), suspects that most studies have not gauged the full extent of the situation. Kinsey found that half of all married men and one-quarter of all married women could be expected to have had extramarital affairs by the age of forty. Given this extensive "problem," many sociologists have reacted by speculating that adultery may actually not be harmful at all. Lonny Myers and Hunter Leggitt, reporting in a sociological journal in 1972, contend that "the occasional, casual affair . . . . need not threaten a good marriage." Indeed, they claim, adultery can enhance marital relations in a variety of ways: (1) reducing the sexual demands of one partner on the other; (2) improving the adulterer's performance; (3) motivating the other partner to improve his/her appearance or behavior; (4) holding a marriage together until the children are grown up; (5) offering diversion, excitement, and so forth. A similar contention in the same journal was made by Herbert A. Otto, chairman of the National Center for the Exploration of Human Potential: "New variety is sometimes introduced into the sex life," and "the other member may make a greater effort to please." Going beyond what anyone might have guessed, Otto found exceptional curative powers in "playing around": it could lead to "greater appreciation and love for the spouse," and even "greater openness in communication." Lynn G. Smith and James R. Smith of the University of California at Berkeley added to this that an affair "tends to make life more exciting," and for good or bad "it certainly intensifies" all aspects of a marriage.

How much of this is rationalization by subjects and researchers alike is difficult to determine. There is no good test of the common contention that woman is monogamous and man is polygamous, and the bias which this may exert on men wishing to justify their behavior and women wishing to "liberate" themselves. Albert Ellis concludes that the evidence is insufficient to warrant a valid result, since existing studies rely heavily on subjects who are, by the very nature of inquiry, predisposed to take a liberal view. In contrast to the typical sociological researcher, family counselors base their opinions on in-depth experience with individual cases, and their findings are harsher on the causes and effects of adultery. According to James L. Framo, chief of the Family Training and Therapy Unit at Jefferson Community Mental Health Center in Philadelphia, the results of an affair can be therapeutic or disastrous. But "it is rare for the affair itself to break up the marriage." However, marriage counselor Carolyn Simonds reports, "If the woman has one and is found out, it may dissolve the marriage." (We'll deal later with this implication that the husband cannot handle his wife's affair psychologically, whereas she is expected to "kiss-and-make-up" after *his* affair.) Leon Salzman, deputy director of the Bronx State Hospital, contends that the basic cause of adultery is not "the more popular rationalization regarding man's innate polygamous tendencies which cannot be satisfied by a monogamous social arrangement," but rather "the failure of marriages to fulfill the needs of partners." Ira L. Reiss reinforces this conclusion in *The Family System in America* (Holt, Rinehart & Winston, 1971): adultery is generally the way out "for those who are unsatisfied with their marriages and those with narrow self-involvement in their marriages."

In short, adultery appears to be more of a symptom of a basic failure of a marriage than a cause; a manifestation of a problem rather than a neutral or curative device. In the terms presented in this chapter, we would call it the triumph of sex over sexuality.

The taboos which sociologists argue have plagued the sex lives of married couples are more likely to be taboos of sexuality rather than of sex. This reasoning might help explain the paradox of increasing sexual "hangups" in an era of unprecedented attention to sex in all forms of media. Even when serious medical problems would seem to require utter sexual honesty, failure to communicate remains a central problem in diagnosis and treatment. Social worker Janice Onder, University of Michigan, reported in 1973 that the divorce rate of arthritic patients was higher than that of any other group with major medical problems: "The trouble is that, even today, sex is so shrouded in taboos few arthritic patients or their doctors admit to the existence of problems."

The difference between sex and sexuality is also underlined in recent studies of "sexist" child raising. Jean Lipman Blumen, a sociologist at Stanford University, concludes in an article in *Scientific American* that sexuality still tends to limit a woman's occupational aspirations. The point is that this same thing cannot be said of sex. It is the total relationship between a man and a woman which tends to dictate that a woman would rather marry a doctor than be one. The finding that the majority of women are *vicarious* achievers was based on a study in 1968, and may require updating. Yet here again sex emerges in our culture as an *enemy* rather than an agent for personal growth.

The epitome of the confusion of sex and sexuality is the attempt to treat sexual dysfunction as a thoroughly mechanical problem. Drs. William Masters and Virginia Johnson of the Reproductive Biology Research Foundation in St. Louis are the leading exponents of this approach. For a basic charge of $2,500, they conduct an intensive two-week program in ironing out the physical kinks in lovemaking. The success of their methods, which is reportedly high, is probably the result of careful screening of their clients. This level of care goes far beyond normal counseling, and indeed involves a highly specialized area of medicine. Masters and Johnson nevertheless claim that 50% of all marriages suffer from sexual dysfunction. Sheldon Mitchell, vice-president of the Family Law Section of the American Bar Association, agrees with their clinical approach to problems of sex: "Lawyers must learn to talk with their clients about sex as they would about digestion, or a runny nose, or any other bodily function." The fact that the word "sexuality" cannot be substituted in that sentence for "sex" exposes the over-simplification of the issue. Sex was Public Enemy Number One for the Victorians because it was feared; it is Public Enemy Number One in the minds of those who choose to live together rather than marry for the same reason. In one case, sex was feared as the cause of immorality; in the latter case, sex is feared as the cause of "bad choices" in the selection of a spouse. But Germaine Greer was right: "The orgies feared by the Puritans have not materialized on every street corner, although more girls permit more (joyless) liberties than they might have done before."

Perhaps we need another word for sex. At the moment, right or wrong, it can mean intercourse, gender, sexiness, sexuality. It isn't the misunderstanding of words, of course, which lies at the heart of the problem. But we won't learn to treat sex as a friend instead of as an enemy until we come to appreciate the inseparability of sex and Man, and of sex and Woman.

Legacy IV
What Money Does to Marriage

For every survey showing that money is the leading cause of marital breakup, there is a sociological study to prove that money forces couples to stick together. On one hand, the failure to "bring home the bacon" creates envy in the wife and frustration in the husband. On the other hand, financial problems often weld a faltering relationship when either party previously felt he or she could have survived alone.

Money, or the lack of money, can profoundly affect a marriage, but only in the direction already established by the participants. It is, in short, a catalyst. It can be the adrenalin which causes a strife-torn couple to say "now," or the coagulant which forces a drifting couple to say "never."

Up until recently, money has had a clearly determined role in the balance of forces in the marital agreement. In the cruelest terms, a man barters his income for his wife's companionship. This may not be an idyllic conception, but it should be noted that (1) such a bargain is not the result of a conscious choice by men to enslave women; (2) it has followed an economic pattern which has been consistent throughout civilization; and (3) it has served passably well in preserving the family unit (presuming that is desirable).

With accelerating speed, however, the function of breadwinner is falling onto the shoulders of the woman. This is not the place to argue the reasons for or benefits of this change. There is obviously much that is debatable about total equality in employment. Lucille Duberman says, "Except for different biological processes and functions, there is little difference between men and women that is not socially induced," but the *exception* in many occupations is greater than the rule. Men do not assemble tiny electronic parts as well as women do. Women do not kick footballs as well as men do. Nevertheless, between 1900 and 1970 the proportion of women in the labor force rose from 18 to 37 percent. According to the President's Commission on the Status of Women, by 1965 one-third of all mothers in the country were working. Incidentally, a number of studies, such as Nye and Hoffman's *The Employed Mother in America*, (Rand McNally, 1963) showed that at least in sociological terms the children of employed mothers fared no worse than those of "housewives." A 1973 survey of family sociologists (Jayne D. Burks, "The Delphi Study") revealed that more than half of the respondents predicted a totally balanced male-female work force by 1990.

There are those who have fought a rearguard action against this trend on the grounds that the distribution of the breadwinning and homemaking functions is biologically motivated. In *Sexual Suicide* (Quandrangle, 1973), George Gilder went so far as to predict that once the male forfeited his preeminence as provider society would collapse. What most anthropologists overlook in their dire warnings is that the forces of the marketplace and of biological differences cannot long be manipulated by public sentiment, protests, or the most stringent laws. Those who believe in the ultimate difference between men and women need only wait.

The Equal Rights Amendment and various equal-pay-for-equal-work rulings will undoubtedly combine with an expanding female work force to shake the *socially* dictated role of men as economic combatants. Women may discover before they expect it that the price one pays for economic independence is competition, and competition takes its toll in nerves, heart attacks, and emotional stress due to anxiety and insecurity. Already there are signs of a narrowing of the difference between male and female life expectancies.

Our heritage of male economic dominance, therefore, seems to be undergoing a salutary change. No longer does a male enter college with the single purpose of carving out for himself a career based on what the salary scales happen to be in various fields at that moment. A whole generation of college graduates have discovered that the call for teachers and engineers and research scientists when they entered the field could not be turned off before a glut of teachers and engineers and research scientists developed. There are now conspicuous numbers of male telephone operators and male "cabin attendants"—a phenomenon the previous generation could only laugh at.

And no longer does a female enter college with the single purpose of attaching herself to a "winner" and basking in his success. There will always be gold-diggers, but that type of person is no longer commonplace. The stereotypes of Broadway comedies of the twenties and thirties are anomalies today.

The source of money—from the husband or the wife—and the amount of money—identified with blue-collar, white-collar, and "executive" jobs—are no longer the clear-cut distinctions they used to be. As *Fortune* Magazine points out in its own promotions, it is difficult to say that "management" starts at $15,000 when plumbers, truck drivers, and automobile salesmen can easily make more per year. Even a recent study, *Sex, Marriage, and Social Class*, by William Simon and John Gagnon (1972), now seems outmoded. The financial arrangement of the "Upper Middlebrow" is epitomized in joint checking accounts. The Lower Middlebrow way of treating money is characterized as "She budgets." The Lowbrow system is "He gets a weekly allowance."

In former times there were a select few at the upper end of the economic scale who made "antenuptial agreements" when they married. In effect, a contract was inked which protected the assets of the wealthy party from distribution in the event of a divorce, in return for which the other party agreed to marriage. This accepted legal practice has been carried to extremes by women's liberation advocates, who propose contracts specifying who does the dishes on which day of the week. Marriage is, of course, a contract—and in a wide variety of forms (see *The Love Contract*, R. E. Burger, Van Nostrand Reinhold, 1972). But the reliance on legal mechanisms to assure performance in ethical and emotional areas is an ancient fallacy.

Gilder in fact argues persuasively that there is no real bargain in marriage *ideally;* as soon as it becomes a mere contractual relationship of money for services rendered, marriage loses its fundamental force. For the easiest way to dispense with an institution is to reduce it to a law, and then change the law. Most of the apologists for women's causes continue to argue that women have perennially been the victims of the purse-strings. Without economic clout of their own, they have had to go along with unfair marriage interpretations by the courts; they have had to subject themselves to discriminatory credit practices; they have had to offer their housewifely services dutifully under penalty of being turned out to a hostile economic world. Yet it is one thing to point out that all of this is changing. It is another thing to ask whether the admitted economic superiority of the male was consistently and consciously used to the detriment of women as a class.

Have women been denied the opportunity to develop their full talents because of the club of money wielded by men? Or are the two conditions unrelated? It is true that women have been systematically excluded from various professions. It is true that they have had to struggle to gain such elemental rights as the ability to open charge accounts in their own names, to finance a home purchase on their own incomes, or to file bankruptcy on their own debts. Yet there is a large gap in sociological studies which might be able to show *why* these conditions have existed for so long. The evidence seems to be that the accumulation of wealth has been better accomplished by women than by men, in spite of the above handicaps.

One of the paradoxical effects of money on marriage is that those who decry the malevolent uses of economic power the most are the first to seek economic power as a remedy. Men have dominated women too long with money, they say; and money is a despicable force. But now it's our turn. And if we can assert our dominance, well and good.

From the evidence it seems to us that money and its misuses are more the symptoms of other maladies than the causes of the crime. Money sometimes represents success. Often it becomes a symbol of accomplishment, substituting for sexual or artistic or personal achievement. Conversely, its absence can signify failure, impotence, disgrace. It costs $10 to get a marriage license generally and $1,000 to get an "ordinary" divorce. In between, most married couples make decisions in much the same way; the financial cost is nothing compared to the personal cost.

Legacy V
What Divorce Does to Money

Several people we interviewed began the discussion with a question: "Do husbands really run away from their alimony and support payments in great numbers?" Why this question? Simply because divorced parents generally remarry soon (at a far faster rate than the unmarried marry), and often remarry other divorced persons with children. Then the stark reality hits them. One man applied for a renewal of his home construction loan, and listed his new wife's support payments as income. The bank said no. Another man was turned down by a department store on a credit card application. The reason: his wife's support payments could not be considered part of his income. Clearly, financial institutions have taken the realistic view that alimony and child support are more precarious than a first-time job. Back-breaking payments to an "ex-family" are the easiest obligations to rationalize away.

For the word "money," substitute "survival." Money is a means of exchange; the exchange is almost the whole of the human condition. When we talk about money, the implication is that someone is trying to make a fast buck, or to "take" someone, or to aggrandize himself. But in the context of mere survival, "money" means the ability to live with a certain amount of dignity, somewhat commensurate with one's previous background and talents.

The decision to divorce is likely to affect both parties financially at the outset; it will certainly change their lives economically for several years. And it may become the major obstacle to regaining a sense of social balance with the rest of humanity, simply because money has been and will continue to be mistreated in the trauma of a divorce.

Here are some of the factors to consider in deciding to divorce or not to divorce (the disputes and dollar amounts are considered later under the chapters on alimony and child support):

1. *Legal costs.* Few people if any "shop" for a lawyer. And lawyers have a convenient code of setting a fee based on the ability to pay—but *with a minimum.* There is a rising tide of protest that is common among all the divorce reform groups springing up throughout the country: why are lawyers allowed to profit so heavily from divorce actions? The minimum fee just to start talking is about $200. Once started, there is no turning back. Every conference brings a new bill. And the lawyer collects first.

2. *Disruption of income.* Divorce is such a blinding experience the first time around that the ordinary realities of making a living go by the boards when the breach is made. Men lose their jobs because they miss too much time at their desks or stations. Women lose their incentive to support or help support a family that is failing. The divorce proceedings become, in effect, a full-time job.

3. *Separate maintenance.* Even before the divorce comes, one party usually has to move out of the household. Bills go unpaid. Necessary repairs and upkeep on the family home are ignored. Wild spending to satisfy emotional needs becomes the regular order of business. Savings accounts and other hedges against the future become bargaining points rather than pledges.

4. *Costs of "honor."* Under the adversary system that has been our heritage and still is in most states, no amount of money is too much to spend to prove one's case. Often, a husband "gives up" in an emotional release, and signs away the fruits of his previous labors to build a family for little reason other than that he does not want to seem pecuniary. Wives hire private detectives to prove they are not at fault, as much as to prove that their husbands

are. The mere spending of money becomes equivalent to "doing something about it."

5. *Alimony.* When the divorce becomes final, it is the expectation of society that the husband will continue to support his ex-wife at a level equal to her previous situation. (No-fault legislation has altered this condition somewhat, but has not changed the concept, based on the economic facts of life, that the male continues to be the provider in American society.) There have been numerous organized protests against "alimony jail," the only vestige of "debtor's prison" in this country. Yet the fact remains that a man can be put in jail for failure to make alimony payments, but not for any other debt. The pros and cons of alimony are discussed in detail in later chapters.

6. *Child support.* There are great misconceptions in the public mind about the difference between alimony and child support. Alimony ceases when the ex-wife remarries. Child support does not cease until the child reaches 18 years of age. The abuses of child support are on both sides. From the man's point of view, the support of children he sees only once or twice a month, in perhaps another family which can easily handle additional mouths at very little additional cost up to the college level, is merely a burdensome formality. From the woman's point of view, unless she does remarry she is faced with a double burden of trying to support herself and trying to wrest money from her ex-husband. Statistics on the desertion of ex-husbands from their support payments confirm this fear.

There are also many psychological factors which tend to make separated or divorced people particularly vulnerable to economic disaster. When the emotional shock of divorce hits, money becomes a secondary consideration to most people. The cost of legal action becomes a matter of little importance. Money becomes a superfluous commodity. Like the emotional involvement that occurs when a couple buys a home, the traumatic involvement of a breakup blurs financial considerations to the point where a difference of several thousand dollars is of less concern than the price of a pair of socks a few weeks before. In this sense, divorce clouds a man's financial evaluations for months or years after the event. He is either so relieved, or so distressed, by the separation from his mate that his physical and economic condition become totally irrelevant. Divorce lawyers, like realtors, prey on this unhappy circumstance.

In its first issue, *Money* magazine presented a state-by-state analysis of the financial consequences of divorce. This was several years ago, when no-fault divorce was still on the horizon in most states. Nevertheless, the estimate then is about the same now: *a man has to be prepared to live on about half his former income after a divorce.* This fact simply won't sink in to a man or woman emotionally splintered by all of the other shocks of separation.

Much of the resentment of husbands who have to carry the double burden of alimony/child support and the support of their second families is that it is becoming increasingly easy for an ex-wife to "live together" with another man rather than remarry, merely to continue to receive alimony. As we shall see, divorced men in Chicago and New York have organized special campaigns against this abuse.

Very often, the divorced pay the price of their folly out of a sense of their guilt, a guilt nurtured by a morality that goes back into the nineteenth century. Divorce changes their entire outlook on financial matters: money is nothing compared to the "crime" they have committed. They will run to any extreme to redeem themselves, and money is the easiest commodity to use to assuage their feelings of failure.

It is not likely, as we have intimated, that no-fault divorce legislation will alter this emotional involvement and its consequences. It is true that lawyers may have less and less to say about the terms of their payment. They will no longer be able to profit from the open warfare that has usually characterized divorce proceedings. And alimony payments will be made more often from wife to husband. Yet the psychological pressure will remain, the pressure that says, "Get out of this at any cost." We may say blithely, "It's only money." But our whole social fabric is predicated on what money represents: sufficient stability in the necessities of life to enable people to spend more of their time improving their lives than merely feeding themselves.

If the fearsome aspect of loss of income really had an effect on the divorce rate, one would expect low-income groups to have a higher incidence of desertion than higher income groups. But the facts are otherwise. For all the years in which statistics have been gathered on this subject, *there has been no appreciable difference in desertion rates among all income levels.* Divorce blinds us to the realities of money, because our legacy has been to let every man pay for his "sins" against society.

Legacy VI
The Religious Absolute

"The shock of the law's intrusion into the innermost recesses of the human heart is as primitive as surgery without anesthesia." A marriage counselor was talking, in frustration over a court battle that had left husband and wife emotionally devastated. "Even worse is the intrusion of *religious* law, because the devout have an attachment to their spiritual guidelines that no one can have to a civil code. When a priest pretends to banish a divorced woman from her church, he is really turning the knife."

The pretense of marriage without divorce and separation without remarriage is no longer maintained in even the most Catholic of countries. When Italy's 1970 divorce law was ratified overwhelmingly in a 1974 referendum, two messages were sent throughout the world. First, legal divorce would not topple the framework of society: during the first six months of the law's operation, there were less than 5,000 divorce decrees granted, and the number has not spiralled to anywhere near equalling the dissolution rate in other countries. Second, religious authority must from now on take its cues *from*, not give direction to, popular sentiment.

Ireland, Spain, Brazil, and Chile show no signs of passing a divorce law, and Argentina is on the fence. But it is not so much the authority of the Church in these countries—strong though it is—which has held back legal acknowledgment of dissolution. Native religious feeling, sustained by centuries of custom, undoubtedly continues to buttress an ideal of lifelong marriage even when the reality is an underground of "living together arrangements" for those who cannot legally remarry.

Religion and its organized bodies are undergoing a revolution which may in the hindsight of history mark another reformation as important as that of the Middle Ages. This is a reformation of attitudes rather than of organization. "Churching" has already moved far to the left in a swing of the pendulum toward personal morality rather than observance. It will swing back in time, but the impact will remain. Sin is no longer epitomized as masturbation or fornication; it is also the failure to pay taxes and to be honest in one's feelings to one's spouse. It is no longer "How many times?" but "What is your attitude toward your fellow man?" The absoluteness of religious strictures was formerly the strongest hand the church placed on the shoulders of married couples. The vestiges of this heritage remain, but both the theoretical and practical support for observance of the letter of the law have fallen.

In 1973 the Episcopalians relaxed their divorce canons to permit their members to remarry within thirty days, with only the consent of a bishop to certain minimal requirements. Previously, the church had followed the general rule of the Catholic tradition that annulment, and not divorce proper, was permitted; and then a year waiting period was necessary. A dissolution by a civil court is now recognized by Episcopalians as satisfactory evidence that the previous marriage is "dead." Noteworthy in the formulation of requirements for remarriage is the phrasing of the church's attitude toward the duration of the new marriage (which presumably also applies to first marriages): the couple must come to the marriage "with intent" that it be a lifelong union.

What this shift in emphasis signals is the new interpretation that monogamy "till death do us part" is more an ideal to be strived for than a literal absolute. Within the Catholic Church, the formulation is not this simple, but theologians and parish priests are moving more closely together to find an interpretation of marriage which squares with the pressures of living rather than with glosses on the Bible. Father John Dolciamore, head of a Catholic

Marriage Tribunal in Chicago, finds a justification for a more liberal attitude in a broad interpretation of the gospel message: "I think we are understanding more than ever before that mercy and understanding, after all, are the heart of Jesus's teachings, and while valid marriages are still considered indissoluble, there is a great deal of new thought on what makes a marriage 'valid'." There are really two rationalizations here in one: the message of mercy supersedes the law of indissolubility, and the word "valid" may not be applicable to marriages which contained the seeds of their destruction from the beginning. Father Dolciamore enumerates serious personality problems as being such seeds: alcoholism, homosexuality, mental disturbances.

These go far beyond the traditional grounds for annulment—absence of consent, which was virtually impossible to prove to the "Rota" except in certain highly publicized, high-society examples; impotence; and consanguinity. The new grounds are really a widening of the interpretation of "absence of consent" to include anything which might impair consent.

The Baton Rouge, Louisiana Diocese announced in 1973 that it would offer the sacraments to divorced and remarried Catholics, and was censured by the president of the U. S. Conference of Catholic Bishops. But later the Vatican announced that a Catholic funeral would no longer be denied even ex-Catholics who were excommunicated when they remarried outside the Church. Msgr. Stephen J. Kelleher calls for a reform that would allow Holy Communion for all, and goes far beyond sacramental matters in his *Divorce and Remarriage for Catholics?*. The former head of the New York marriage tribunal says, "A Christian man and woman who have suffered through a marriage that painfully died have a right to divorce, and to marry a second time." His reasoning attacks the question from several sides. First, as a practical matter it is extremely difficult for a Catholic couple to receive a fair hearing before the prescribed tribunal: "Only one-tenth of the broken marriages among Catholics which are brought before the church court are ever heard, because the system is taxed to capacity." Second, there is widespread unfairness in ecclesiastic decisions as a matter of geography: "The Washington and Newark tribunals grant few annulments; on the other hand, annulments are rarely denied in the Brooklyn tribunal." Finally, in his opinion, the real test of the "validity" of a marriage is whether it is working: "In almost every instance (of requests for annulment), the marriage had broken up because each party was upset that they were destroying themselves and each other. Only rarely was a third party the initial or primary cause of the breakup. Their approach was 'my marriage has ceased to exist . . . it has become utterly intolerable.' "

In a letter to *America* magazine in 1973, Msgr. Kelleher suggests that the most suitable tribunal on marriage and divorce should consist of the parties themselves: "In the resolution of the problem of the intolerable marriage, the couple *are* the Church. Only in the case of a most flagrant indecency is their judgment to be overruled."

Discussion of the subject in Catholic publications continues to turn on theological distinctions, and words like *a toro* and *a vinculo* (from bed, from the bond) are tossed in with interpretations of what Jesus really meant and what the Jewish *ketubah* (marriage contract) required. On the counseling level, there is a decided avoidance of this sort of deductive approach, and instead an attempt to find a theory to fit the facts only after the human problem has been solved. This is, of course, the type of situation which alarms the traditionalist. The implication that marriage may not be the indissoluble bond the Church has always maintained is feared to be a self-fulfilling prophecy. The wavering of supposedly absolute standards smacks of "situational ethics." In contrast, most divorce counselors seem to view the prospect of easy marriage/easy divorce becoming the dominant pattern as more the concern of premarriage counselors than of theirs. The incidence of divorces among churchgoers is currently highest among Protestants with those of the Jewish and Catholic faiths increasing rapidly. Dr. James J. Rue, general director of the American Institute of Family Relations, states: "There is a trend in evidence that within the near future there will be a comparable incidence of divorce among all faiths." In the words of one divorce counselor, "There is no reason to believe that success in marriage should depend on one's faith, rather than on the general development of human qualities. Is it better to punish those of one faith as a way of maintaining respectable statistics, or to help them become better persons?"

There is convincing evidence that cultural and social factors play a stronger role in decisions on marriage and divorce than do the apparently religious influences. In *Family Design: Marital Sexuality, Family Size, and Contraception* (Adeline, 1969), Lee Rainwater reports on various studies of lower, middle and upper class families—with the not surprising conclusion that income level, education, and family tradition were determinative of sexual practices. There are, of course, many large families at the top of the social scale (and large generally because they are Catholic). But the overall attitude toward sex and its importance in marriage is only loosely related to religious persuasion at every social level except the lowest. The vision of rebellious masses kept under the thumb of any American church is a throwback to the nineteenth century.

More emphasis in all churches is currently being placed on programs to help alleviate the hazards and distress of divorce than to punish the "guilty." In the past, many Catholics chose civil ceremonies for their first marriage, later to be "solemnized" in the Church, to obviate problems of divorce and remarriage if the first one "didn't work out." The tension among Catholics over divorce is now so great that even some clergy are not aghast at this alternative. The head of the Archdiocesan marriage tribunal in San Francisco, Msgr. Richard Knapp, concedes that teenagers who don't want to face the stricter marriage preparation requirements of the church are turning to civil ceremonies. "Although we don't like to see this, perhaps in the long run it's best. If the counselor's evaluation proves right and divorce follows, as Catholics they are free to remarry." (Civil ceremonies are not recognized as valid for Catholics; apparently "living in sin" is to be preferred *before* a religious marriage than after it.) A phenomenon that is becoming commonplace in most dioceses is the formation of organizations, headed by priests or ministers, to help the divorced. Msgr. Frank A. Maurovich, who heads a group called GEMS, composed of divorced Catholic women, is typical of a clergy more concerned with healing than laying down the law. "Most of these women," he says, "are doing heroic jobs—working, taking care of the home and trying to play the role of both mother and father." They are often bitter about priests who take a legalistic attitude, "like the divorcée who asked me, 'What do you do with sexual thoughts and longings when prayer doesn't work?'"

Attention is being focused by the churches on greater marriage preparation, going far beyond the "Cana Conference" program, which is required in many areas as a condition for a Catholic wedding. In the San Francisco area, as in 20 other dioceses, teenagers are now required to complete a program of evaluation by a counseling agency, and then receive a passing recommendation by the agency before the ceremony can be set. The hope is to decrease the rate of divorce by Catholics under the age of 24, an alarming 56%. More than 90% of teen-age "shot-gun" marriages by Catholics end in divorce.

Efforts are also being made to cushion the shock of separation which is legal and physical, but not emotionally complete. Where children are involved, the battle to "prove" who was wrong or to punish the other party by means of the children is traumatic. In Los Angeles County, it is estimated that 90% of the fathers do not take advantage of visitation rights which they have received in their dissolutions, and which they hold out to their children as a promise. Religious groups of divorced fathers and mothers take aim at the emotional reaction that is likely to follow this abuse: to poison the children against the errant parent.

The legacy of religion, which once seemed to take its first task to be to dispense guilt to offenders, now shows a helping hand. Theologian Peter J. Riga of St. Mary's College, Moraga, sums up the current feeling of his peers: "Any sort of official approval of divorce and remarriage within the church is years away. Meanwhile, there are millions of divorced Catholic people hurting. Can priests be content simply to say to these people that it is a difficult law of God but it is nevertheless the law. . . . even if this second marriage is not properly sacramental, but is simply a situation which they believed was humanly the best for them?" When priests themselves are wrestling with another "ideal" made into law—celibacy—it is a question to which a theological answer would seem least appropriate.

Legacy VII
The Liz & Dick Syndrome

Married couples are currently encountering a dilemma which the previous generation knew only vicariously—in the never-never land of Hollywood stars and the social 400. That dilemma is the price of the "new freedom." When an adult, especially a woman, sees trouble in a marriage, should he or she "cut the losses" quickly or risk hanging on to a losing cause and thus jeopardize a "second chance?"

Margaret Mead sees this dilemma as a leading cause of early divorces: "Today, particularly for young wives and mothers, it is the fear of what divorce implies for their own security and their children's that drives them to divorce while they still have a chance to make a life of their own, instead of waiting to be abandoned." Such a fear is the other side of the coin of "liberation." Now that women are increasing their opportunities to be self-sufficient, they are also expected to be willing to take those opportunities. As we have seen, there is even legal recognition of this fact in the spreading practice of limiting alimony to shorter periods of time in the case of obviously employable divorcées.

Organizations favoring men's causes in divorce have made quite a bit of hay out of this apparent imbalance in the social structure. Noting that the awarding of alimony still favors women in most localities—and it is a matter of local discretion—the strongest of the pro-male groups, A.D.A.M. in Chicago, has gone to the Federal Courts to attempt to sway judicial opinion. A.D.A.M. (American Divorce Association for Men) takes a hard line on the issue; says President Louis J. Filczer, "Only when women's rights groups effectively work for an increase in marital and postmarital responsibility will they succeed in getting out of a male-dominated society." Sponsors of the Equal Rights Amendment and other women's groups feel, on the contrary, that women have a long way to go to achieve economic equality, and until they achieve it completely they cannot afford to work for men's causes as well.

So the dilemma is not only a personal one, but one for society. The well-to-do of the previous generation solved the problem simply by jumping from one marriage to the next as rapidly as possible. Elizabeth Taylor, Judy Garland, Ava Gardner, Rita Hayworth, Marilyn Monroe, and Lana Turner were married a total of 29 times (as of this writing!) to 28 husbands. There was little personal problem, because they were not only quite employable, but quite marriageable. And there was only the social problem of scandalizing a small percentage of the population. Most of us, no doubt, laughed at the "Liz & Dick" syndrome without worrying about its consequences for society. Dr. Joyce Brothers recently gave the typical shrug of the shoulders to this phenomenon: "The reason so many Hollywood marriages are brief," she said, "is that most women there spend more time with their hairdressers than with their husbands."

In a more serious vein, however, Dr. Brothers put her finger on the seriousness of the Hollywood-type serial monogamy. No longer are economic freedom, personal independence, and easy remarriage the sole prerogatives of the wealthy and the famous. "In Hollywood, you don't have the joint effort of child-raising . . . the community pressure isn't there . . . . the man doesn't have to stay with his wife for a regular sexual outlet . . . she doesn't have to stay married for sex . . . so you end up wondering what held the marriage together—except for community property." Today, all of these characteristics of Liz and Lana and Ava and Rita are commonplace for the Mary Lous of the world as well. When parental and community pressure eases, when sex and children are no problem, what *does* hold a marriage together? This apparent laxity, added to the fear of missing out on a second chance, has propelled thousands of "nobodies" into a Liz & Dick type of experimentation with mate-swapping.

Reno, Nevada currently handles about 3,000 divorces a year—and one suspects that most of them fall into the category of easy mate-swapping. The duration of marriages that are ended in the "quickie" divorce mills is typically less than three years. At the other end of the social ladder, excluding Hollywood, the marriages seem to last longer and the trappings of the divorce are much more elegant. Sun Valley, Idaho serves as a pleasant locale for about 30 out-of-state divorces a year, and what is lacking in numbers is easily made up for in amenities. Happy Murphy, now Mrs. Nelson Rockefeller, Pat Kennedy Lawford, Charlotte Ford Niarchos, and Amanda Burden put in their six-weeks' residency here. Comfortable housing can run up to $75 a day; add private ski instruction at $50 a day, entertaining, and shopping and the divorce bill can soon make outrageous legal fees seem reasonable.

For the famous or the wealthy, indeed, the dilemma of divorce is a thing of the past. The last politician to suffer from the stigma of divorce was Adlai Stevenson—and he never remarried. Perhaps the last prominent Catholic to "scandalize" the faithful with a divorce and remarriage was Henry Ford II. Social or financial prominence hasn't been a barrier to a change of mates for a good part of this century. The attitude of Bob Crompton, whose divorce was casually explored in a front-page interview in the *Wall Street Journal* in early 1974, is revealing. An affable 36-year-old "who married a woman so wealthy that he could spend his days hunting foxes instead of working," Crompton candidly told reporters that the settlement, rumored to be $2.5 million in his favor, could support him in the style to which he was accustomed for some time. An acquaintance remarked, "Each time I see Bob, he has a smile on his face and a different, good-looking girl on his arm." His ex-wife, a soup company heiress, was meanwhile reported to have married her divorce attorney.

Such stories are grist for the gossip mills, and they may dismay traditionalists, but they are no longer serious news and they certainly cast no adverse reflections on the parties involved for the

vast majority of Americans. The fact that they can afford the luxury of sumptuous settlements and uncomplicated dissolutions is
more a matter of envy with most people, than it is a matter of
moral or social concern. For most people, Toulouse-Lautrec's
characterization of marriage applies: "a banquet with the dessert
at the beginning." Those who can afford to have dessert also at the
end are growing in numbers and in community respect.

To what extent is the Liz & Dick syndrome reaching down
into the ranks of non-celebrities, non-heiresses, non-famous? The
fashion among social scientists is to see fundamental changes just
around the corner. Alvin Toffler, in *Future Shock* (Random
House, 1970), thought the changes had already occurred. "In one
sense," he confides, "serial marriage is already the best kept family secret of the techno-societies." He argues that polygamous
societies today produce fewer "plural marriages" than our se-
quential marriages. But this fuzzy thought is trivial alongside his
basic message about the inevitability of serial marriage: "Serial
marriage—a pattern of successive temporary marriages—is cut to
order for the Age of Transcience in which all man's relationships,
all his ties with the environment, shrink in duration. It is the
natural, the inevitable outgrowth of a social order in which automobiles are rented, dolls traded in, and dresses discarded after
one-time use. It is the mainstream of the marriage pattern of
tomorrow."

Despite such grandiose formulations, in which car renting
becomes part of a rush to Armageddon, serial marriage does not
seem to be a secret to most Americans. In the last five years since
Toffler stated his case for the compression of events and knowledge that would overwhelm our capacity to deal with them, divorce legislation has, if anything, become more rational and more
humane *than at any other time in our history,* albeit a decade or so
behind the times. The fears of many traditionalists and religious
bodies—that no-fault dissolution would make the Liz & Dick syndrome a parlor game—have not materialized. Few of us live in the
world of Myrna Odell Firestone, the fourth wife of the tire heir,
who was granted a $60,000 annual alimony settlement with a
cost-of-living escalation clause. Few of us will even be able to
avail ourselves of the 24-hour divorce proceedings in the Domini-

can Republic, "a quick flight from Atlanta, Miami, or Washington, D.C.," according to their advertisements. What we have inherited from the past is a sort of healthy distaste for the shenanigans of movie stars, hopping from bed to bed, and at the same time a smiling acceptance of their peculiar predicament. More recently, we have inherited the demands as well as the benefits of "liberation," and this if anything is the dilemma that still may make serial marriage an attractive escape in the tumultuous years ahead.

Legacy VIII
The Financial Showdown

The greatest obstacle to runaway serial marriages continues to be the devastating cost of jumping from one partner to another. We have already seen how the emotional shock of dissolution blinds most couples to the realities of maintaining separate households, liquidating assets, paying double taxes, and doling out fees to counselors and accountants and clerks. The two largest burdens, the ones that make divorce virtually impossible for many couples, have always been legal fees and alimony. Even the welfare of the children seems to take second place to the financial deterrent.

In the recent past, there has been a palace revolt launched against the abuses perpetrated by attorneys, courts, and ex-spouses in the setting and enforcing of divorce payments. And, of course, there are two sides to the story.

From the man's point of view, legal fees and alimony are set arbitrarily high, with little regard for services rendered or ability to pay. In the most extensive recent study of alimony payments, in Indiana, it was found that *payments were in arrears in nine out of ten cases*, and had stopped after a year in about half the cases. Men cite such studies as evidence that the demands were too great; women reply that the statistics merely show enforcement is lacking. Men object to the automatic division of assets accumulated during marriage in the eight community-property states (generally in the West). Women point out that, in the remaining 42 states, men keep everything that is not specifically placed under both husband's and wife's names. (Yet in stringently conservative states such as Pennsylvania, men can lose everything.) Men object to "alimony jails" as the only remaining vestige of debtor's prison, supposedly outlawed in the Bill of Rights. Women object to being put in the position of being bill collectors, with the humiliating prospect of being unsure of when and how much money is coming.

The sensational stories of improbable fees and settlements mean little to the average couple, but they illustrate how severe the financial crunch can be. Our survey showed that an outrageous 45.3 percent of the divorced persons interviewed found the monetary burden unfair and "near-disastrous." In 1964, New York newspapers gleefully reported that Patricia Anne Shephard was awarded a record $3,000 a week in alimony, doubling the previous record held by the ex-wife of lyricist Alan Jay Lerner. Patricia's attorney was allowed the round sum of $125,000 for his services. On the other side of the fence, when a Cleveland woman and her attorney attempted to collect a $4,278 fee from her ex-husband, the latter sued for $350,000 in damages for harassment. A Vietnam POW, reunited with his wife and family after six years in captivity, was promptly served with divorce papers; his wife, who allegedly had been living with her attorney, also claimed his back pay. In community property states, the retirement pay of career servicemen is currently being treated as joint property, and by a quirk of interpretation a man could be required to pay $5,000 a year to his ex-wife five or six years before he was eligible to retire. Money magazine reported in its first issue several years ago that legal fees can work out to $100 an hour, since a lawyer has to be simultaneously "mother, father, and surrogate husband to our clients. They call in the middle of the night to say that the husband is pounding the door down, that junior has been picked up for possession of marijuana, and the story never ends. In contested custody cases, the sky's the limit for legal fees." For the average couple, a fee of $25 an hour would work out to $1,000 for a typical divorce, according to a specialist in divorce law at New York University. More recently, Harry F. Bain, Chairman of the Child

Custody Committee of the American Bar Association's Family Law Section, estimated a low of $35 an hour and a high of $750 a day for time in court. *The Annual Price Survey*, a report on budget costs for moderate standard of living in New York City, estimated that a divorce would require an increase in annual income of the husband of 25%.

It's clear that although there can be variables that would make any exact calculation meaningless, the only cheap divorce is one that is (1) uncontested, (2) involving little joint property or business interests, and (3) settled out of court without benefit of attorneys. Unfortunately, none of these conditions is frequently encountered. The common sense question that seems to be asked more and more of younger and older couples alike these days is: Is it not true that the longer, more bitter, more drawn out and obscure a divorce litigation becomes, *the more the attorneys benefit and the litigants lose?*

A key question that is being answered more by trial and error than by logic or tradition is: "Just how important is an attorney?"

The American Bar Association has consistently opposed no-fault divorce laws, as it has no-fault automobile insurance, and for the same reason. The laws are changing so rapidly from state to state that there is no point quoting the current status of no-fault divorce. But there is no question that within a few years most states will have adopted some form of nonadversary proceedings. In the meantime, do-it-yourself divorce kits have become popular, and free or low-cost legal-aid groups have made their presence felt in major U.S. cities.

Men's groups have naturally been the most outspoken in attacks on the traditional adversary system, and their focus is on the alleged favoritism of judges toward wives and the alleged collusion of attorneys to avoid confrontations with judges and with fellow lawyers. The range of protests is from the sophisticated to the unabashedly crude.

The National Council of Marriage and Divorce Law Reform and Justice Organizations is currently composed of a dozen regional associations, whose titles give a good idea of the thrust of the men's causes (and those of second wives). In California there is the American Family Council, which has successfully filed a child custody case with the United States Supreme Court *without benefit of an attorney;* and In Pro Per, Inc., whose title derives from the legal expression for appearing before the court on one's own behalf. In Minnesota there is the Men's Rights Association. In Washington, D.C. is the headquarters of Parents Without Partners, Inc. The Second Wives Coalition was established in New Jersey. There are chapters in almost every state of the "United States Divorce Reform" with the general theme: "Take divorce out of the courts." Other statewide groups call themselves "Fathers United For Equal Rights," or "For Equal Justice," etc. Regardless of their titles, the proliferation of these groups is clear warning that ex-husbands have taken up the battle against courts and lawyers with a vengeance.

In spite of the apparent bitterness and wild-swinging charges in the literature of many of these groups, their chief goals are well on the way to being accomplished. As long ago as 1970, the model Uniform Marriage and Divorce Act (the work of a federally-sponsored commission) contained the key concept of no-fault, nonadversary divorce proceedings, and the elimination of the traditionally automatic awarding of alimony to women. The presumption that the man should pay legal fees for both parties has also been challenged. And judges, whose discretion has always been great in family law cases, have taken a decided swing in favor of men's rights. If one were to read in detail the earlier cases involving men's protests against alleged discrimination in divorce hearings, he would marvel at the persistence of men fighting with little legal knowledge or little of the customary tactfulness and respect that have always been a requirement in a court of law.

A basic case often cited in support of avoidance of lawyers is that of Wilbur Alsup vs. his attorney, in a divorce action in 1965 in Chicago. A bill of $335.70 was presented by the attorney, representing office and telephone conferences, preparation of petitions, and court appearances. Mr. Alsup objected: the attorney had not given him any justification for the fees. The attorney duly threatened suit to collect the fees, finally subpoenaed Alsup, who then replied. Alsup demanded a trial by jury, and claimed in his formal answer to the suit that "the Plaintiff is an Attorney as only attorneys use and accept the warped degenerate money-making criminal system of the Bar Association members, including working in collusion with each other, which only Bar Association members stoop to do, and that the Plaintiff should be ashamed to admit that he is an attorney, as it is only an admittance of being a member of an unconstitutional and illegal organization. . . ."

Alsup then turned his wrath on the judge: "The Defendant paid $50 to the Plaintiff to petition the court to restore the Defendant's visitation rights with his son; the Plaintiff for about four months made various excuses for not petitioning the court; some of these excuses were that the Plaintiff had to talk to Judge Robert L. Hunter, whom he called 'Bob,' and after talking to 'Bob' the Plaintiff stated a court report was necessary (for another $35)." Finally, Alsup prayed that the court would investigate a conflict of interest in having a member of the Bar Association sit as judge in a case where the plaintiff was also a member of that association. The hapless attorney (whatever the merits of the case) sought to dismiss the answer as a "malicious harangue and attack on the integrity of the Judiciary." Nevertheless, the unceremonious but heartfelt language of Mr. Alsup carried the day, as the attorney withdrew his suit within a few weeks.

A whole series of "pro se" (for himself) or "in pro per" filings in Cook County, Illinois have been recorded since then by various rights groups. Harriet Sherman, calling herself "Victim Defendant," asked for "the lawyer/judge to abstain from any ruling and for a judge to replace him who is not or has never been a lawyer." She then launched into a multipaged complaint against judges and attorneys, associates and underworld figures, right up to Mayor Daley and Meyer Lansky, leaving no doubt that her case was based less on discrimination against any group than on the collusion of an entrenched legal system. The tenor of the remarks in these and other filings "pro se" is that the law has been used as a sort of priesthood on an unwitting populace. As Wilbur Alsup concluded in one of his "different" motions, "the United States Constitution does not require a victim to fill out fancy forms and experience any hocus-pocus to get justice."

No law school could have anticipated the type of argument that Fred Labern brought in answer to his wife's suit to enforce child support: "The victim defendant was illegally ordered to pay ransom and extortion under the guise of child support . . . and is being victimized by a conspiracy of all judges and lawyers involved in the divorce racket . . . all working together to extract juice for the judges' and lawyers' personal luxurious support and not for the children . . . and for any crooked sociologist, crooked psychologist, crooked lawyer, or crooked judge to conclude that the victim defendant is crazy and in need of psychiatric treatment is only a part of the overall divorce racket . . . and for lawyers to promote litigation and extort money from the husband or wife is indirectly taking money from the children, *making lawyers child molesters. . . .*" (our italics).

Harold W. King began his defense against his wife by stating that her attorney "is again petitioning the Circuit Court of Cook County to commit another felony." Later, he speaks directly to his adversary as "you child-molesting, warped, perverted, degenerate, profligate, completely given to dissipation, shyster, snake-in-the-grass lawyer and kidnapper of innocent and helpless children." In a following motion to recover expenses from the attorney, King states that anyone who objects to the arrest of the attorney would be guilty of obstructing justice. This type of diatribe reaches hysterical proportions in the nonlegal fulminations of Arthur R. Gawin, who has made it his personal crusade to nail the Bar Associations as "the International Communist Party and International Crime Syndicate, owned and operated by the Zionists."

Whatever the original motivations of this attitude, it obviously overshoots the mark of reform of the divorce courts. A more balanced view is taken by A.D.A.M., whose president states that the "purpose of divorce should be to preserve, not destroy, human values, and this goal can better be achieved by a family arbitration board that would include a lawyer, a professional counselor, an accountant, and, ideally, a person who has already been through divorce; the present adversary system just doesn't work."

It seems clear that the legacy of the adversary system is an albatross that can not be tossed overboard without also overturning a good part of our legal system. The financial showdown that has no doubt been abetted in the past by the personal interests of lawyers need no longer be justified as an obstacle to easy divorce, nor countenanced as a normal legal procedure.

The minutiae of alimony and legal fees are best exemplified in the contortions of the IRS and the Tax Courts. *The Wall Street Journal* regularly reports on rulings on tax deductions due to separation agreements, property settlements, and alimony. In one recent case, the IRS held that, after an annulment had been granted, all subsequent support payments were taxable since there never was a marriage nor a divorce. A lower court overruled this decision because it was four years retroactive and hence out of step with the way the government customarily dealt with corporations. We seem to be moving out of the minutiae, and into the mainstream of the problem.

And as we shall see in our survey, bobbing to the surface of that mainstream for those contemplating divorce is the growing feeling *that divorce attorneys are more harlots than heroes.*

Legacy IX
Growing Out of Marriage

"I don't have the courage to make a move. Say it louder: I AM A COWARD. Is divorce, after the investment of all our young years, an act of courage or the act of a fool? I don't know. But I want to be one of the survivors . . . on our fiftieth, I want to dance The Anniversary Waltz first with my husband and then with our son. Is that a reason to stay married? Well, *is* it?"

The most persistent dilemma of the "middle-aged" marriage—with a life of between seven and twelve years—is the fear of "growing apart." We are told by marriage counselors and divorce experts writing in the women's magazines that either the wife or the husband can be expected to outdistance the other intellectually, artistically, or socially, and that the inevitable result is dissolution. On the other hand, psychologists tell us that significant changes in the personality or abilities of a person generally do not occur after attaining adulthood. The mid-thirties wife who summed up her dilemma in the paragraph quoted above from a recent magazine article is typical. She wants to hang on, but she is not sure that she might not find on her fiftieth wedding anniversary that it was all a chimera.

The increasing incidence of divorce after twenty, thirty, forty years of marriage seems to support the worst fears of the skeptics. The pattern is familiar: after "the kids are grown and gone," if only off to college, the parents decide there is nothing requiring them to stay together except economics. If the husband can afford a comfortable alimony schedule, he settles with his wife and marries someone half her age. The traditional economic advantage of men obviously has helped perpetuate this pattern. A man of fifty or fifty-five years of age can attract a woman under thirty because of the security and prestige of his job or social position—if not because of any physical attributes. His discarded wife generally must content herself with the company of friends of her own age, to whom she can offer only her abilities as a bridge player.

Dr. Rose Franzblau, columnist in the *Chicago Jewish Post and Opinion,* among other newspapers, frequently deals with questions of the "older" divorce. She believes that a divorce in later years, after a long marriage, "raises many more questions than in the case of younger couples." On the surface, the decision to separate is easy to make: "Now that the children are married and on their own, they have done their duty as parents and can at last break away from the mate for whom they have no respect and love." But this rationalization hides a briar patch of conflicting emotional ties and secret yearnings. The father will generally be cast in the role of the villain by the grown children. The mother will resent socialization between the father's new friend or wife and any of the children. As one distressed daughter reported to Dr. Franzblau, "Our eldest son spent a weekend at my mother's house and she recounted every detail of her 40 miserable years with my father. He was shocked. She pestered him about my father's visits to my home . . . Now she refuses to visit her other children's families if she finds out I will be there." The complexities of in-fighting at three generation levels are almost impossible to unravel, and the apparently easy dissolution of the grandparents becomes a nightmare for a dozen or more people.

Other sociologists believe that this pattern has changed substantially in the last few years of women's liberation. Dr. Jessie Bernard echoes a common feminist feeling nowadays when she says, "So many women used to be frightened by divorce dreariness. But now they see their friends leaving home and surviving. Women are not aging the way they used to, and are finding out that living alone and being free can be great." Dr. Alfred Messer, director of the Family Institute in Atlanta, agrees: "There are growing numbers of women who are no longer socially and economically dependent on the male, aren't afraid to say 'my husband is a bore,' and feel perfectly free to move on to another relationship." Yet Dr. Messer had to report, as a result of a three-year study of 40 couples whose marriages were terminated after from 18 to 42 years, that most of these older marriages seem still to be held together primarily by the presence of children at home. Three-fourths of the couples were divorced only after the last child had left home. There is also disagreement among the experts about how emotionally free a woman is nowadays even after the children are gone and after the first blush of the liberation movement has passed. Dr. Esther Fisher, marriage and divorce counselor with the American Foundation of Religion and Psychiatry, senses that the old pressures are still very much at work, and that the new freedom brings hardships of its own: "Women aren't all that marriageable at that age, and finding a new man still is difficult. If a woman isn't working, she might feel a certain futility and, of course, money will be a problem. Sexual attitudes have changed considerably, too, and some women may have trouble adjusting to the new standards."

Whatever the increase in later divorces may mean for older women, there is no question that the increase is a striking phenomenon even against the background of the upheaval of American marriage. More than one out of four divorces that now occur involve marriages of 15 years duration or longer. One out of six involve marriages of 25 years or more. According to the Bureau of the Census, the pre-World War II figures for these same categories were infinitesimal. In spite of the current problem of young marriages and divorces, the statistics on divorce are being fattened far more by dissolutions of older marriages.

Jurate Kazickas, writing in the *Long Island Press*, reports that "divorces that tarnish silver anniversaries" are often twenty years too late. Among the women she interviewed were two fiftyish types who adjusted quite easily to their new found freedom, regardless of the problems of lack of companionship and security in a male world. Their only regret was that they had to wait half their lives to discover that they were unhappy in marriage. "From the moment we decided to split," says Flory Barnett of Manhattan, "I came to life . . . I was shocked out of my mind as to how well I could manage. I mean, I never knew I could be smart, competent, and successful. It was a new me I never dreamed of." A story that could be repeated in the same words by thousands of women was told by another Manhattanite: "We grew apart. We simply had nothing to say to each other anymore. I wanted to leave him 15 years ago, but he begged me to stay and I did. But love had been dead a long time. When my two sons went off to college, I left." Already employed, she had no trouble surviving alone, and didn't even ask for alimony. On the subject of male companionship, she is typically realistic about her chances for a permanent and satisfying relationship, and perhaps there is a little cynicism in her rationalization, "The world has too many things to offer and enjoy to get tied down again. Marriage is something everyone should experience once, and I've tried it already, thank you."

The older divorced woman tends to reap unexpected benefits from her new assessment of herself: she tries harder. Knowing she has to depend on herself, including her appearance, she watches her weight, her makeup, her clothes. Frequently, she becomes an object of envy to her married friends. "I run into women I knew from the suburbs and they all say I look fantastic," confesses a New York promotional consultant. "But the way they say it I know they'd be happier if I looked dead. They look so terribly old and tired and, I think, 'There but for the grace of God go I'." Another says, "At least now my wrinkles are just from age and not from worry and unhappiness."

There are conflicting theories for the apparent sudden increase in older divorces. The dilemma of aging, which we have discussed here and in Legacy VII, may be part of the answer but it doesn't satisfy the sociologists. Men who start worrying about their graying temples and who sport the clothes of the younger generation have always been around. The "frigid forties," in which one or the other spouse seems to lose interest in sex or turns totally toward being either a homebody or a "company man," have not been so altered by sexual liberation to explain the rash of late divorces. Kenneth Kruger, director of the Family Service Agency in Fort Lauderdale, Florida, believes that there may be an historical explanation: "We've probably seen more divorces in that age group over the last ten years because of the World War II marriages." The problem of quick marriages on leave and after returning from three or four years abroad may now be coming home to roost. Yet the increase in divorces is across the board, with some of the most dramatic changes occurring in marriages that were formed before World War II.

Our survey has turned up additional evidence that older marriages that fail are usually just shells of an earlier relationship. The sentiment repeated again and again is the wish that the divorce could have been seriously considered ten or twenty years earlier. It seems to us, therefore, that the major reason for the increased incidence of older divorces may simply be the general openness and honesty that have become widespread in modern personal relationships. There need be no conclusion that we are more tolerant or forgiving or permissive in our relationships; but it is undeniable that the taboos of communication of an older generation have been brushed away. Divorces that could only be discussed after years of agony and frustration are now apparently being entertained, for better or worse, at the onset of marriage problems.

Divorce for the older couple may shock onlookers, but it is generally smoldering for years before it reaches public attention. Dr. George P. Dunleavy takes a more optimistic view of such marriages: "As a marriage counselor, my job is not to save marriages, but to help the couple decide if it's worth saving. I would say that 75% of the middle-aged people I see need only to learn to relate . . . to learn how to grow with one another."

We have been left with the legacy of believing that at forty or fifty years of age we can be drastically different people than we were at twenty. Some people grow, some stand still. Some are content to settle for security and love, some want prestige and wealth. The question to be answered is this: if a couple grows apart, wasn't there a time perhaps early in the marriage when they failed to see—or chose not to see—the opening of the chasm?

The Mercenaries

The depredations of lawyers have been a persistent theme of English literature ever since William Caxton, the first English printer, departed from the text he was translating to cry out, "Alas! and in England what hurt do the advocates, the men of law, and attorneys of the court inflict on the common people of the realm . . . how turn they the law and statutes at their pleasure; how eat they the people, how impoverish they the community!" (*The Game and Play of the Chesse,* 1475.)

The sentiments of many opponents of current divorce practices could hardly have been put more forcefully. Typical of the protest of men's groups is a pamphlet and book entitled *How Lawyers Have Made a Racket Out of Law,* by William Thomas. His point of view is underlined by such titles as "Justice Under Free Enterprise—The Great Delusion," and "Wake Up! America, You've Been Had!" Another is headlined "The Shakedown Racket In Our Divorce Courts." Newspaper headlines read: "Divorced Men Cry Discrimination." As we have seen, most of the protests are aimed at a fee system that encourages a wholesale handling of what should be individual cases; and when the cases are obviously not ordinary, there seems to be a tendency to churn up controversy just to multiply fees. The protestors see a conspiracy of lawyers and graduates from the legal ranks: judges. Yet the mercenaries in a divorce battle are not limited to the legal profession, nor is the profession always the hideous villain that it has been pictured.

The following description of an encounter with a divorce specialist is the unhappy vision that has been created by years of experience with the adversary system, now on the way out. The writer is a woman, the magazine is the Canadian monthly, *Saturday Night*; the protest against mercenaries is not limited by sex or nationality.

The attorney, a flamboyant type recommended by a friend, "took no notes but listened as a cat does, eyes closed, ears perked. He could help me, he said, and, further, he would help me . . . He would now pass me on to his assistant who would arrange details of paying the retainer. . . . He shot his cuffs, pushed a buzzer, shook my hand, said it was a pleasure doing business, and bared his excruciatingly groomed teeth in a feral smile." Time passed while installments were paid on the retainer and grounds for divorce, such as a "little innocent adultery," were discussed. Then suddenly, the new divorce laws went into effect, and a court appearance was set. "The great man would appear himself . . . he said we'd have a brief refresher on the facts of my case. He seemed confused over several details, others he failed to recognize at all. I took a large breath and recapped at length." Finally, with a few quick questions before the judge, the divorce was granted. But the story isn't over. "A few days before the three months of waiting on the final decree was up, a letter arrived from the great man. He had been temporarily suspended from the bar on some minor thing and . . . would I kindly pay forthwith as he needed the cash. The figure mentioned was several hundred dollars more than we'd agreed upon."

Many lawyers, of course, have proved this example to be an exception rather than the rule in their practice. On balance, the attorneys we have talked to in the course of completing our survey have been conscientious and in some cases grossly underpaid. They must often put themselves through the same stresses and conflicts which they have to deal with in their clients. They must act as counselors when that isn't their training. Yet usually they are the only visible villain when costs start to mount and things begin to go wrong.

Veronika Kraft, of the law firm of Kraft, Lefcourt & Libow, is in favor of simplified divorce laws to reduce "the distrust and paranoia that sometimes crops up between a client and a divorce lawyer." The firm has gone so far as to devise a do-it-yourself divorce packet, the kind that bar associations initially tried to ban as illegal. A new generation of attorneys, such as Arthur I. Hirsch and Howard Bass, subjects of a story in *Town & Country* magazine, deliberately search for the human factors in a divorce case. "A good divorce lawyer is someone who helps a person in this situation straighten out his life," says Hirsch. "I push for counseling right away," Bass adds, "so the client can go through the whole divorce process with a clearer perspective and then, when it's over, be in a better position to reconstruct his life. . . . sometimes the couple calls off the divorce." Despite the fact that new, simplified divorce laws will cut heavily into the income of some attorneys, the reaction of most seems to be that expressed by Kraft: "The main problem is that the legal machinery for divorce is ridiculously complicated."

Some of the complexity has been taken out of divorce proceedings simply by reducing the "waiting period," and lawyers readily concede that this sort of simplification does not weaken their roles. In Virginia, attorney John C. Towler has campaigned for several years to get legislative approval for a one-year separation as evidence of a marital failure. The effect of this idea is that the waiting period is less a punishment than a demonstration. Like California's former six-month requirement, the separation period establishes no-fault evidence that the union no longer exists. Lawyers must still deal individually with cases where adultery, incompatibility or some other ground is alleged—in which circumstance no waiting period is required.

Foreign governments, tourist boards, and even travel agents have perennially tried to share in the divorce market by offering attractive competition to divorce codes. Recently, the out-of-state divorce mills have had to concentrate their efforts on those states where the laws are still relatively complex. Predictably, their most vocal opponents are not legislators or churchmen, but those who stand to lose from the shrinkage of the local market—divorce lawyers.

In Memphis, Tennessee, a typical furor developed over the promotional activities of an independent travel agent, Charles Harrelson, Jr., who offered a package three-day tour to Santo Domingo for the divorce-bound. The $750 fee included air fare on Pan American World Airways, accommodations, and the services of a Dominican Republic law firm. Several Tennessee attorneys, including a representative of the Memphis Bar Association and the state attorney general's office, sought to undermine this venture by challenging the legality of divorces arranged by a travel agent. A spokesman for the American Bar Association could not quite put his finger on the legal fault of such an arrangement, but simply said, "For any divorce obtained in a foreign country, there will always be a little bit of a question." Yet the divorce decrees come back bearing the signature of the minister of foreign affairs in Santo Domingo, authenticated by the seal of the American Consul. And a local attorney specializing in Mexican divorces accurately predicted the outcome of the rhubarb: "There is not a thing they can touch him with."

The fear of a state becoming a divorce mill has been the primary deterrent to more liberalized divorce laws—and those lawyers whose interests are at stake readily summon up visions of Reno-like operations in any discussion of the subject. A federal panel of three judges recently used this reason to deny a class action suit in New Mexico, which contended that the six-month residency requirement was unconstitutional. At the other extreme, lawyers have often used technicalities in the law to prolong the granting of a final decree—either to force the payment of fees or to pressure a haggling couple to agree to a property settlement. In Ohio, Domestic Relations Judge Francis Pietrykowski brought this curious phenomenon into the public spotlight by granting final decrees not properly documented by the attorneys involved—and pointing out that some of them had been "open" for as long as four years. The attorneys had failed to file a "journal entry" of the judge's decision to grant a divorce, in some cases because of simple negligence. The "divorced" parties could easily have been involved in bigamy without knowing it.

The question of what constitutes a reasonable time of residency in a state before a divorce can be granted was tentatively defined on the "high" side by a federal panel in Rhode Island similar to that cited before in New Mexico. There it was ruled that the state's two-year requirement was "unconstitutional on its face." The statute, which was enacted in 1956, was finally successfully challenged in 1973, and the Family Court has been enjoined from enforcing it since then. Again the "divorce mill" argument was raised, this time unsuccessfully. In Missouri, the residency period was lowered in 1973 to 90 days, without any apparent rush to the state by prospective divorcées.

There is no clear relationship between residency requirements and the legal complexities of a divorce—despite the fact that "divorce mills" tend to offer the best of both as far as the couple is concerned. The Missouri code, in attempting to tighten the reins on husbands, seems to have added to the corps of mercenaries between husband and wife. Marriage counselors, including those in the court's own domestic relations division, now play a secondary role to attorneys, if any at all. Wage assignments and garnishment to insure alimony payments and child support can now be ordered by a judge. In effect, financial matters as well as other individual concerns have been taken farther out of the hands of the couple and placed under the authority of the court.

The adversary system, and the evils caused by its complexities, are on the way out. Certain broad interpretations of what "no-fault" means are coming clear—such as the fact that most states are following Iowa in agreeing to a one-year residency requirement without fear of becoming divorce mills. But the problem of policing court decisions and keeping voracious lawyers in hand will always vex the couple who only wants to "get out" as honestly and fairly as possible.

Most people approach divorce as a once-in-a-lifetime decision. They don't want to be experts in the intricacies of the law. But they want to be protected. As a divorcée in Hawaii noted, "Why not publish a booklet on what to expect in one's own state—listing the names of the attorneys who specialize in the field? This would prevent finding out after it is all over that the reason your attorney did such a lousy job is that his specialty is real estate. . . . And it is about time attorneys were required to put their fees in writing. Too many of us naive people have been ripped off. . . ."

In short, *familiarize yourself with the local and state laws, and retain an attorney only after all other alternatives have been explored.*

Legacy XI
Children in the Balance

No other area of the divorce question attracts so many platitudes as the "children of divorce." This theme is a surefire subject of newspaper columns and women's magazine features. Yes, children are affected by divorce or separation. But the volumes of material that have been written year in and year out don't seem to have advanced our understanding of the question beyond the mundane fact that "children of divorced parents face special problems."

Yet there are significant questions, some quite practical, some more theoretical, which have not been answered adequately:

1. How and when should a child be told his (or her) parents are divorcing?

2. Is it worse to be raised in a "broken home" or in an unhappy home?

3. Is the finality of separation the worst shock in a divorce?

4. At what age is a child likely to be adversely affected by divorce?

5. Does the lifestyle of the parents have much to do with the reaction of the child to divorce?

6. At what age does a child deserve legal aid in a divorce?

7. Do "children of divorce" fare any worse in the long run than progeny of an uninterrupted marriage?

Everyone seems to assume that the answer to the last question is obvious. Dr. Lee Salk, a syndicated columnist who writes regularly on the emotional behavior of children, says simply, "Divorce generally causes children anxiety and concern because most children love both parents and feel somewhat caught up in the midst of an incompatible arrangement." Others are more pragmatic, like New York attorney Diana DuBroff, who emphasizes the sheer physical hardships, including starvation, which "divorced children" must face. Dr. John B. Reinhart, director of the psychiatry department at Children's Hospital in Pittsburgh, found in extensive studies that "children of divorce are harder to manage, sadder, angrier, more possessive, noisier, restless, and pushy. They kicked, they hit, they occasionally bit. Some couldn't play anymore and seemed quite depressed." At the same time, Dr. Willard Abraham reported that "constant bickering, tension, coldness, and hostility [on the part of the parents] may be more detrimental for children than not having one of the parents around all the time."

Who's right? Both. It seems clear that *it is the failure of the parents, rather than the failure of the marriage,* that harms the children. Indeed, a "friendly" divorce can actually improve the development of the child. Dr. E. James Anthony, Professor of Child Psychiatry at Washington University School of Medicine in St. Louis, says, "It is therapeutic to see the friendly reconciliation of battling parents. When a divorce is not an absolute rupture of a relationship, when the parents remain fairly close, the children are helped to preserve the idea of a good marriage, which they themselves can achieve some day."

The answer to Question (7), therefore, is that children of divorce probably do *not* fare any worse in the long run if the divorce is the honest answer to a marriage problem. *Parents who fail to make an early decision to divorce, when divorce is the best answer, may well do more damage to their children by remaining together.*

This answer leads directly to a central fact about children which has surfaced in many forms, in many circumstances: they are not to be underestimated. Dr. Anthony recalls in this connection, "I had one mother come to me to ask how she could keep her children from suffering from her coming divorce. When I talked to the children, I found that they knew what was coming, even though they had not been told. They had assessed those looks between their parents." Some believe this sensitivity comes to the fore in children in the pre-teen years. Dr. Joseph Fischhoff, director of psychiatry at Children's Hospital of (Detroit) Michigan, states that children between 6 and 11 "probably have the most traumatic reactions to divorce because they are learning to bury their feelings. The younger child will fight, cry, whine, and return to bedwetting. The teenager may feel lonely and sad but will be better able to cope with his feelings. . . . " Dr. Anthony sees children affected by divorce at a far younger age: the *pre-school* age: "A child intensely attached to one parent, a clinging, fearful child who does not think well of himself, is especially likely to be hurt. So are handicapped and adopted children, and youngsters with chronic illnesses."

Dr. Anthony's pre-school age group and Dr. Fischhoff's pre-teen-age group exhibit much the same symptoms: stomach pains, sleepless nights, headaches, bedwetting, nausea, vomiting, clamming up, and hyperactivity. Though they haven't settled on the same age parameters, both doctors, among many other researchers, agree that society has neglected the rights and awareness of the child for far too long. At a recent family law section symposium of the American Bar Association in Washington, D.C., panelist Doris Jonas Freed summed up the legacy of our judicial system: "A child is not in all respects considered a person." Others on the panel noted the similarity between the condition of women until recently and the present plight of children, "both outgrowths of the chattel system of feudal times." They called for two radical reforms in the courts' handling of children: to offer legal aid to children, and to allow them more of a voice in their own custody. Attorney Henry Shain of San Francisco feels that judges are already leaning in this direction, even though there is no particular age of consent for a child. Ralph J. Podell, a circuit court judge of Milwaukee, Wisconsin, believes that "those courts that are not appointing independent attorneys for children during adoption proceedings are going to find those proceedings tainted one day." Dr. Freed, of the American Bar Association panel, has authored a bill of rights for children along with law professor Henry H. Foster, Jr., of New York University, who predicted that kids "damn well better be heard and we had better give them the right to independent counsel during divorce proceedings."

Many judges are not sure children would benefit at all from a greater say in their parents' divorces, but they are sure the suggestions of "kids libbers" are impossible to implement. Chief Judge Jean J. Jacobucci of the family court of Brighton, Colorado, scoffs at the idealistic notions of the ABA panel: "I hear 20 cases a day and there simply isn't enough time or money to appoint an independent counsel for every minor in custody cases. Most of the kids I talk to say, 'I love my mommy and I love my daddy and I wish they'd get back together.' That's no help at all. A child just can't make an adult judgment."

Psychologists would amend that to read, "A child can't make an adult statement; adults need help in deciphering a child's judgment." Perhaps if money were available for the child, instead of it being in the hands of the husband (and occasionally the wife), it would be more feasible for attorneys and judges to spend the time listening to the child's plaints. This is part of the idea behind divorce insurance, the chief program of NOISE (National Organization to Insure Support Enforcement). When NOISE founder Diana DuBroff explains her brainchild to people, the immediate reaction is skepticism: how can you insure against something which the beneficiaries can cause to happen at will? But further examination makes the idea seem highly practical. The beneficiary is the child (who is then no longer a burden for mother or father). If a couple go to the trouble of having a child, there is little likelihood they will get a divorce merely to reap the benefits of the policy. First, the other high costs of divorce make this an unprofitable venture; and second, the greatest benefits accrue when the child reaches college-age and the policy pays off like an annuity. Some of these ideas are embodied in policies being offered by American International Group as "family security bonds."

But it will be a long time before anything as practical as this—and as necessary as automobile insurance—becomes mandatory for any significant part of the country. In the meantime, the psychological threats to the child are an area of concern that can be dealt with as a matter of better education and understanding. Dr. Fischhoff and Dr. Denis Walsh, of the University of Michigan, list the common *faults* in taking children over the rapids of divorce:

1. *Blame the child for the breakup.* Instead, as Dr. Lee Salk says, when the divorce is first announced, at the very same time the child must be assured it is the parents' problem alone.

2. *Keep the child in the dark.* Instead, if another woman is involved, say, the child will know or soon find out: so the husband must come clean from the start.

3. *Berate the other parent.* This is a major fault because hatred expressed for an adult can easily become hatred for a child, the child reasons. Apart from this selfish attitude, the disturbing effects of open hostility on the child are reason enough to avoid the outpourings of bitterness.

4. *Play the lollipop game.* This is a form of using the child as an indirect attack on the other parent, in contrast to the direct attack above. [See Legacy XII.]

5. *Change the child's physical surroundings.* Instead, realize that the environment adds to the drastic change of the loss of a parent-in-residence.

6. *Avoid outside help.* It is not surprising that divorce counselors would caution against this; but competent professional advice can never harm the parents, and offers the child an outlet when his lines of communication may be reduced to a single adult.

Surprisingly, one of the most natural tendencies of divorced parents—to treat the child in more adult terms—has its serious dangers. According to Dr. Anthony, the most destructive aspect of divorce for the child is not the loss of a parental figure for identification, but the *forcing of the child into the missing role.* This is most often displayed in the "You're the man of the house, now," or "You're Daddy's little helper, now" kind of fuzzy reasoning or amateur child psychology. In effect, the remaining parent chooses the child as a source of identification with the absent spouse. The result is often a reenactment of the divorce, or an intensification of the bitterness toward the "villain" who has left the family circle. Dr. Louise Bates Ames, of Baltimore, Maryland, points out that while "parents do not divorce their children" and the child can be assured of the support of at least one parent, *the child must not be pushed headlong into an adult role.*

There are now more than 9,000,000 children living with divorced parents, and probably 20,000,000 including separated or deserted parents not formally divorced. They have experienced the finality of divorce or estrangement. Their presence in our society is a legacy that will be with us for generations. It's time we accept that legacy and deal with it responsibly.

The Price of Custody and Support

There is no economic law which says a man's income will continue or increase after a divorce. Yet alimony and support figures are based on such a supposition. There is no legal framework to assure receipt of alimony and support payments. Yet the courts rely on the regularity of such payments in handing down their judgments.

This, in a nutshell, is the reason why both sides in a divorce often claim to be the victims of "blind justice." Justice is blind to the vagaries of the economy and to the wanderings of spouses.

The price of alimony is accordingly set either at impossible levels—to insure some kind of a payment—or else at paltry levels—to encourage some kind of compliance. In either case, divorce courts (variously called Family Courts, Domestic Relations Courts, and various kinds of Welfare Department Courts) have exacted a tremendous cost in hardship on wives who believed that support payments could be enforced like traffic tickets, and on husbands who thought that debtors' prison was outlawed in the Constitution.

The scandal of ducking child-support payments reached such proportions that Senator Sam Ervin, Jr., in pre-Watergate days, sponsored a bill to make nonpayment a federal crime. As it is, a delinquent father, out of a job or disenchanted for any other reason, can easily skip out of the state and thumb his nose at the form letters requesting payment. A destitute wife must either hire a bill collector (at the cost of a retainer in advance) or pursue her ex-spouse through the toils of civil law (either cumbersome legal aid or ambulance-chasing attorneys). As of now, Senator Ervin's proposal remains merely a good idea, while an estimated 50% or more of absent fathers are substantially behind on or oblivious of their payments.

Practices vary from county to county, and from state to state, but generally there is no good machinery to guarantee alimony and support payments at the local level. In Cook County, Illinois (Chicago), for example, a mother who fails to receive a child support payment has her first recourse at the Circuit Court. Judges David Linn and Robert C. Buckley of the divorce division of that court estimate that they spend half of their time on the bench in hearing child support cases. On the other hand, in Wayne County, Michigan (Detroit), failure to make payments for child support is flagged by a computer printout, and the sheriff's office is immediately authorized to bring the offender into court. The difference is that Wayne County collected almost $40 million last year for the benefit of the children of divorce, while Cook County, with a larger population, was able to recover only $3.5 million through its public aid legal service, or less than 9% of smaller Wayne County. The Detroit system is unfortunately still a rarity.

Central to the problems of enforcement of support payments is the fact that nobody can make any economic hay out of such cases. A typical husband caught in the legal flytrap, John Preston of Chicago, recounts his turmoil: "I am not willfully in contempt of court, but all the judge can ask is, 'Did you pay the money?' I could petition the post-decree court to decrease the payments, but if I could pay the lawyer's fee to do this, I could pay the support. It would cost $500, and I'd rather pay that in child support than to a lawyer." Preston had tried to start a new life after his divorce by going into business for himself; now he's barely making expenses. "All the court can do is decide I'm in contempt of court, just like someone who skipped bail, and send me to jail." John Preston was sentenced to 30 days in jail, and given a month's reprieve to do something about it.

There is little incentive for lawyers to become involved in such cases, and surprisingly there is hardly any incentive for local government to raise its eyebrows. As Patricia Moore stated in a series on the support problem in the Chicago *Daily News,* the cynical fact of political life is that the city or state office which keeps tabs on traffic violators "is rich in patronage and power. The money collected from traffic violators goes unto government treasuries and helps support these same local governments. Child support merely feeds and clothes kids."

The rule of thumb of the legal profession is that there is money in divorce but only work in collecting *after* divorce. A financially abandoned mother relives *Catch 22:* She calls the local Legal Aid Society and finds the agency no longer takes nonsupport cases. Referred to Public Aid offered by the courts, she is told the payments must be three months in arrears before it is worth their time to act. Perhaps the state Bar Association can help; no, they have no referrals to offer for the amounts involved. After a year of waiting, scrimping, seeing her plight build to desperate proportions, she goes to a lawyer picked out of the telephone book. "You're out of luck kid," he says, "if you don't know where he is, you can't get any money. You should have acted right away, when he was around."

Parents who skip out on their support or alimony payments are not necessarily proved by that fact to be irresponsible. Yet this logic seems to have a sinister influence on judges who must decide both custody and support agreements. If a judge "gives" the children to the mother, he seems likely to place a punishing burden on the father, as if to insure that his first decision was the correct one. Yet the fact is that failure to continue payments to the spouse is related more to economic conditions than unwillingness to pay or lack of concern about the welfare of the children. It is well known that a major strike in Detroit or Cleveland or Los Angeles floods the courts with nonsupport cases. A California study in 1973 found that the father's previous occupation and income level had little to do with payment habits: even fathers on welfare struggled to make payments as long as their economic condition did not take a sudden dive.

Men have typically been the villains in the custody-alimony-support controversy, and even now the case of a woman charged with delinquency makes headlines. The Milwaukee *Sentinel* devoted major space to a story in early 1974 of a woman who failed to keep up support payments for her child living with the father. The local Welfare Department, which brought the complaint, stated "There's only been a handful of cases like this." In Ravenna, Ohio, a husband making $880 a month was awarded $50 a month child support for the five sons he received custody of, even though his ex-wife was earning only $350 a month as a secretary. But the public as well as the courts are beginning to realize that there is no longer any monopoly on parenthood by mothers, or on livelihood by fathers. We can now accept the pathos of the parent in this example as not unbecoming a father: "She was a good mother. I don't know why she left. The boys keep asking when she's coming home, and it's hard to answer the little ones."

The growing realization that men and women can no longer be treated as types—providers and homebodies, respectively—has forced the courts to look afield for counsel in custody and support cases. In ruling on the obligation of a parent to provide a college education for a "divorced" child, a Family Court in Rhode Island held that "it is necessary that an advocate should be appointed who will make decisions for the best interests of the child, and consider his health, personal, and educational needs."

Such an advocate is seldom employed in family courts in most states. A model for the rest of the country is the Domestic Relations Court in Nashville, Tennessee, presided over by Judge Benson Trimble in divorce cases involving children. He is to a child custody case what a pediatrician is to a child medical problem. In 1973 the *Nashville Tennesseean* reported on the special steps Judge Trimble took to insure he had "all the facts" in a typical custody action.

The star of the story was a Mrs. Marshall Barnes, described as a "special master" for the court, whose job it is to investigate all aspects of the divorce action which have a bearing on the child's future welfare. When an investigation must prove which parent is preferred for custody, Mrs. Barnes studies the "physical set-ups," such as where each parent lives, the bedroom space, which parent claims to want the child, who will stay with the child if the "winning" parent works, hygienic conditions in each abode, social practices of each parent, and so forth.

"Judge Trimble expects me to visit the school and find out how the child is getting along, and how adaptable he is to the programs and school work," the *Tennesseean* quoted Mrs. Barnes. "These are the facts I find out and take back to Judge Trimble. He studies them. He has rules to go by. He has waiting periods before decisions are made."

Few of the precautions insisted on by Judge Trimble showed up in the hundreds of cases investigated and reported on in the latter half of this book. The *Tennesseean* noted that Judge Trimble's court was the only one of its kind in the state—in itself a tragic disclosure. At the time of this writing, we must report that few other attempts at thorough investigation of the *child* and his or her needs precede judicial action.

In spite of the efforts of several pressure groups, such as A.D.A.M. in Chicago, court practice in divorce cases involving children is changing slowly, if at all. More depressing is the apparent unwillingness of parents to insist on higher standards from the courts. Mrs. Barnes' own testimony, after studying hundreds of cases for Judge Trimble's court, reveals the selfishness that pervades emotionally charged custody hearings. "Yes, personally I think couples are thinking first of themselves. I have talked to them privately. When they realize what the waiting period is going to be—what they stand to lose—they have been known to come full circle."

The price of custody and child support is high—in dollars and in emotions. We have inherited that price from a male-dominated society, with its fixed roles for husband, wife, and child. For the couple with children, the changing dilemma of custody is the most serious of all.

Legacy XIII
Is It Worth the Price of Submission?

Alimony and support are commonly confused by anyone who has never really had to consider divorce. But when the time comes, the difference becomes quite clear. The crux of the distinction was underlined recently when a Midwestern woman was awarded custody of the children but had to pay alimony to her ex-husband.

Alimony remains on the law books more as a punishment or a reward, a matter of vindictiveness or successful gold-digging, than as an economic necessity. As we have seen earlier, the price tag on divorce is seldom appreciated until after the fact. When alimony looms large in that price tag, one party typically must make the decision whether to *submit* to the wishes of the other. When alimony is not a big factor, it is usually a divorce by mutual consent.

The payment of a settlement has come to mean a humiliation for the woman involved, either because she has been "discarded" or "left behind" or is presumed to have "taken" her "ex." At the rarefied atmosphere of six or seven figures, however, ex-wives apparently are shielded from such feelings; and the dollar amounts are more interesting as gossip-column items than as sociological grist. For example, we find it hard to relate to the $11.5 million which Reuben Fleet settled for in 1945; the $6 million Winthrop Rockefeller handed over in 1954; the $9.5 million Edward J. Hudson paid in 1963; or the like amount Dean Martin parted with a few years ago. But when an old friend collects a few thousand plus a few hundred a month, we can sense the meaninglessness of this "tribute," and the constant stab the monthly payment, even though welcome, must inflict on the emotions of the recipient.

Alimony is a legacy which is on the way out. The evidence seems to be that this passing of a dubious custom can only benefit women. Paradoxically, "women's libbers" have clung most tenaciously to the money, while piously disavowing the principle of the thing. According to Burton Rudnick, an eminent New York divorce attorney (and consistent with our survey findings), there are two prominent reasons why one party "asks out" of a marriage: another woman (adultery—in which case either the man or the wife forces the issue), or a new career for the wife (immaturity when married). In both cases, according to Rudnick, the woman is practically forced to seek alimony to protect herself at all. When that necessity ceases to exist, alimony and the sense of submission that goes with it will be things of the past.

In the meantime, the debate goes on over the rights and wrongs, the abuses and the benefits, of the rapidly changing institution of alimony. This is not the place to draw conclusions; perhaps the best way to view the passing parade is to listen to the combatants:

Paying alimony is like sending oats to a dead horse.
                                        —Anonymous male

Alimony is back pay . . . severance pay for a job that is not recognized.
                            —Elaine Livingston, NOW leader

Remove the bounty and you'll see the divorce rate hit a plateau.
                        —Sidney Siller, co-founder, Committee
                                for Fair Divorce & Alimony Laws

If we want to keep our women soft, silent, and supportive, then we've got to protect them.
                                —Burton Rudnick, attorney

Twenty years ago women took support for granted and, twenty years later, these same wives are called parasites. Many of the current statutes are unfair to wives who became wives twenty years ago.

—Doris Sassower, president of
the New York Women's Bar Association

You can't think a man's ghastly and at the same time think of him as someone on whom you depend. Alimony is a condition of dependency.

—Diana DuBroff, founder of N.O.I.S.E.

How free is a woman when she lives on an ex-husband's money?

—Patricia MacDonald Fahey, writing
in Town & Country

Divorce is a luxury only the rich can afford.

—Judge David Linn, Chicago

You can't ask for so much from a man that he loses his incentive to work.

—Donald C. Schiller, attorney

When a man doesn't want to pay, he won't pay. You can bring him to court and bring him to court and you still won't get that money.

—Betty Dwyer, NOW leader

If I hadn't taken that settlement, I would have had to work, and I would never have had the time or the money to do the things that interest me.

—Socialite, after receiving a
large cash settlement

I would like a job like Barbara Walters!

—Charlotte Ford, after divorcing
Stavros Niarchos

In theory, alimony should make it possible for the woman to maintain the standard of living she experienced during her marriage. In fact, the amount generally falls far short of that goal. Infrequently, instead of alimony the husband is required to make a cash settlement at the time of the divorce.

—Lucille Duberman, Marriage
and Its Alternatives

The cash settlement is the tidiest way out of marriage.
                                                    —Fahey

Alimony NOT Welfare.
                                          —NOW slogan

Women say they come off the worst, and the men claim they have been taken. It's not so. Both come off worse than before and it's not the court's fault.
                                          —Judge Linn

Alimony is no more certain than a roll of the dice in Las Vegas, and the consequences to the litigants may be just as disastrous as they are to the gamblers.
                                          —Marya Mannes

Will the Equal Rights Amendment groups and supporters also work for the elimination of alimony to capable women?
                    —Louis J. Filczer, president A.D.A.M.

If you do not get a complaint from time to time about the amount of your fees, chances are you are not charging enough.
        —Attorney, writing in the *American Bar Association Journal*

Divorce is creating a new poverty class—of divorced women.
                    —Louise Raggio, Dallas attorney

· *F. Lee Bailey was my lawyer and I still lost.*
                    —Nat Denman, A.D.A.M. leader

And so it goes. When the dust settles from the current overturning of divorce legislation throughout the country, alimony will have taken on a new name: support. Like the current child support concept, "ex-spouse" support will probably be based on a more realistic consideration of need and capability of working than on arbitrary divisions of property. Alimony has never been a pleasant word for the husband or the wife, and as a concept it has been little more than an ad hoc measure given our economic system. As alimony fades out, or changes to another form under another name, it will no longer present the dilemma that it has traditionally raised at various stages of a marriage: Is she marrying me for my money? Is he sequestering assets before he sends me packing? Can I afford to free myself from this unhappy union?

But it hasn't faded out yet.

After It's Over

"What happened to notions like commitment, responsibility, and an even more discredited concept, suffering?"

This is a divorced man talking, a man willing to put his case in a daily newspaper under the headline, "I am one man, hurting." His hurt is compounded by the sense of having been betrayed by a society—and a person—who didn't believe marriage was worth the work and the suffering that are part of being a human being. He also makes it clear that he is one of almost two million men hurting, from divorce, each year. The theme of the suffering of divorced people has been a popular one lately—with books alternately telling the divorced that it can be an enlivening experience, and that it can be a suicidal experience.

Divorce therapist Mel Krantzler, himself a "victim," tried to make a case for "creative divorce." And apparently a lot of people were willing to believe that a disaster could be turned into an enriching opportunity. But what are the facts about post-divorce? Can we make any sense out of the confusion of freedom and alienation, hurt, upheaval, and contentment—contradictory emotions that follow in the wake of divorce?

We know that we can dismiss at a glance the petty grievances. Dr. Walter Alvarez writes a typically sanguine column in major newspapers about family problems. He advises that "the strain (of divorce) causes inattention while driving, resulting in accidents, traffic tickets, and other difficulties;" and "people with chronic diseases like diabetes and epilepsy should tell their physicians about their divorce problems." The doctor seems to be interested only in the *surface* of a deep-seated problem, for he closes his analysis by saying, "When they came to me, I would have to spend enough time talking with them to earn their confidence and eventually learn of the sorrows of a divorce or of some other trouble that was the cause of their physical symptoms. How much less expensive for them, and less time-consuming for all of us, if they had told me right away that they had a personal turmoil which was tearing at their heart." What is this turmoil?

It is becoming much easier to bare one's soul, even in public. Novelist Dan Wakefield did it effectively in *Starting Over* (Delacorte Press, 1973). Here he talks about more difficult matters than traffic tickets. In the end, he comes to a familiar plaintive theme: "Holidays are the most psychologically torturous times of the year. I can feel Thanksgiving coming on like a migraine." Twice married, twice-divorced, he admits to having found a "detachable" relationship. But the past, which includes children, won't let go.

After it's over, neither party to the divorce wants to be alone. This is the crux of the matter. And the legacy we have been left with is that it's just too bad for the guilty party, usually assumed to be the man. Let him take the consequences. If the consequences are loneliness, so be it. "There's nothing quite as lonely as a bachelor pad," confessed a Daytona Beach, Florida man. "Men cry, feel, and bleed inwardly just like women; but they are supposed to pick up and go on as though nothing has happened."

Contrast this with the picture jealous married men conjure up: "I've been divorced for nine months and I'm really having a ball. I'm a real swinger. I go out every night with a different girl. I come and go as I please. Finally, I have some money to spend on myself. I'm really living it up!" Then the speaker sighed, and looked straight in the interviewer's eyes: "I feel lousy. I miss my children and, I hate to admit it, I miss my wife. . . . I even miss fighting with her." We see this experience duplicated over and over, with men and women, in the interviews reported in the final part of this book.

Perhaps because men are not supposed to be as emotionally

affected by divorce as women, a wave of sympathy has swept over the revelations in print of troubled men trying to recover from the shock of separation. Call it the "Mel Krantzler syndrome." It reads the same in a book or in a Sunday tabloid: "I looked around at the dingy orange walls, the dirty windows, the packed boxes. Well, this is it! I said to myself. I tore open the first box I could get to, and started to arrange my books, put away the pans and dishes. Anything, right then, to keep from thinking."

Then the confession turns to life as it was before separation, the gradual drifting, the shock of divorce. The hopelessness of an alcoholic/divorcée/unemployable hits bottom, then rebounds: "Things are mending. I have painted my apartment, and have found a new job at a bowling alley. At this moment I am drinking iced tea, and think it'll be my drink from now on. . . . A new and better life lies ahead." (From an interview with Randall Rogers in the *Seattle Times,* 1973)

So far, all this is predictable. But lately, a new theme in the lament of the divorced has surfaced. As one Albert Martin, of Stamford, Connecticut, confides to a newspaper reporter, "At some point, doesn't a counterrevolution have to take place? Don't the excesses in favor of the individual have to be met by a consideration of the needs of families? Doesn't a psychology which hands a license to a wife to do what she wants to in these times —fueled by the themes of women's lib—have to be called to some accounting of responsibility?"

This is the complaint that will be heard more often in coming years. There is now a villain in the story: women's lib. Women are sacrificing social and familial concerns to achieve their individual rights. And women are getting the best of both worlds. They can reap the same old benefits of alimony and cash settlements, and not miss out on male companionship because of the "in limbo" status of a living together arrangement. Alimony is supposed to stop on remarriage of the wife, in most cases; the laws confer an unexpected financial blessing on nonmarital cohabitation. Men's groups have another name for it. Real or imagined, these are the complaints.

A Chicago judge says that a woman's characteristic emotional response "may breed greed . . . not because she really wants money, but because she wants to punish her husband." But whether an ex-wife wants to hurt her "ex" or not, the mechanism is there to be used for her advantage. And this is another major point for men's divorce groups: men don't want to pay for the happiness and success of their ex-wives, and they especially don't want to pay for the happiness and success for their ex-wives' paramours.

The emotional impact of divorce is almost totally defined by the pressures, or lack of pressures, of society, of parents, of economic equals. As the steam has been let off all these pressures in recent years, so the emotional distress of divorce has slackened. What happens after divorce for the younger generation is now not much more than what happens after a teen-age boy-girl summer infatuation fades into the fall. In this sense, the dilemma for the unhappily married has been palliated. Parents now understand. Peers take it for granted. Society moves further and further aloof.

We will see fewer stories in the general press, in years to come, about the oppressive emotional punishment of divorce. *It just isn't there.* "Friendly" divorces are on the rise. Over the past thirty years, divorced partners were able to say, "Of course we're still friends," muttering under their breath, "You son of a bitch." Now the last part of that communication can go. The venom of divorce has been cut in the impersonality of legalities, as we have seen. Although experts still hover to collect their retainers, the parties to a divorce are taking more of the substance of it into their own hands; the emotional shock has been cushioned by the knowledge that divorce is something they can handle as well as they do their own income tax.

Blame in divorce has gone, and with it, both psychological and physical punishment. Our culture says that suffering is an unmitigated evil. But we have yet to discover whether we have mitigated the grief of personal estrangement by easy divorce, or just driven it to some other corner of our psyche.

PART TWO

Our Emerging Solutions

The temptation is irresistable to approach divorce reform with an analogy in hand. Those who favor easy divorce or serial monogamy compare marriage with choosing a career: you keep trying until you find something that fits. Those who think the fault lies with easy marriage say that the prospective bride and groom should have to study and take examinations, as you would if you wanted to cut hair or drive a car. Those who favor no-fault divorce point out that if you don't need a trial to get married you shouldn't need one to get unmarried. Because marriage is some sort of a contract, you can make just about any point you want by comparing it with other contracts.

A contributor to the "Letters" column in *Newsweek* took issue with the idea that the marriage contract can be wiped away because it isn't working well: " . . . . I have a car I bought two years ago and still owe two years of payments on. Bessie (the car) and I got along fine at first, but as she grew older she developed annoying squeaks and began to miss on the hills. I think I ought to be able to drive Bessie back to the dealer and dump her. I don't think I should be liable for the rest of the payments I agreed to two years ago because—well, because it just didn't work out between Bessie and me. I'm sure the vast majority of thinking car owners agree with me, but alas, we lack an effective lobby . . . . "

Too many of our decisions, public and private, are based on analogies. Marriage is like a banquet—but every now and then one needs to try a new dish. Or divorce is like a graduation. Or alimony is like severance pay. Alimony is like making payments on your car—after it's been wrecked. Marriage is like sitting in a bathtub—after you get used to it, it's not so hot. The other side of the story is "But this is different." And parties to the debate are right back where they started.

The essential questions that have to be answered about marriage and divorce, on the contrary, are *unique*. There is nothing else in human experience quite like these two basic institutions.

Just in the last few years some profound changes have taken place in these institutions. At the moment, it is difficult to see a pattern in the emerging solutions to our domestic ills. But what we are witnessing is the beginning of a vast sociological experiment; to use a more serious analogy, the laboratory of the family is seething with activity. The pressures of tradition, inhibition, religion, restrictive legislation, parental and social control, and plain ignorance are now being taken off married couples. There is now an unprecedented freedom in the land to marry or not to marry; to sleep around and to set up a living together arrangement; to use contraceptives; to abort; to have two or more families; to have a childless marriage; to have as many children as the pocketbook will bear; to mate-swap; to have a homosexual or bisexual relationship; to be a parent without ever having married; to have a family of mixed races; to marry across racial and ethnic lines; or to court and wed a virginal childhood sweetheart, raise a traditional family, and eventually celebrate a silver wedding anniversary.

Ten or fifteen years ago, books were being written about the future of the American family, the family in crisis, the coming patterns of society. But we can now witness the future all around us. *Never before in history has mankind had the opportunity to test his beliefs and expectations about society so thoroughly against experimental facts.*

Some of the reports are in. The following pages summarize what is being printed, what is being talked about, and what is being done in this great social experiment. The reports are based

on newspaper and magazine stories, radio and television debates
and talk shows, and especially person-to-person interviews across
the country. This is what is happening; these are the solutions—in
the sense of what is being *resolved*—for better or for worse.

Is Commitment Still The Key?

The first wave of experimental marriages (arrangements, relationships, or whatever one wishes to call them) has now passed over
us, and we are left with remnants of promising ideas and the
pieces of abandoned projects. The impression grows that whatever is worthwhile in marriage also exists and is the motive force
in some other guise in all of its experimental imitations. And a
central part of what is worthwhile is that elusive notion of
commitment.

What we call the "imitations" of marriage fit into several
categories. There are the "unmarrieds," the group marrieds, the
divorced marrieds, the life-stylists, and so on. Many divorce
counselors point out that a certain form of marriage goes on long
after a divorce becomes final. Psychiatrist Clifford Sager notes that
when people "continue to behave in a terribly hostile way, they
aren't really divorced. These are mutually destructive ways of
continuing a relationship that no longer exists. In a divorce, there
is a sense of being abandoned. . . . Then anger gives way to grief,
frustration, depression. These are all attempts to gain what has
been lost—until one sees that it can't be done. And then one
begins to repair." The commitment to another person can express
itself as either love or anger—anger when a legal or formal threat
to the commitment appears. Until the commitment ends, the
"marriage" remains some sort of a reality.

Even in the "civilized" divorce, the apparent absence of outward emotions is no sign that the commitment has ceased. Dr.
Tilla Vahanian, a New York marriage counselor, describes a "Let's
be friendly" divorce situation as generally unhealthy. A wife
confides to the counselor, "I would like to make our marriage
work, because I think the children should have a father at home. I
love my husband, but if he wants a divorce, I will respect his

feelings. I love him enough to want to make him happy . . . . " The counselor asks, "You say you love him, yet he wants to leave you. How can you not be angry?" According to Dr. Vahanian, the repression of expected anger leaves the commitment unresolved: "Until people confront their real feelings, they've got unfinished business. Everything may seem fine, fine, fine—and then all the pain comes bursting in on them the first night they're alone."

In the late '60's, group marriage in several variations was popularized by Robert Rimmer's *The Harrad Experiment*, and other books searching for a marriage structure involving more than two people. In an extensive interview in *Psychology Today* (January, 1972), Rimmer attempted a rationale for bringing more people aboard a single connubial bed: "It is an adventure and we have very little adventure in our lives. It enlarges your life. Four people are not so likely to turn on television as an escape . . . With the breakdown of the family, people will realize that they want to live with more people than the nuclear family—they just want to be with somebody." Another sample: "Watch an average monogamous couple out for an evening. They go out to dinner and they eat in virtual silence. Put four people together and you force verbal exchange." The thinness of these explanations underscores the fact that group marriages are little more than an attempt to give some sort of formal sanction to adulterous or bigamous relationships (as they are traditionally known). The essence of communal living, where it has been successful, is a well-understood commitment of *short duration*: while going to school, moving around the country, changing careers, fighting depressions of any substance. There are few *sustained* examples of a structured "Bob and Carol and Ted and Alice" relationship. Anthropologists who have discovered communal living arrangements in primitive societies have effectively demonstrated the universality of the normal marriage form—by showing us the rarity of the exceptions.

The commitment that exists in a commune, in addition, would seem to be far more demanding than that of a conventional family. The sharing of common facilities, the division of duties, and the delicate balance of emotions between four or more adults in a group marriage can only multiply the already complex conflicts that exist in the nuclear family. Rimmer quotes with approval the speculation of psychologist Abe Maslow that the pressures for limiting the population might "cause couples to merge just to share children." This implies some sort of innate need in adults to live with or raise children—an anthropological thesis that is certainly debatable. Rimmer flatly states that "If a couple limits itself to two children we have the nuclear family with all its defects. A nuclear family of husband and wife and one or two children is a very tenuous relationship." But he doesn't tell us why. He sees the traditional family on the way out, the one "where aunts and uncles and so forth come together." He caps his sociological report by saying, "I know at least a half-dozen couples involved in two-couple arrangements."

The living together arrangement is, of course, far more of a reality and a vital development in current sociology than is group marriage. Its popularity seems to hinge on the very opposite extreme of commitment that is required in communal arrangements. The "life-stylists," as we might call them, for this is the phrase that comes most readily to their lips in various forms when describing their point of view, seem to exhibit the traits of a conventional monogamous union—but without the "possessiveness" and legal overtones of a formalized marriage. It is the form itself which they believe stifles the marriage.

The typical gossip-column interview is not likely to elicit a serious evaluation of the LTA. Peter Bogdanovich says, "Living together (with Cybill Shepherd, by the way) is so much sexier." Actress Brenda Vaccaro makes a more pointed comparison: "I lived with a guy for two years and was married to him for three. I was made to feel more responsible after we were married with that little bit of paper—another contract. When you're married you try harder. Who needs that kind of pressure? It should be a spiritual thing." Michael Douglas, son of Kirk and the man Brenda is currently living with, emphasizes the difference in psychological pressures between marriage and the LTA: "Why is it that if you live together, everybody thinks in terms of day-to-day, whereas when you're married, it's got to be forever?"

Most of us would agree that living each day for itself is a romantic and philosophical ideal. From another point of view, the need to prove oneself to one's companion on a daily basis is psychologically far more demanding than having the security of knowing that a balance of the good times and the bad times is all that matters. We have interviewed scores of couples who chose marriage after a brief period of living together. When we asked them why they chose to be "tied down" to each other and to the state, by law, they did not give the expected answers about pleasing the parents or saving on taxes. In a variety of expressions, they seemed to be saying that the formality of marriage was psychologically reassuring. They wanted their friends to know they were making a commitment to each other; they wanted the community to know; they wanted a way of saying to each other "we really mean to live together and grow together until the unforseeable happens." Indeed, it is this rediscovery—perhaps "recollection" is a better word—of traditional values and their implied significance to future relationships which is the bright, shining light at the end of the "New Morality" tunnel. We reprint here an article by Judith Nielsen in a very aware and socially perceptive weekly newspaper in California's Marin County, The Pacific Sun. It is entitled, "I Now Pronounce You Old Man and Old Lady," and its message speaks for itself:

I NOW PRONOUNCE YOU OLD MAN AND OLD LADY
by Judith Nielsen

Five years ago, Deryk Hunt was sharing his bed with three women and selling underground newspapers on street corners. Today he drives a Cadillac, is devoted to his wife Louise, and is investing in a business project which will hopefully guarantee them a yearly income of $10,000.

Deryk is 31, Louise is 23. They are part of a yet uncompleted cycle of their generation which has brought many people from the free and loose days of sporadic lovers for the permanence of marriage; they deserted a "hand-to-mouth" existence for the pursuit of material goals. Their transformation may prove to be prototypical of the children of the Woodstock age. The couple felt that Yippiedom and all it implies is a thing of the past, and that most of their friends will eventually follow suit.

But what does "follow suit" mean? A discussion with Deryk

and Louise indicates that to follow suit is to discover that the traditional values you once rejected are too deeply imbedded to be rejected for long. In the following interview, they explained the process of that discovery and its implications in their lives.

Why did you marry?

DERYK: *We lived together for two years and marriage seemed like the only step left. I got to a point where the relationship just had to go in another direction and there were only two possibilities—to leave or get married.*
LOUISE: *For me, it was really just a solemnization of what already was.*

Has marriage changed you?

DERYK: *I feel more confident in the future now.*
LOUISE: *I think we're a lot kinder to each other. We try to be kind so the other person won't have any regrets about marrying. For instance, the house has been a lot cleaner since we married. We're more organized and business-like. We believe in making an effort to be kind. When you're just living together you don't have to make that effort because there's really nothing to lose if it goes wrong. It's almost an ego thing, too—you're glad the other person married you and you want to show appreciation to him for it.*
DERYK: *The drag with living together is that you can't make any plans for the future. As our joint plans began to evolve, we realized we'd better make some sort of plan for the future or else forget plans altogether.*
LOUISE: *I think our marriage affected other people more than it affected us. People ask us now: "How's married life?" Which is strange to me. I mean they never used to ask "How's single life?" When we were living together, people, especially our parents, ignored it. Now my mother-in-law makes jokes about our sex life. Before, it was a taboo subject in spite of the fact they all knew we were sleeping together.*
DERYK: *There are practical reasons behind the marriage, too. First of all, we both reached what we thought was about the right age. Secondly, Louise got out of school. As soon as you're out of school, your life becomes more settled and has a chance to take a*

direction. That had an effect on why marriage suddenly looked feasible.

Has your attitude towards marriage changed?

DERYK: I've come full circle. As a child I thought it was inevitable and natural. Then the flaws and built-in stumbling blocks became more apparent than the joys. There was a time when the middle-class family was held up to mass ridicule—and I was one of the ridiculers. Then came the experiments. Since I was 21 I've lived with about eight women. I once lived with three women at the same time. We all slept in the same bed. I was faithful to them but they had other lovers besides me. There was no sense of permanence and no interest it it either. Then, relationships were expected to have a definite end. Then I got tired of ends.
LOUISE: I thought marriage might be in my future but then I went to college and got interested in a career and I also discovered feminism. It convinced me a good man is hard to find. I never lived with anybody because I thought it would be an infringement on my freedom. I thought I'd end up washing socks and also it would be so awkward if someone else interesting showed up. I thought that those living together were bigger suckers than those who were married because the emotional breakups were so traumatic.

What made you want to live with Deryk?

LOUISE: Eventually it seemed ridiculous not to. We'd go to his house and there would be moldy granola all over because he hadn't been home in so long.
DERYK: It was the granola that did it.
LOUISE: My books were getting scattered between his place and mine and it was all just inconvenient. When we moved in together I wasn't thinking of marriage. But after awhile I couldn't see a separation either. My parents had a lousy marriage in which I feel my mother got the shaft, so I was wary of men and of marriage.
DERYK: I think the marriages that have resulted from people living together will be better than marriages have been. My father told me he married my mother because he had never been alone with her and wanted to know her better. But what if you don't like

what you come to know? It seemed to me they used to do things backwards. So when we rejected the idea of marriage we were really just rejecting the traditional form of marriage. I used to think it was alright for the old folks but not for the new folks. Now I think the new folks just need something better.

LOUISE: In a sense, marriage brings more of a sense of freedom than being single does. You can stop worrying about whether the other person will suddenly take off and you can begin to live your life like there's something organized about it. It might sound strange to my single friends but I feel freer now than I have in the past.

DERYK: Her interest in feminism put me through some changes that made marriage look better. I was determined not to be like my father. He dominated my mother so much that she never learned to drive and never had the furniture she wanted. I decided not to marry so I wouldn't be like that until feminism raised the point of view that there was an alternative. Marriage took on a new meaning.

LOUISE: I almost felt guilty when I decided to marry. I felt like I was betraying the cause and was a little hesitant about telling women friends about my decision. Then I realized that liberation and love were not incompatible.

DERYK: I had tried everything but marriage and I suppose it was all that was left.

Why didn't the other experiments work?

DERYK: Well, for one thing, the scene just began to pass and I didn't have the energy to follow it. Often times, it didn't work for basic financial reasons. I began to understand where I fit in society and it was depressing to remain constantly on the out-fringes of society. I guess I realized that I was basically too traditional for that.

LOUISE: I didn't love all my lovers like Deryk did. I had sort of a cavewoman complex—I call it my Don Juanita phase. I was getting drunk and dragging them off to my apartment. It was so silly. I began to feel too much like the Cosmo girl. There comes a time when you realize it's simply not worth the effort. Especially after the idiotic conversations that took place in the mornings.

DERYK: When things start to take shape in one area of your life the other areas seem to follow suit.

LOUISE: Things started to gel. I finished school and was interested in a career. Deryk and I began to buy things together and our finances started to flow together. I was chronologically older, too, which is important. The other times I would say I was in love, I was simply too young to consider marriage.

DERYK: Students drift around but when you plan to begin to become conservative which fits with the definition of the middle class.

LOUISE: Also, I wanted children. There are too many challenges to raising children alone.

Do you regret your previous life styles?

DERYK: I lost too much time and energy the other way. I was distracted from thinking about what I should have been thinking about which was basically what to do with myself career-wise.

LOUISE: I was too young to have lost time, but it did make me cynical about men and I regret what I did because I deserved better. So many times it turned out to be just sex-for-the-sake-of-sex without any communication on any other level. I used to think that was fine but after you experience a relationship where both people are giving emotionally, anything less is unsatisfactory. Someone said it's like settling for hamburger when you can have steak and I suppose that's right.

Are the friends you knew then married now?

DERYK: Almost all.

LOUISE: Very few, yet.

There are ex-Jerry Rubin devotees cloistered in little offices all over the country. There are upcoming young business people who once dressed in jeans patched with the American flag. And there are couples like Deryk and Louise who are trading communal water beds for one double bed.

To all of them, the way of life they once rejected has suddenly taken on a new meaning. To Deryk and Louise that meaning is clear and simple:

The sixties were exciting but they offered no sense of direc-

tion. They offered a sense of freedom but no security. The whole decade may go down as one of the most stimulating, adventurous, and unfulfilling eras of our time.

So the debate goes on. The formality that rankles some couples reassures others. The legal bond that one woman needs to "protect herself from desertion" is to another woman a way of offering herself more completely to her loved one. Your choice? Its basis is as unique as your personality.

It is symptomatic of the chasm between the points of view here that some LTAers cringe at the phrase "loved one" and would like to keep unknown quantities like love out of any discussion of a relationship. Artie Shaw once said of his relationship with Evelyn Keyes, "I'm incapable of jealousy and I want the same freedom I give her. You marry someone who sings 'The Man I Love' all day—forget it! We see each other when we want to. In her I've got something important—friendship and trust. I'm very concerned about her. Is that love? I don't know what the word means." Evelyn, for her part, would throw all of the trappings of marriage out the window: "I worked very hard not to have children. . . . If I had any I couldn't have lived the life I've led. Falling in love, that silly thing, is the worst reason there is to get married. . . . Marriage belongs to another era."

Tony Perkins and Berry Berenson are typical of LTAers who react violently to the attempts at setting up codes and formulas for the nonmarriage relationship. Whether or not they can define it, they rely more on the traditional concepts of love, romance, infatuation. "It's love, absolutely," says Tony. Berry gives in to an old-fashioned sentiment: "I'm very domestic these days, but then I never really had anyone to do this for before." The highest compliment she can pay to her arrangement is, "What we have today is as good as a marriage."

Marriage continues to be the standard of comparison for man-woman relationships, the cumbersome, flawed institution which most of us pass through, cling to, or shy away from. What is it that impels people to strive for some kind of a continuous sharing of intimacies, of aspirations, and even of domestic drudgery? As we have sketched it above, there seems to be no common theme of children, careers, sexual satisfaction, love, or social concern which runs through all the forms of cohabitation . . . except commitment. This broad concept is easier to see in particular critical moments of a relationship: it shines in the eyes of bride and bridegroom at the altar, just as it surges through a community of young people combining their talents to create a self-sustaining farm.

The "unmarried marrieds," as Eunice Fried has dubbed those who live together part-time, resist the commitment of any of the types we have considered. In a sense, they are an older generation of daters; they're going steady. Their credo is expressed by New York psycholanalyst Barbara Koltuv: "No matter how liberated a woman is, she still has need for a love relationship. But there is no reason why it need be a full-time relationship." Other observers have created the phrase "singular person" to describe the type of indivudual who is most likely to want an intermittent arrangement with a person of the opposite sex. The singular person supposedly is self-contained in his or her interests, work, and goals. Typically they are women from 30 to 60, widowed or divorced, who are "faced with a new challenge in life." They maintain their own addresses, spend several evenings alone by choice each week, yet want to "complete their reverie by adding one special man." Few of these cases, which are reported regularly in the women's magazines, from which the above quotes are taken, have actually been documented. They may be the fantasies of inventive editorial staffs. They are all too believable and predictable: "They have a strong sense of responsibility and disdain for the superficial and meaningless affair." Their attitudes toward marriage spring from a previous unsatisfactory experience or from the necessities of the marketplace and the society in which they live: "We do so much together," one fiftyish woman is quoted, "without pressure and with a sense of humor. Marriage would bring up so many different problems. They could probably be worked out, perhaps with a flexible open-marriage kind of arrangement. But would marriage with its nitty-gritty pettiness change all the loveliness we now have?"

One is tempted to throw up one's hands over the proliferation of catch-words that attempt to substitute for serious analysis. Are you a "singular person" or a "dual person?" "Sometimes the singular period of one's life happens in youth, often in middle age. But it can happen also in the later years," we are assured, which is not very much of an objective guideline. About all we are left with, after dozens of anonymous interviews, is that some people opt for an unmarried commitment, without permanently shared living quarters.

Los Angeles divorce attorney Marvin Mitchelson, noted for his representation of celebrities as well as hard-nut causes, put the case clearly for a more basic understanding of the realities in marriage and in all its competitors: "I believe the trend of the law may and should move away from the classic concept of marriage and divorce. It's time to have a national set of principles relative to marriage and divorce and *to emphasize the relationships between people that produce obligations and responsibilities, rather than just licensing.*" (Emphasis added.) Mitchelson's point of view is understandably affected by the fact that he gave his interview to support his contention that his client, Michelle Triola, was entitled to a divorce settlement from the man she had lived with for six years without benefit of a marriage license, actor Lee Marvin. "Divorce without marriage" was the way the newspapers headlined the court battle, but the concept is that marriage and divorce, by whatever other names should be handled not as legal transactions but as human realities. Mitchelson argued, "It costs $3 to get a marriage license. I say that for a $3 license one should not have different rights than one who has the same relationship but doesn't pay the $3." The Marvins' agreement was oral, but none the less binding, according to the suit. "They agreed to combine their efforts and earnings, and would share equally any and all property accumulated. It was further agreed that plaintiff and defendant would hold themselves out to the general public as husband and wife, and plaintiff would further render her services as a companion, homemaker, housekeeper, and cook." Lee Marvin married his childhood sweetheart, Pamela Feely, in 1970, still supporting Michelle. When the support stopped, Michelle sued for half his assets. Mitchelson, who in 1963 won a landmark decision before the United States Supreme Court on behalf of indigent defendants in an appeal case, had hoped to be the first to bring a divorce case before the country's highest tribunal. But the case was settled out of court.

The acknowledgment of a commitment, which is inherent in the application of law, is the common thread which is helping to bring together the apparently diverse and contradictory forms of "coupling." If legal bonds create psychological problems, perhaps society will learn to dispense with the legalities and simply honor the commitments. The upheaval in our divorce laws is a direct manifestation of this principle, in reverse: where there is no commitment, where the marriage is dead, the hurdle of legalities posed by divorce has been knocked down.

We are fast approaching a point in marriage law where the codes are symbols of commitment, but not the commitment itself. We are reaching a balance with the purely symbolic religious ceremony, which is somewhat more appetizing than city hall.

The Contracts of Coupling

Here is a document sent to us by one divorced person in our survey. Show it to your spouse, or boy (girl) friend and see what reaction it elicits.

AGREEMENT

This agreement, entered into this _____ day of _____ by _____, Husband and _____ Wife, who reside at _____ · _____, _____.

WITNESSETH

That the parties hereto are husband and wife, having been married to each other on _____, in _____, _____, County _____ in the state of _____.

That each party has made full and complete disclosure, before a witness, of all debts and obligations contracted before marriage and of any and all property possessed before marriage.

That although they anticipate a long and happy married life together, the parties nevertheless desire to enter an agreement expressing their state of mind about the marriage contract, the appropriate rights and duties of each party, the proper care and custody of any children who may be born to this marriage, and the settlement of property upon the death of either or both parties, or upon dissolution of this marriage.

NOW THEREFORE, in consideration of the love and affection which they hold for each other, and of the mutual promises herein contained, the parties hereto agree as follows:

I. Debts and Obligations

a. Each party shall be responsible for any and all debts and obligations incurred prior to this marriage, and shall not look to the other party for payment or assistance.

b. Each party shall contribute to the family economy to the full extent of his or her ability; and insofar as is consistent with the statutes of their place of residence, each party shall be responsible for his or her own personal debts and obligations after marriage.

II. Property

a. Separate

1. Each party shall be deemed the sole owner of whatever property he or she possessed prior to the time of marriage.

2. Each party shall be deemed the sole owner of any property he or she acquires by gift or inheritance, from whatever source, during this marriage.

3. Any property acquired during this marriage, unless specifically acquired as mutual property, to be used and enjoyed by both parties equally, shall be considered as being solely owned by the party whose principal use it was acquired.

4. All property acquired principally for the use of one of the parties shall remain forever separate. Each party shall have full right to enjoy, and to dispose of his or her separate property, and each party agrees to execute any documents which may be required to effect any transactions involving the separate property of the other.

b. Mutual

Any property acquired for the use of both parties shall be owned equally by both parties. Disposal of such property, when necessary, shall be done in such manner as will insure equitable division of proceeds to each party.

III. Wills

Each party shall, within thirty days from the date shown hereon, execute a will making the other party sole beneficiary, and providing for the care, custody, and support of any children who may be born to this marriage.

IV. Divorce or Dissolution of Marriage

a. As between the parties hereto, the sole ground for divorce or dissolution of this marriage shall be its irretrievable breakdown.

b. No action for Divorce or Dissolution of this marriage shall be filed within sixty days of separation. During said sixty days waiting period, there shall be at least one meeting, attended by both parties, with a qualified marriage counselor.

c. In the event of divorce or dissolution of this marriage, neither party shall demand payment in the nature of alimony or maintenance.

d. In the event of divorce or dissolution of this marriage, the care and custody of any children which may be born shall, insofar as is consistent with statutes then in effect and the orders of any court having proper jurisdiction, be as follows:

1. All children under six years of age shall remain with the mother.

2. All children over twelve years of age shall have the right to choose the parent with whom they wish to live.

3. Male children between the ages of six and twelve years shall remain with the wife, unless she declines.

4. Female children between the ages of six and twelve years shall remain with the husband, unless he declines.

5. The parent not having custody of a child shall be permitted to see, visit, and be with that child at all reasonable times, as agreed between the parties hereto.

e. In the event of divorce or dissolution of this marriage, each party shall have the right to take his or her own separate property, as hereinabove defined.

f. In the event of divorce or dissolution of this marriage,

either party may buy the interest of the other in any mutual property.

g. Any money received from the sale of any mutual property shall be divided equally between the parties hereto.

h. The terms of this contract shall remain in force, regardless of which party originates the action for divorce or dissolution

V. Conclusion

Nothing in this contract is intended to permit either party to avoid duties imposed by statutes of any state wherein the parties hereto may reside, or to avoid the orders of any Court having proper jurisdiction.

Executed in two copies, each to have the full force and effect of an original, this the day, month, and years first shown above.

_____   date _____
witness

_____   date _____
witness

The idea of a contract has often been substituted for the somewhat more elusive concept of commitment. Under the law, marriage is indeed a contract. Exceptions and additions to the standard terms expected by the state must be filed at the recorder's office in city hall, and there you will find the agreements between aging financiers and their nubile nurses, between the Jackies and Aris of the world, and between dowagers and their consorts—to protect the relatives in the will, to keep capital accounts separate, or to remove anyone's fears about gold-digging. These are the standard "antenuptial" agreements, dealing entirely with finances. In recent years, there has been a wave of interest in other types of contractual changes to what the state expects in a marriage (it expects the couple to live together, provide the number of children society needs, and generally maintain a stable family unit). Women's liberation groups seem to take the greatest delight in plumbing this new opening in the legal bulwarks. In all seriousness, Norman Sheresky and Marya Mannes included a long, detailed sample contract in their book *Uncoupling: The Art of Coming Apart*. The contractual stipulations they recommend, like those of Susan Edmiston in *Ms.* Magazine's premier issue, seem diabolically designed to take a marriage apart. Frankness and full disclosure are admirable and can be promoted by the form of a contract; but preoccupation with set times and dates and minute observances only compounds our present legal complexities and provides excuses for scuttling the whole contract.

Russell Baker has provided the *reductio ad absurdum* of the "women's lib" contract in a piece on *Ms.* in *The New York Times.* He envisions a divorce petition beginning, "Wife the plaintiff disposeth that husband the defendant did, in willful violation of the contract, refuse, neglect, and fail to tuck in Jennifer and read her 'Peter Rabbit' on Sunday night, the 26th of December last, wherefore. . . . " Further complications ensue when the kids get the message, and in response to male chauvinism exercise their expression of their rights, *kiddismo.* When the father arrives at his child's bedside at 3 A.M., with the explanation, "I know you called for Mommy, Jennifer, but this is Sunday night, and under the terms of my contract with Mommy it's my turn to get up when you call," to avoid a confrontation over the parental contract the father's lawyer might call Jennifer's lawyer and threaten to get an injunction unless she settled for her father at her bedside. The only real justification for such specific contracts is that they get communication started. They should not be drafted or approached as legal instruments. But they do serve to bring up such subjects as birth control, careers, children, housing, travel—*before* the wedding, when most couples shy away from serious discussion in the belief that their love would wilt in the hairdryer of reality.

Typical courting customs and post-marital practices, moreover, provide ample opportunities for solid nonlegalized agreements. In *The Love Contract* (Van Nostrand Reinhold, 1973), a half-dozen forms of contracts are explored in the courting-marriage process, which are ordinarily neglected as having no permanent value. For example, the exchange of letters between lovers (before or after marriage) is a ready-made occasion for discussion of subjects difficult to handle face-to-face. Love poems, now a rarity, can convey a sense of basic values that no legal document can define. The discussion of movies, books, art, or even the day's news provides a springboard for revelations of one's attitudes toward virtually any subject likely to be covered in a formalized document. But the couple must realize they have this open-ended opportunity.

Men and women previously divorced have been the chief advocates for a more complete disclosure of views and assets in entering marriage. Many have been badly burned financially. Attorney Louis Nizer points out that 94% of all divorced and widowed women, according to the Department of Labor, are employed. Further, a divorced woman at any age and regardless of the number of children "has a better chance for remarriage than a single woman has for marriage." She approaches the marriage decision with greater independence and assurance. She is aware that even the custom of taking her husband's name cuts into her sense of individuality—in some cases—and usually works against her financial position. If she happens to be in the social register, she will experience the further discrimination of being tagged with all her former mates—whereas their marital record is not revealed.

Marriage contracts in a formal sense will probably come into greater and greater use as a way of avoiding the hazards of costly divorce settlements, rather than as a checklist of grievances designed to give either party grounds for divorce. Antenuptial agreements have been tested successfully in states like Colorado, where attorney Richard O. Pittam says: "they work well in court. They substitute for the permanent order. . . . they save a lot of grief." Howard Rosenberg, head of the Denver legal aid service, reports that agreements for division of assets are not agreements to get a divorce, but to keep property separate. "They're not legal in some states," he says, "in other states, some aspects have legality." As more cases come to court, it can be expected that advance agreements on the terms of a divorce might eventually become part of the "fine print" in the list of "I do's." As it is, the way assets are divided is an accident of the state you happen to be married in or live in—common law states or community property states (as well as a function of the mood of the judge, the craftmanship of the attorneys, or the whims of a jury—all poor substitutes for social and moral justice). Why not give couples the option of three or four reasonable alternatives, to be checked off like a shopping list at the time of marriage? "At the time of divorce," says attorney Frank Bryant, "emotions are running too high for rationality."

Grief Insurance

The temptation to use analogies in wrestling with the problems of divorce has led to other interesting ideas for taking precautions against the failure of marriage. Living together arrangements are essentially precautions against either emotional involvement, the possibility of being "trapped," or the entanglements of divorce settlements. As we have seen, Diana DuBroff has pioneered what is generally called "divorce insurance"—a method of paying alimony and child support when marriage breaks up. Just as there is a built-in paradox in antenuptial agreements (are they really *divorce* contracts?), it seems ironic that a couple would take out an insurance policy, to protect the wife against a husband who would skip out on alimony payments, at the very moment they are making vows for better or for worse, for richer or for poorer.

Partly because of this emotional inconsistency, Ms. DuBroff has placed most of the emphasis on the hardships on children when a father thumbs his nose at court orders. And state Senator Donald Halperin of Brooklyn has also taken this tack in the New York Assembly, where his proposed bill legalizing divorce insurance died in committee. He now favors a long-range study of the problems of child support. Judging from the response of insurance companies, there are so many practical problems—such as couples who might divorce just to spite large corporations—that the whole concept may be a decade away from any final form.

But analogies continue to intrigue the advocates of insurance. Australia and New Zealand have a state-sponsored system. Life insurance was only a pipe dream 75 years ago, and now it is considered a necessity. Health and disability insurance are newcomers. Unemployment insurance was once thought to be impossible because it would encourage people not to work—just as divorce insurance might make it profitable to split. How about the high risk of divorce? As we have seen, when the divorce rate is figured the same way the unemployment rate is arrived at, divorce comes off favorably. We are already paying a large part of the cost of divorce insurance, it is argued, in the welfare rolls swollen by abandoned mothers and children.

Private companies have not rushed into the divorce field. The risks are a potential nightmare, and there is no easy "handle" for the whole concept. Again the analogies: "I can only compare it to Van Cliburn having his fingers insured," says John O'Connor, executive secretary of the Casualty Insurance Companies of Massachusetts, admitting that only someone like Lloyd's of London might tackle the job. Payson Langlely of Aetna compared it to crime insurance in high-risk locations, but "the government is subsidizing crime insurance."

One New York company that has made a move, on the urging of Ms. DuBroff, is really offering a bond—"like a Christmas Club, but with interest." But this sort of thing is already available as an ordinary annuity policy or a U.S. Savings Bond—the payor never gets out more than he paid in, except for interest. So far, only Metropolitan Life has worked out a genuine insurance plan—with premiums of $28 a year and benefits of $100 a month for three years after a divorce.

Despite this discouraging picture, the gap between the need and the solution is narrowing. The grief of children of divorce going to school hungry, of young mothers trying to live on welfare, of women struggling along on menial jobs that pay little more than the cost of their babysitters—all because of the high deliquency rate in alimony and support payments—is documented in every daily newspaper with regularity. The public is aware of the problem. But is insurance a likely solution?

It seems to us that there is an increasing body of evidence that changes in alimony requirements, better enforcement, antenuptial agreements, and basic financial protection for wives from the beginning of marriage will come much sooner than "grief" insurance. Not the least of the good ideas that have come along in this direction is that of a Portland, Oregon high school student, who visited a divorce court as a class project and proposed to the

Domestic Relations Division that prospective brides and grooms should be required to spend a morning in such a court. Such an eye-opening experience might be far more beneficial than a blood test.

But if education and contracts and laws fail, the last resort will undoubtedly be some form of shared-risk insurance under the Social Security program, with payments too low to encourage easy divorce and high enough to establish a floor for reasonable living conditions. What will always remain in the residue of a marriage is the conviction that what two people put into an enterprise must have been of some value. There must have been a sharing. Whether it was for better, or for worse, both parties must continue to share that outcome. Until all people are placed on an equal dole, alimony will be a fact of post-marital life.

The Debate Over No-Fault

"Somehow the process of legal change is like divorce—fear of the unknown deters action even where one's strongest feelings make one know what the action should be." New Jersey attorney Theodore Meth was commenting on the delays in his state's divorce reform laws. Yet his "strongest feelings" about what is right for marriage and divorce in New Jersey are not universally shared. At this writing roughly half of the states have leaned in the direction of "no-fault" divorce, while a debate goes on in a good many of the rest.

There is little disagreement over the major feature of "no-fault." Story after story in national magazines has primed the American public to the idea that the abuses of old divorce laws flowed directly from the adversary system. Now that either fault or guilt no longer has to be proved, the acrimony, the deceit, the litigious delay and costliness of contested divorce cases are things of the past. People forced to live out miserable marriages because of the spitefulness of one party ("I won't give you a divorce") or because of the financial disaster of a court battle ("I can't afford six weeks in Reno") can now gain their freedom. We have discussed in detail the hideousness of our legacy of having to set up an adultery scenario or poison the children against one parent. A Washington legislator announced, as his state entered the no-fault rolls, "We've put a lot of private detectives out of business."

However, the simplicity of the no-fault idea masks a lot of popular misconceptions. For the person who is eagerly eyeing the no-fault route, the following facts should be considered carefully:

1. There are two main avenues to no-fault divorce. Both are embodied in some state laws; one is sufficient to achieve the liberalization of splitting. First, there is the abolishing of all grounds for divorce except "the breakdown of the marriage" or some similar phrase. Second, while keeping some traditional grounds for divorce, there is the adding of an all-purpose ground: separation for a given period of time. Obviously, if the separation period is too long, it is not a very useful ground. Therefore, a state's divorce law can be *relatively* no-fault.

2. The availability of a no-fault divorce does not eliminate considerations of relative guilt or responsibility from divorce proceedings. Judges must still take into account, in most cases, who was responsible for the breakup—in establishing alimony and custody, for example.

3. California is generally given credit for being the first no-fault state, but Delaware actually had a no-questions-asked ground for divorce—after a separation of three years—as long ago as 1958. Recently that was lowered to six months, then put back to one year "to keep Delaware from becoming a divorce mill." Accordingly, Delaware has been an excellent case history in the relative success of the liberalized laws.

4. Divorce is on the increase dramatically in the most lenient of the no-fault states, but this does not mean that the law is creating unwanted divorces. When the New Jersey divorce laws were relaxed in 1971, the number of decrees promptly doubled—but no one bothered to find out if half of these couples might not have gone out of state if the New Jersey laws were stricter. As Mike Barrier of the *Arkansas Gazette* put it in an excellent summary of the changes caused by no-fault: "The idea that laws can lure a couple into divorce—or, alternatively, save a marriage by forcing the couple to stay together—is farcical. What really matters, where preserving marriage is involved, is getting couples to take

marriage seriously before they get married, and no law can accomplish that."

5. Alimony has been weakened and eliminated in many cases by no-fault laws, but not in a significant way in proportion to the total number of divorces. According to a study in the *Hastings Law Review* ("Women as Litigants," by Stuart Nagel and Lenore J. Weitzman), alimony was generally awarded in 10% of all divorce proceedings. Now that figure is closer to 5% in no-fault states. Yet one of the main arguments raised against no-fault is that it is threatening the economic survival of women; more likely, it is the automatic, unnecessary alimony award that no-fault has dispensed with.

There is no question, as we have seen, that the simplification of divorce proceedings for the average couple has spawned a new field of do-it-yourself law. Divorce kits are popular in Canada and several states. In Contra Costa County, California (across the Bay from San Francisco) a couple can get divorced by mail. A typical advertisement (from a Vancouver, British Columbia newspaper) begins, "It's true! You can now get your divorce and legally remarry within 14 days after visiting our office! No money down . . . Kits: regular $75, now only $12.95." Under the company name, a credit firm, is the slogan: "the only company that allows you to pay AFTER your divorce."

The whirlwind of recent change is not the result of a sudden drop-off in concern for the family or the ascendancy, overnight, of the new morality. The National Conference of Commissioners on Uniform State Laws was given the task of drafting some sort of divorce law reform way back in 1882. Eighty years later they came up with a no-fault provision (after Delaware, it should be noted, had established a direction). This proposal failed to win the approval of the American Bar Association, but neither did that group vote to oppose it actively. The "irretrievable breakdown" concept has won the respect of most counselors, lawyers, and judges, *and appears to be the backbone of a truly national divorce law*—some five to ten years away.

The merits and disadvantages of no-fault, after conceding the hypocrisy of the old law, are not clear-cut. Trial lawyer Al Julien says, "I think there's an angle that has been overlooked. I believe

that women are not getting their fair share of alimony and property in the settlements. And I feel that Women's Lib may be partially responsible. Our judges are mostly male and some of them
are irritated by 'the more militant sex,' and often feel that the wife
is either working, or can get a job. Therefore, they cut down the
settlement accordingly." Edward Schaeffer, president of the New
York chapter of the American Academy of Matrimonial Lawyers,
rebuts, "I don't think Women's Lib has any effect on judges. Most
women these days are gainfully employed. They're getting their
slice of the economic melon. It is these things that influence a
judge. He does consider her ability to support herself, and should.
But that doesn't mean that Women's Lib has any influence on the
court."

    As far as the effects on children are concerned, matrimonial
attorney Eleanor Alter feels that the impact of no-fault on children
is not so damaging as its opponents would have it: "It is no longer
quite true that children of broken marriages are looked upon as
'different' from other children nor that they necessarily suffer
from neuroses . . . In homes where tension and strife are forever
present, the children are better off without parents. I think such
marriages should be dissolved if for no other reason than the
children's sake." Margaret Mead agrees with part of this: "Each
American child learns, early and in terror, that his whole security
depends on that single set of parents who, more often than not, are
arguing furiously in the next room over some detail of their
lives . . . But we have never made adequate social provision for
the security and identity of the children if that marriage is
broken."

    The accolades for no-fault are almost excessive. Columnist
Louis Kohlmeier finds no-fault "civilizing the divorce arena."
District Court Judge Lawrence C. Krell, of Omaha, Nebraska, said
he is "delighted with the law," even though the mandatory provision for attempts at reconciliation actually reduced the number of
successful tries. University of Washington law professor Luvern
V. Rieke says that under his state's new dissolution law, "the
hassle potential has gone down substantially." Philip H. Corboy,
president of the Chicago Bar Association, acknowledged that "It
might seem iconoclastic for a Catholic lawyer who has never

handled a divorce case and who has been married for 23 years to the same woman to recommend this legislation . . . but it will take the hypocrisy and embarrassment out of divorce. It makes divorce much more sane, much more moral." As "dissolution" replaced "divorce" in Arizona, Judge Irwin Cantor commented on his first day with the new system as encouraging: "The new law encourages couples to avoid name-calling and to try to save the marriage through conciliation." Assemblyman John W. Donaldson of Indianapolis commented on the dissolution bill he co-sponsored, "It brings Indiana into the twentieth century. . . ."

Some reactions are guarded. In Tennessee, several years of debate resulted in a compromise dissolution law, which Nashville's Judge Benson Trimble succeeded in strengthening with the proviso of judicial discretion. "Over the years I have been on the bench," he said, "I have seen many cases wherein one of them feels that the marriage can't go on, yet the other feels it can. . . . At a later date the parties do become reconciled and make a wholesome life for themselves and their children." In Delaware, this loophole was not covered in its early legislation of a relatively no-fault character. John T. Gallagher, reporting in the *American Bar Association Journal*, noted, "A problem then arose that had not been anticipated. For the first time, spouses (usually wives) who did not desire to be separated or divorced found that in many instances they were powerless to prevent the granting of divorce decrees."

More surprising is the view that no-fault may not really make divorce any easier. Attorney Al Ambrose made this analysis of the Michigan dissolution law: "Most of it is just semantics. When you examine the number of cases actually affected by no-fault, you'd have very few." Only 5% of the divorce cases under the old law were contested to begin with, according to best estimates. Says Ambrose, "Many were contested because of a dispute over the property or sheer mental imbalance. So what have you accomplished with the new law? Nothing that I can see, except that in the past the so called non-guilty party might have gotten a little more in the settlement." Attorney George E. Snyder of Detroit discounts the no-fault effect in stronger terms: "Most people think that 'Gee, since we have no-fault, you just go into court and get your card punched.' Anyone who's been involved in divorce knows it isn't easy. The custody problems, the financial problems, the emotional overtones continue to exist in full measure."

No one should expect miracles in the ability to deal with the normal demands of marriage just because the law has changed. This is the message of Theodore Meth: "As far as sex is concerned, most parties to an unsuccessful marriage have been inadequate and constrained in sex in the past and will continue to be so in the future. Forty-five orgasms later and the second or third marriage starts to look uncomfortably like the first, unless some change is made as a result of appropriate therapy." The other side of this coin is the laconic observation of Saul Tischler, standing master of the New Jersey Supreme Court. Liberalization of the divorce laws, he avers, actually promotes the marital institution because "most divorces are preludes to a new marriage."

Opponents of no-fault have been strident but not convincing. The most direct observation is that of Barbara B. Hirsch, a Chicago attorney who has seen the problem from both sides: "It's extremely unfair that a voluntary decision can end a marriage. For the woman who has made her 'career' marriage . . . it's a terrible thing. When women achieve real equality—equal pay, equal job opportunities, equal educational opportunities—then no-fault will make sense. Now it's an insult."

The National Organization for Women is currently turning its attention from job discrimination to family law, and has outlined a program of divorce law reform. A conspicuous feature of the program is the justifiable complaint that women have been left behind in the job market in deference to the husband's job. San Francisco attorney Anne Diamond says, "The woman who married at 19 and stayed home while her husband studied and trained will never catch up when she begins 20 years later. If she's wise, she'll prepare herself for possible termination of the marriage. That means she won't be able to go 'all-out' as wife and mother. . . . "

Other N.O.W. arguments are less convincing. It is claimed that "no-fault conveys the idea of no responsibility, permitting a person guilty of wrong doing to profit from it." As we have seen, as long as a judge exercises the right of final determination, this is a specious argument. "Fault" is not equated with "wrongdoing." A better phrase might be "no-accusation divorce."

No-fault will not solve the problems of hasty marriages—yet this is a standard condemnation of the new laws. Under a headline "The Case Against No-Fault Divorce," Vera Glaser writes in the Chicago *Tribune,* "America's shocking divorce rate is not likely to be cured by rewriting divorce laws. It goes much deeper. Should it be tougher to get married?" In another story she deplores "Deadbeat daddies who walk away from divorce settlements." But there has yet to be shown any connection between a change in the grounds of divorce and an increasing incidence of delinquencies in alimony.

A 55% increase in divorces occurred in the British Isles when a no-fault law went into effect in 1971. The divorce rate in ten other European countries was *still* higher than that of England. American divorce is *not* an isolated phenomenon. It seems logical that laws merely reflect what society already demands. The handwriting on the wall seems to be "no-fault."

No-Hate Divorce

Does no-fault divorce treat the symptoms or the disease? Is it a way of clearing the court calendar so judges and lawyers can go on to more enjoyable or profitable cases—or is it for the benefit of husband and wife? By depriving a couple of their day in court, have we silenced the hate only to sharpen its cutting edge of impersonality, venality, and repression? These fears have apparently not materialized.

This is how the new divorce procedure works in a typical no-fault state. In St. Petersburg, Florida, a "court master"steps in to screen the cases before bringing them to the attention of the circuit judge. He is an attorney, working one day a week, hearing twenty cases—a surrogate judge pressed into service to help clear the backlog of cases. He conducts an interview with each couple, one by one, across a polished table, with only a court reporter in attendance to take down the responses on a shorthand machine. The questions are direct and unloaded. Where do you live, Mr.

Brown? And Mrs. Brown? How long have you lived there? I see. And you have how many children? Now do you both believe that this marriage has irretrievably broken down? Mr. Brown, how long have you felt this way? This is the way it has been for both of you? Did counseling occur to you at that time? And since then, have you thought of getting some help? So you both have satisfied yourselves that nothing further can be done to restore your relationship?

The essential points have been covered. If there is no argument between husband and wife over the questions and answers, the documents are passed on to the judge for his signature .

In many cases the couple's lawyers have prepared the answers, including the important agreements on property settlements and custody. A smartly dressed society matron (the stereotype in newspaper accounts) answers in a clipped tone: "No, further counseling would not help. The marriage has been over for some time. We saw a psychiatrist but there was nothing he could do." A marriage of thirty years. . . . divorce granted.

The simplified court procedure makes no pretense at changing the psychological background of a marriage. It can only palliate the public outbursts and, by removing the spoils of a contested divorce, keep in-fighting to a minimum.

No-fault seems to have meant no-hate for most couples who have thus far tested the liberalized laws. The empirical results match the prediction of Judge Clarence C. Case, who in 1950 made this profound distinction which is at the root of no-fault: "Matrimonial suits are in some respects *sui generis*. Their reflex consequences are rooted deeply in the home, in society, and in human relations generally. They ought not to be permitted to take on the aspects of a game wherein wit, speed, daring and finesse prevail over elemental right and justice."

The whole legal system in modern, Western civilization is based on the value of advocacy as the best test of justice. (For "advocacy" read "game.") What Justice Case is saying is that perhaps marriage is so different in kind from performance contracts and personal injury and property rights that it cannot be tested properly in the furnace of adversary proceedings. It is not a game. The step from a legalistic to a humanistic handling of divorce may be as important as that first step toward the rule of law which Will Durant delineated: "To transmit greed into thrift, violence into argument, murder into litigation, and suicide into philosophy, has been part of the task of civilization. It was a great advance when the strong consented to eat the weak by due process of law." We are now ready for an advance beyond due process.

Some of the hate of divorce is a distillation of years of refusal to permit one's spouse a divorce, psychologically or legally. No-fault has at least done away with that. And the spitefulness of "digging up dirt" to make points in court has also gone. This is the "pain" that a divorce conference in Wisconsin sought to define as the first negative element to be eliminated from court actions before the merits of a case are discussed. "Divorce is becoming more and more the norm," says Dr. Samuel D. Stellman, director of the University of Wisconsin Extension Center for Social Research: "We have reached the point where there can be some stability in it." As a result, Stellman argues, divorce tends nowadays to be used less and less as a weapon, either as a threat to the weaker party or as a punishment for the stronger party.

The message that is emerging from these points of view is that no-fault does not *confer* the benefits of a less hostile divorce. It is rather the *possibility* of less hatefulness that makes no-fault feasible. "No-fault will work only if there is an adequate cooling off period, and a time for conciliation and reconciliation," says Milwaukee Circuit Court Judge Ralph J. Podell. Without the premise that a couple has tried to work out problems together amicably, and only then has come to court, no-fault divorce would be a license for the strong to take advantage of the weak. The strength of no-fault is in no-hate.

The efforts of a court, therefore, should be to encourage the climate of conciliation rather than to simply streamline its procedures to make divorce less time-consuming and costly. Judge Benson Trimble of Nashville is one member of the court who has moved slowly into no-fault procedures, because of his reluctance to abandon the chance for judicial review of a couple's actions. In his court, he has been requiring a 60-day waiting period between the filing of an answer to a divorce petition and the actual setting of a trial date. He attributes the dismissal rate—the rate at which divorce petitions are abandoned—to this period of reflection and debate. About half of the petitions filed in his court never come to trial.

"Divorce with a smile," as one newspaper headline summed it up, is already gathering its own type of supportive rituals. Announcement cards, showers, and parties now accompany some divorces in some social circles as casually as they do marriages. A religious divorce ceremony, which calls for forgiveness and charity, has been celebrated for several years in some San Francisco churches.

While everyone is in favor of reducing or eliminating bitterness, acrimony and spitefulness, the law is really helpless to encourage these goals. Divorce-headed couples must assume the burden themselves. They can no longer use lawyers, judges, and bar associations as surrogate villains—at least not in the no-fault type states. The legal system can only help them reduce the hostility factor when *they* decide it is not what they want.

Cost and Responsibility

"I would like to see legislation come out of this *permitting people to get back in control of their own lives.* Couples who agree on all matters should be able to go to court and have their agreement looked over by, say, a panel of independent people. Then, if it's OK, you're dissolved." (Emphasis added.) The speaker is attorney Phyllis Eliasberg of Canoga Park, California commenting on the legal turmoil surrounding the proliferation of do-it-yourself divorce projects in Southern California.

Her point, and that of a new breed of lawyers and judges wrestling with the divorce problem, is that the real benefit of lawyer-less divorces is not economy, but a greater sense of responsibility by husband and wife. They are forced to take their problems in their own hands. And the task of forging their own agreement is a necessary first step toward any attempt at reconciliation.

When the first divorce kits made their appearance, they were considered an opportunistic fad. A Rochester, New York barber,

James A. Winder, got the idea for a kit in 1971, spent four months poring over law books, and began turning out legal forms and instructions on a press in his garage. He was soon enjoined by the New York State Supreme Court on the grounds that even mail communication regarding legal matters constituted an illegal practice of law. But the precedent of Norman F. Dacey's *How To Avoid Probate*, which much earlier had received a clean bill of health from the state's top appellate court, effectively broke down the rigid interpretation of what "practice of law" means. In state after state, bar associations have had to backtrack on the hard line that any form of communication about legal matters is advice or practice. In California, a socially conscious attorney, Charles Sherman of Berkeley, pioneered a serious attempt at popularizing do-it-yourself divorce. His book, *How To Do Your Own Divorce in California*, was an instant success, and led to his formation of "Wave Project," a network of 20 offices throughout the state. Here consultants, not necessarily lawyers, supplement the advice in the book with explanations of forms, counseling, and moral support.

Sherman's rationale for limiting the use of lawyers in divorce is simply that dissolution "isn't all that much a legal problem." Attorney Eliasberg would go further: "Attorneys' own excesses have brought about this attitude. I've never seen a reconciliation come out of a lawyer's office, but I've seen many people ripped off by lawyers." According to Sherman, once an agreement between a couple is worked out, "the rest is just red tape." As for the red tape constituting "the practice of law," a divorce consultant argues, "If transferring information to papers is practicing law, then every legal stenographer in the state is practicing law." Nevertheless, the state bar association has brought enough pressure in Southern California to harass, at least, the operators of consultation services. The owner of the California Divorce Council, which offers a complete divorce service for $55, was fined $100 after plea bargaining to a misdemeanor charge of unauthorized practice of law. Similar cases were appealed, and it now appears that Sherman's opinion of the amount of law involved in divorce cases has been vindicated.

The instant success of divorce self-help and "avoiding probate" has led to numerous other attempts to get around lawyers —in the field of adoption, change of name, and bankruptcy. John Slavicek of San Francisco established the American Bankruptcy Council in 1972, and offers a kit for *pro se* (on one's own behalf) filing of personal bankruptcy, homesteading, chapter XIII (the wage-earner's plan), and even business bankruptcy. But lawyer-less divorce has become far and away the most popular legal action brought by laymen.

In Michigan, the cause of do-it-yourself divorce was first championed by a persistent woman whose own divorce from a lawyer many years ago left her bitter and disillusioned. Virginia Cramer, who went to jail rather than comply with a court order banning her $50 divorce kit, says, "There's no such thing as a good lawyer." But her dogged campaigning has won her the respect of a good part of the legal profession. A Wayne County Circuit Court judge, who preferred to remain anonymous, agreed with the substance of her complaints: people can represent themselves in many divorce matters, and lawyers have been overcharging their clients for years. A lawyer sent by a bar association to inspect her forms reported back that they were quite good. Finally, the Detroit Bar paid her the ultimate compliment of starting a low-cost, assembly-line divorce system of their own, with a cut-rate fee of $125 for families with incomes under $8500. Mrs. Cramer was not impressed or appeased. "All they are saying is that they are not going to overcharge poor people anymore, but they will continue to overcharge others."

The restrictions announced by the DBA were so severe that there is little danger of laymen practicing much law under their plan. In addition to the income requirement, couples wishing to qualify must have no children, seek no alimony, and have no property beyond household goods, automobiles, and personal effects—and these they must agree to divide up without outside help. Mrs. Cramer continues to press for an over-the-counter type of divorce service, operated by clerks. When Wayne County Commissioners began expressing interest in her proposal, the Detroit Bar reacted with its compromise $125 fee program. Ivan Barris, Mrs. Cramer's nemesis at the DBA, explained, "It was always presupposed that we could never embrace the idea of having laymen at a counter dispensing divorces like hamburgers." Unexpected support for Mrs. Cramer then came from attorney and law professor Wilson Hurd, who set up a system using legal assistants and charging a uniform fee for all income brackets. Hurd is aware of the danger of an assembly-line process "where you don't counsel, go into problems, try to reconcile." His answer is that the one couple out of ten which needs legal or family counsel can get it elsewhere, and will be so advised. At present, this is the crux of the dispute between pro-legalists and pro-do-it-yourselfers. Allen B. Gresham of the State Bar of California insists that "divorce consultants give legal advice when they make the decision whether it's a simple case or not."

Women have been in the forefront of the battle for do-it-yourself divorce for more than the obvious reason; men have traditionally had greater access to lawyers and to the family finances. In addition, women have found that they have a more sensitive feeling for the issues in a divorce case, and work more effectively in volunteer groups. Mary Borstad, who obtained her own divorce through the Women's Divorce Group in Milwaukee, says, "It would be the greatest thing in the world if men would form their own group—but they are just too inhibited." This Wisconsin group has made particularly successful strides toward a low-cost, fully responsible dissolution procedure. A judge advised one of the group's members, who was on welfare, that she should be going to law school. Another judge was so impressed with a woman's handling of her own difficult case that he commented when it was over, "If I was getting a divorce, I'd want you to handle it." An experienced Milwaukee divorce attorney, a male, said he thought it would be only a matter of time before "laypersons" were handling even contested divorces. In the Family Court Commissioner's Office in that city, women are often observed filing their own divorce papers under a sign reading "Attorneys Only."

In other parts of the country, attention has thus far been given first to the problems of cost. In St. Louis, the $45 filing fee is now waived for "indigents," whom a study showed to be mostly women. In Chicago, where court fees are $70, various low-cost or no-cost programs are available, but so far all are in connection with legal aid, referral services, or group lawyers (American Society of Divorced Men, ADAM, EVE, etc.).

The opposition of local legal groups to do-it-yourself divorce has been a brake on exploitation of the poor or uneducated by fast-talking opportunists. In Canada, where a liberalized National Divorce Act went into effect in 1968, the entrepreneurs were not so closely watched. Divorce kits were offered by finance companies, by underground newspapers, and by known bunko artists—even in the more traditional eastern provinces. As bad as they were, these attempts at self-help apparently filled a crying need; previously in Quebec and Newfoundland, divorces had to be approved by the government in Ottawa.

The fears of some judges that low-cost divorce would mean low-responsibility divorce have not been confirmed. The proponents of assembly-line dissolution even claim that the absence of a lawyer almost automatically guarantees more involvement by couples in their own affairs. It is certain that the "quickie" divorces that used to be the only other option—in the Dominican Republic, for example—combine the worst of no personal counsel and legal hi-jinks. If George C. Scott and Barbara Streisand found this route effective, why not John Doe? With Mexico currently uninviting as a divorce mill, Santo Domingo (as we have seen) has been quite popular. One man, whose wife had given him the necessary power of attorney for her and so could remain at home, found that "It was like the old days when I was a paratrooper, only in this case I wasn't worrying about the chute not opening. Every thirty seconds the line moved forward. In four minutes flat we were through the door. I held up my hand, gave my name, said 'yes' to two questions ('do you want a divorce', 'does your wife agree?') and that was it." In England, where irretrievable breakdown and two years of separation are now the sole grounds for dissolution, the process is almost as simple, and the cost is only $31.50. But the separation period and a generally cautious governmental attitude toward the use of lawyers have kept do-it-yourself divorce the exception rather than the rule.

The most hopeful sign of all, behind the flurry of kits and crusades and injunctions, is that cheap, convenient divorce has not, so far, been irresponsible.

Shunning the Siren Call

The siren call of easy divorce—is it one of those inevitable consequences of modern life, of social and economic mobility, of a more
sensible morality? Or is there still a case for old-fashioned marriage?

The availability of a way out of a bad marriage makes the
decision to *stay* married all the more commendable. So a rising
divorce rate does not at all mean that this generation's couples are
undedicated, unstable, or irresponsible. If long-term monogamy is
less in favor today, it may only be because the alternative was
lacking in other eras.

The unpopular position that marriage and fidelity and con-
stancy are worth keeping around for a while has been receiving
more support in recent years. Dr. Carlfred B. Broderick, of the
Marriage and Family Counseling Center at the University of
Southern California, presents some interesting statistics to back
up his somewhat optimistic view of marriage. Will marriage be
replaced by the living-together-arrangement? More than 95% of
all Americans marry before the age of 40; LTA's are usually a short
prelude to marriage. How about the future of communes? "The
half-life of most communes is less than 18 months," another
spawning ground for marriages. But surely the sexual revolution
has uprooted the ideals of marriage, hasn't it? "The institution
seems to have survived millenia of premarital sexual experience
by males without sinking . . . and the one big study of swinging
showed that the average couple tired of this pattern after two
years and dropped back into a monogamous pattern." The present
average length of marriage is a little more than 20 years. You can
win many a bar bet by asking what percentage of marriages end in
the death of one or the other of the spouses, rather than in divorce.
The answer is 75%.

"It is not marriage that is despised," says Dr. Broderick, "but
that detestable ex-spouse."

The general theme of other recent defenses of traditional marriage has been an appeal to values. "The art of staying together,"
according to a typical piece in the Canadian magazine *Maclean's*,

is a deeply human art: "There is that impulse in all of us, maybe stronger than it's ever been before: find somebody who will know you and trust you more than you do yourself. Find the missing part of your body." Shifra Nussbaum of the Jewish Family and Child Service in Toronto speaks of growth and independence and self-awareness as the saving values in a marriage: "I really distrust *techniques* for a happy marriage, the artificial ones, the rituals." Martha Weinman Lear takes a stand against the easy prescriptions of *Open Marriage* in an article in *Redbook*, "The Case For Loving Just One Man": The right words are all there, the time-tested buzz-words of sociologists and marriage therapists; but the implications between the lines are that you can have that extramarital affair and that swinging time if you only think about it in the right way. Authors Nena and George O'Neill fill their pages with pillow-words like 'relationships' ('it is on the basis of their own internal relationship—that is, because they have experienced mature love, and real trust, and are able to expand themselves, to love and enjoy others and to bring that love and pleasure back into their marriage, without jealousy'). Such a little matter—'without jealousy'." The whole case for open marriage then seems to hinge on whether jealousy is an instinctive or man-made emotion, and we quickly get off the deep end into anthropology. As Ms. Lear concludes, "You can write 'I won't be jealous' on the blackboard 500 times. You can take those marriage manual formulas (The Eight Cardinal Guidelines), study them, memorize them, say them backward and forward . . . the bee will still sting."

In *Marriage Is Hell*, Kathrin Perutz is equally blithe: "Making love with a person not your spouse doesn't have to be a serious breach." Harriet Van Horne comments that readers can't pass that by without remembering the pain of infidelity that has struck so many lives. If marriage can only be kept alive by making it an emotionally barren vessel, inhabited by "let's be sensible" automatons, then it probably doesn't deserve to survive. Dr. Carl A. Whitaker, psychiatry professor at the University of Wisconsin, argues for an old-fashioned idea, that marriage demands self-discipline to achieve a greater value than one's individuality can confer: "When you marry you must sacrifice some of your wholeness for something bigger." And when you think your independence and personality are being stifled by marriage, divorce may only be a superficial, and costly, way to try to regain them. "It is too drastic a step "to use divorce to reassert the right to be a person. It's good to break out of the intimacy of marriage, but not by getting a divorce certificate. Divorce allows you to do only two things; to not worry about the kids, and go back to being 19 again. And then you have to expand your loneliness again in golf, money, or your job."

Dr. David Reuben finds that marriage is not obsolete at all—at least when he is talking to a women's magazine audience in his regular monthly columns. The alternatives to marriage "just don't work—and, besides, none of them is new," he says. The most recently favored experiment, "renewable marriage," denies what most of us want in a relationship: security. "The don't-call-me-I'll-call-you marriage gives both parties all the security of a tightrope walker with a wooden leg."

A survey conducted by *Family Circle* magazine in 1973 identified five types of marriages by asking for ratings on five key factors which hold marriages together. Nine hundred and fifty-two women judged "mutual consideration and thoughtfulness" to be the most important factor by a good margin, ahead of "sexual satisfaction," "being active and interesting persons," "money" and so on. How many marriage manuals come to grips with this simple idea of "consideration?" Among those who rate sexual satisfaction first, consideration was a clear second. "One of the reasons people get divorced," says columnist Nicholas von Hoffman, "is that they forget why they got married. Many men, for example, can't fight off the infection of playboyism, until they go and do it for a while. . . ." Yet we continue to look to divorce as a solution to the problem of marriage, when not marriage, but people, are the problem. He adds, "Perhaps we put too much hope in splitting up because our literature has tended to concentrate on unhappy marriages rather than unhappy divorces." We should add, "and on unhappy people."

The resolution of the dilemma, to divorce or not to divorce, may come in the search for the root of the problem: is it in the institution or in me?

Time To Decide

"The greatest pain in divorce," a panel of Episcopalian divorced people in Cleveland, Ohio, concluded, "is the decision to do it." Because we do not want to face that pain, psychologists warn, we unconsciously procrastinate—hoping that time can heal what sacrifice and self-examination have failed to. (As we'll see later, more than 20% of those surveyed related timing (sooner or later) to what they would do differently.) At the same time, no one is urging married couples to conduct a weekly probe of their marital happiness quotient.

Most marriage counselors agree that couples come to them with problems much too late to do any good. At that point, one party or the other is really looking for confirmation of his or her decision to divorce, rather than for help. "Divorce counseling might be more helpful," says a Los Angeles psychiatrist, "because in most cases any attempt to save a marriage which is already on the rocks is just formality." The director of Christ Church Marriage Guidance Council, New Zealand, Mrs. Eileen Saunders, says, "Our greatest concern is that people should come to us much earlier than they do. If they would come when things begin to go wrong we can often stop the breakup before there is too much bitterness between the partners." In that country, counseling is now mandatory before a separation can be granted.

Second marriages, contrary to the popular image of divorcées jumping from the frying pan into the fire, are statistically more successful than first marriages. And a random survey of "two-time losers" indicates why: the first marriage is a crash course in human survival when the parties are too young or immature, and that's where most of the divorces come from. The second time through, husband and wife know the ingredients of a successful relationship and the grief of a divorce. This is not so much an argument for trial marriages as it is for earlier attempts at working at the relationship. "It may seem trite," says Dr. Harry Adams, a Burbank, California marriage counselor, "but the main problem in troubled marriages that is the last to be faced is the problem of communication. Couples do not want to tackle disagreeable subjects. Men especially try to avoid fighting at all costs—that is, dealing and negotiating. Such a passive man will avoid a confrontation by walking out the door. His wife typically bitches at him, trying to get him to stand up to her so that she can feel secure."

Some couples among Dr. Adams' clientele are so backward in being able to communicate that they cannot repeat the substance of a message immediately after hearing it from each other. By using tape recorders and playing back both the original statement and the attempted repetition of it, Dr. Adams is able to dramatize the gap in simple listening. After this hurdle is overcome, the next task is to teach men that their world will not end if they fight with their wives.

The American family has been undermined less by the prospect of easy divorce than by blindness to incipient problems. "Divorce statistics," says Rose DeWolf, columnist for the Philadelphia *Bulletin*, "are not good indicators of the state of health of American marriages. They are better indicators of the state of American laws." Our laws have now given us the opportunity to make the freest decisions we have ever had at our disposal concerning marriage and divorce. But the decision to divorce must come from a knowledge of our problems, not a knowledge of the law.

After Marriage, What?

There is apparently no end to the parade of confessional books and articles on the shadowy afterlife of a broken marriage. Men reenter the single state with the prospect of reliving the days of a bachelor. Women have reason to be less sanguine. Both soon come to grips with the realities of loneliness, depression, and hard times.

The great disparity in the fortunes of men and women after divorce has been lessened in recent years by a softening of the distinctions of men's and women's roles. "Apple pie may still be sacred, but not motherhood," begins one newspaper account of custody decisions. Every section of the country has been reporting, with obvious approval, the awarding of children to the father rather than to the mother. Oregon, the pioneer state in non-sexist custody awards, has an encouraging history of well over a decade of single fathers raising their children. The image of the man who "immediately feels a compulsion to live it up, to think he's expected to paint the town red," says Dr. Samuel D. Stellman of the University of Wisconsin, "is fast changing." Unfortunately, the plight of divorced mothers with children may even have worsened in the wake of women's lib.

The Journal of Marriage and the Family several years ago pointed to a trend in families headed by women. They are more likely to be poor, "comprising one-fourth of the low-income groups." And they make up 10% of the total population. This trend has accelerated dramatically with the rising divorce rate, and the number of fathers who win custody of the children is still not statistically significant. In fact, it is somewhat insulting to mothers to observe the adulation and detailed attention devoted to single fathers and their children in daily newspapers.

The "reentry" clubs for divorced men and women are generally separate, and very unequal. A Marin County, California sample of divorced women found the mixed clubs to be "nothing but body-shops—demeaning, embarrassing, the women outnumbering the men six to one. And the men are weird." In a major city like Chicago, there may be dozens of get-together organizations: Divorce Anonymous, UP (Unique Programs), Spares, Singles, Parents Without Partners, Fifth Wheelers, Formerly Marrieds, and so on. In New York, a private club called the Sword Foundation for single, widowed, or divorced men has operated on a lavish scale for a dozen years, with a bar attended by young ladies and with well-appointed club rooms. Dubbed "an ego rehabilitation center" by the *New York Daily News,* the foundation has dues of $400 a year, plus initiation.Members are naturally known as "Swordsmen." Whereas the main problem for divorced men seems to be the "five o'clock drag," women typically talk about the rigors of survival in a world where plumbing, cars, and credit are still a man's domain. There are about 2.8 million divorced, unremarried women in the United States. With only one in twenty now receiving alimony—or even fewer due to delinquencies— economic hardship and resulting loss in self-esteem are chronic burdens on them and their children. It is unlikely that changes in equal opportunities and equal pay will make any headway in the near future against this overwhelming backlog of neglect and wishful thinking. A study of 8,000 high school girl seniors in 1971, conducted by the California Commission of Women, found that two-thirds stated they didn't think they needed substantial preparation for an occupation. Emotional shocks seem also to be typically harder on women. Meyer Elkin of the Los Angeles Conciliation Court believes that women have been traditionally at an emotional disadvantage in marriage, because of past standards of femininity which equated self-esteem with masculinity. "There's nothing so potentially dangerous as getting married," he claims; "the ego begins to die—and for women, faster."

Advice to women in magazines and newspapers typically revolves around how to adjust and how to meet a budget. "You must keep yourself active and busy and in the mainstream of life," they say, in one form or another. And then there is the promise of a new awareness of self, a new chance for "growth." "Most newly divorced people are frightened of their oneness," says the leader of a "creative divorce" group in Denver. "We show them that that's pretty neat—oneness."

However, with all the self-deception and depression there are positive, hopeful signs that the tragedy of post-marriage has seen its worst days. Change has not come from a direct attack on the social problems of the divorced—such as increases in social security benefits or the creation of more organizations. Where improvement is visible is in the greater awareness of those who are now entering or thinking of entering the ranks of the divorced. They are approaching dissolution more realistically, more freely. Their eyes are open to the fearsome prospect of a long separation, a lonely life, a need for self-sufficiency. And because they probably approached marriage, in the first place, with fewer of the legacies of an older generation, they will not be polarized away from a second chance at it by their first mistake.

And, based on our extensive surveys and interviews over the past two years of researching the divorce picture in America today, we make this prediction: *the staggering divorce rate now being experienced in American society will soon begin to decrease significantly and will drop to a phenomenally low point by*

1985. This is predicated upon the incontrovertible evidence—tough medicine for the adamantly conservative older generations or the religiously inflexible—that *young people are no longer marrying for the wrong reasons*. They are no longer marrying for the expediency of sex. They are no longer marrying to legitimize pregnancy, both because of the pill and because of the "new morality" condoning of both abortion and unwed motherhood. They are no longer marrying for fear of being "old maids," or under the spectre of latent homosexuality which used to be conjured up in the presence of a "confirmed" bachelor. They are no longer getting married because of family pressure. And so on.

They are getting married for *positive* reasons, not negative. Friendship is becoming as important as "love." Commitment is beginning to mean more than perfunctory promises. Evaluation of motives for marriage is now a somewhat more mature, responsible process, and no longer a hyperemotional reflection of a movie scenario.

Best of all, young people today—and not an insignificant number of the over 30's, too—are looking at both sides now and choosing to marry or to divorce with their heads held high.

PART THREE

The divorced speak out—
introduction

In researching this book, we spent more than a year interviewing more than 1,000 divorced persons. We felt that in order to achieve a sound statistical base, an acceptable geographical mix, a wide age range, and a balanced male-female response, 1,000 persons would be a significant sample—far more than those samples from which too many other so-called survey books have been written. (One such book in 1973, for example, dealt with the sexual mores of a certain class of adults in suburban communities, and was based upon only 114 interviews! That means, statistically, if only about 11 people in the survey committed adultery, the author could, and did, state on national television—and thousands of people could read as *ex cathedra* truth—that 10% of the nation was committing adultery.) No, we insisted on at least 1,000 persons, and we believe this represents the largest such tabulation of opinion in the divorce bibliography.

We developed a questionnaire which we either filled out during or after a personal interview, or which was mailed to a divorced person somewhere in the nation after he responded to a call for volunteers. During our survey, we took ads in major metropolitan daily and Sunday newspapers explaining what the survey was about and asking for persons willing to complete the confidential questionnaire (permission to quote directly was also voluntary). Each respondent was told that his or her information would be followed in this text only by "Mary, 34, Brooklyn teacher," or "Marvin, 42, Ohio chemist."

The questionnaire, whose statistical breakdown is discussed empirically in the last section, called for replies to seven questions plus the following information: Name, sex, age, address, either high school graduate or "some college," city, state, telephone number (for follow-up interviewing), years married, age when married, date divorced, number of times married, occupation, number of children, and who received custody of the children.

The seven questions were:

1. What do you feel was the underlying reason for your divorce (e.g., financial difficulties, adultery, immaturity when married, alcoholism, etc.)?

2. Did you make a determined effort to "save" your marriage (through counseling, trial separation, etc.)? And if so, how?

3. Did you experience any *unanticipated* financial, social, or emotional calamity as a result of your divorce, and if so, what specifically?

4. Based on the above experiences, what would you do differently once having made the decision to divorce or to separate?

5. What advice would you give others about avoiding certain pitfalls or making the divorce situation easier, smoother, more effective, etc.?

6. What are your thoughts on *alternatives* to divorce, which might circumvent the current legal and financial barriers?

7. What would you like to see investigated in the preparation of this book, and what additional comments do you have?

Each respondent was encouraged to add information wherever possible or thought pertinent, and it was explained that, although the questions weren't as detailed as one would like, they were designed to evoke highly subjective thoughts and opinions.

It should be said here that the questionnaire worked extremely well for what was, after all, a less than clinical conditions study. We were after a *straight-from-the-shoulder* approach to gathering the thoughts of divorced persons with unique stories to tell, and we eschewed at every turn the temptation to "organize" or "analyze" our results in the context of the techniques used by professional survey-takers or incorporated opinion research firms.

A full 97% of the respondents filled in their names and other personal data, and, incredibly, more than 75% used extra sheets of paper or the reverse of the questionnaire to elaborate on their remarks.

Naturally, reproducing every word received would be beyond the physical limits of this book. Books of 3,000 or so pages do not seem popular these days, and we want as many adults as possible to hear the message of the nation's divorced. Consequently, we have edited the findings heavily—and, yes, subjectively—in order to bring you the most cogent responses. Some respondents were terse but pithy; some were verbose but empty of useful information. Perhaps another book will be written after this, with the feelings and advice of the hundreds of thousands of divorced people from whom we have yet to hear, and whose letters we welcome. But now, let these people have their say.

What do you feel was the underlying reason for your divorce?

I was immature when I was married at only 20, and eventually found that I needed personal growth and freedom.

Jane, 34, California writer

Immaturity. I was 22 when I got married, but still far too young.

Mark, 54, New York insurance broker

He drank too much and "ran around" on me. I'm finding it hard not to be bitter, even though I was the "other woman" in his first divorce. I suppose the need to be married was my own downfall, because I kept putting it off and hoping he meant it every time he went on the wagon and took me out to dinner in repentance. Don't put up with any crap, I say. In marriage it should be two strikes you're out—not three!

Sue, 30, California stewardess

We were just too young. She was 18, I was 21 and we wanted to hit the sack, that's all. In those days it was tougher to just screw around and then see how we got along with each other. No pills, fear of motels, nowhere to go—the same old story. I think it's a good idea that kids can now live with each other for a while, provided there aren't any illegitimate babies.

Joe, 42, Texas newspaperman

We were immature, early 20's, and probably had seen too many movies. Anyone who expects rockets, and bells and candybox romancing is doomed.

Tim, 29, California lawyer

What it finally boiled down to was that we just didn't like each other enough to maintain a 24-hour-a-day relationship

Bill, 34, California bartender

She wouldn't stand for being broke for a few years while I worked my ass off trying to make it. Once she took a job to "help with bills" while I chained myself to the typewriter. She thought she'd have more fun than I could show her at the time.

Tom, 46, California writer

I'd say immaturity when married. Neither one of us had decided beforehand exactly what we wanted out of marriage other than sex. It wasn't too long before we discovered that he didn't want children after all, while I wanted three or four, and that I'd have to find a job also to help out for a while. Christ, we didn't even like the same foods once we got over the dining-out phase.

Kathy, 35, Missouri secretary

People fail to realize that this "maturity" bit works both ways. Sure, we were immature when we got married—most kids are—but then the first time we got uncomfortable, or things weren't going right, we weren't mature enough to make a go of it. We rushed right out and got divorced and thought, "Wow! Wasn't that a close one! We really got out of it in time!" Well, a year later we got married again.

Ellen, 34, California legal clerk

Religion screwed things up. Both of us had a hang-up about the religious implications of divorce, so we lived with a bad marriage for as long as we could. It only made things worse.

Don, 36, Missouri commercial pilot

It's probably my upbringing in this part of the country, but when I got married, marriage was a no-choice situation. The woman served the man, made the beds, cooked his food—when he showed up at night!—had the babies, changed, all that jazz. Now, things are different, and as the woman's role changed, I began to feel there was something else to marriage than all that chattel bullshit. So I went to group therapy, initially to cope with his boozing problem, and I remember one night he came home and I said, "_____, as soon as I get myself fixed up I'll probably be so straightened out I'll split on you." And he just laughed and had another drink. Well, I had finally learned that there was something else to the world of marriage than what I called this "Boston Sacrifice" kind of philosophy. I divorced him and haven't heard from him since.

Lilly, 31, Massachusetts artist

Deception on the part of my husband. He was just eager to acquire an attractive wife and have children to reaffirm his masculinity, and I suspect he wanted a full-time servant whom he didn't have to pay. Within three months I discovered he was seeing another woman, but having been married twice before I was determined to make this one work, to do everything to "win" his love.

Judy, 62, New York housewife

If I had it to do all over again, I wouldn't get married so quickly. And I'd be especially careful with a guy who's been married before. It could be a warning sign.

Bernice, 39, California exec.

My husband went slightly crazy during the dangerous 40's. The deepest reason was his insecurity due to a bad childhood—broken home and raised in a Catholic school. My husband changed his entire personality when he began to chase around. He bought a wig, spent hundreds on clothes in one month, became dishonest for the first time, stayed out late and became physically abusive to his children and a raving maniac to his whole family, including his grandchildren.

Mabel, 48, California realtor

After seven years of marriage, there were personality changes by both partners.

Chet, 31, Illinois personnel mgr.

The reason for my divorce was the same as for my marriage: a need for love and for intimacy, for "relating," for security and a shared growth. None of these was a part of the marriage as I lived it. I suppose you could say the reason for the divorce was unrealistic, immature expectations.

Mary, 44, Illinois teacher

An insane female—I misjudged her completely!

Dan, 45, New York restaurateur

My first wife was a German and believed very much in an extremely strict home life and child-rearing. Anything that didn't go strictly according to her rules created a family fight. Probably what hurt the most was not being able to enjoy my children as a result of this strictness and bickering.

Dave, 38, North Dakota engineer

A lack of compatibility and understanding, probably because we grew apart—we matured in different ways.

Agnes, 34, New York R.N.

Character and personality disorder which prevented my husband from assuming responsibility for any aspect to the marriage.

Virginia, 45, New York secretary

Corporation life—the constant moves with long-term separations resulting. It was literally a long-distance marriage with infidelity and weekend alcoholism.

June, 44, housewife (no location given)

My husband was an adulterer.

Joanne, 54, New York housewife

Differences in life-style and values.

Elaine, 46, New Jersey research asst.

I didn't realize at the time that he wanted to continue to be a playboy.

Sally, 39, California housewife

Our careers conflicted, and neither of us could reconcile the differences, neither wanted to give a little for the sake of the other one's future successes.

Larry, 42, New York producer

The underlying reason was alcohol. My ex-husband started to drink more and more the longer we were married, and he became very mean when he drank. After he endangered the children and my life, I felt something should be done. He blamed me for not going along with some of his wild ideas.

Mary, 33, North Dakota R.N.

Immaturity on the part of my wife. She didn't have a realistic view of marriage. She was only 19, and married me just to get away from home. I was 25, but I probably was on the rebound from an affair.

Joe, 31, Caliifornia teacher

My ex-husband is, and always was, to a greater or lesser degree, selfish. He thinks he's more important than anyone else. He had to be "free."

Patricia, 38, California teacher

I married a nut.

Sue, 38, California teacher

Immaturity when married. I am not the same person I was 25 years ago. My husband was an alcoholic, and we had grown at different rates and in different directions.

Susan, 46, New York teacher

My husband had never dated much before me, and was surrounded by the temptations of many 20-year-old students in his classes. He decided that "open marriage" was a better way. I disagreed.

Connie, 30, graduate philosophy student (no location given)

Unfortunately, I married a professional con-man!

Mary, 63, New York legal secretary

My husband became obsessed with living the life of a "swinging" Californian. I had put him through law school and he was with a very prominent law firm. After seven years of marriage we had a beautiful baby daughter, but while on the one hand he wanted a life with us, on the other he envied the "swinging bachelor" life he never got to try. This conflict within him eventually caused a nervous breakdown and was the beginning of the end for us.

Linda, 30, North Dakota homemaker

I was definitely married too young (16) and my husband was very immature. As we grew older he became possessive and jealous of everyone.

Pam, 25, California cashier

First Marriage: When you're young and probably immature you've got the financial strain of making it, and both parties' values are only on the surface—furniture, dining-out, etc. Eventually I think these strains caused a slowly deteriorating mental disease, resulting in institutionalizing my wife for long periods.

Second Marriage: Financial, coupled with immaturity. My second wife was 15 years younger than I was. She loved it when I made forty grand a year and we travelled all over hell. But when the company went bankrupt and we had to make a readjustment, she couldn't change her life-style.

Tim, 47, California advertising exec

Incompatibility of character on the part of both of us. We never stopped to think about whether we really "fit."

John, 46, California artist

Absolutely no acceptance or responsibility whatsoever on the part of my husband. He was unfaithful and blatantly deceitful and had heavy psychological problems.

Sue, 37, California (no occupation given)

Immaturity. I wasn't ready to settle down and felt I had missed out on a lot of things by being married so early (20). He didn't feel the same and wanted the marriage to last, so we separated for three months to find out about ourselves. I still didn't want to be married.

Donna, 30, California secretary

Lack of communication, I guess. We didn't have any interest in each other's activities, and he was away from home on business a great deal of the time.

Joan, 28, California medical secretary

Differences in philosophies of life. One of us placed importance on material things, and the other on intangibles such as honesty and understanding.

Ann, 64, New York R.N.

Sex. My wife felt guilty about it.

Don, 34, North Dakota exec

First Marriage: *Immaturity when married (19). We mistook other feelings for love.*

Second Marriage: *My husband suspected I was still seeing an old boyfriend and his extreme jealousy caused many fights. There were also some financial problems.*

June, 27, California sales representative

His success. His adultery. His difficulty in accepting my work and my becoming a personality in my own right.

Sue, 48, California newspaperwoman

Mother-in-law problems, coupled with immaturity.

Harry, 30, California (no occupation given)

My husband's immaturity—he changed jobs five times in three years!

Anna, 32, California (no occupation given)

My husband was impotent due to emotional problems.

Barbara, 50, law student (no address given)

Immaturity on both our parts, but my husband seemed to grow more childish as the years wore on. We didn't communicate with each other because of it.

Ruth, 30, California teacher

I knew my wife only eight weeks before we got married, when I was 22, and she didn't get a sample of my childish temperament until a few weeks afterward. Even though we saw each other nearly every day during those eight weeks, it was still possible to hide my negative side from her. I wish now that there had been a compulsory waiting period, or else some required premarital counseling. We go into marriage expecting that its termination will come because of old-age death, when the marriage usually dies before the partners.

John, 37, California teacher

My husband really didn't want to be married.

Rita, 38, California homemaker

Lack of communication.
David, 25, California student

We married too young (19). I wanted a family and a husband, but all he wanted was the pleasures of having someone pick up after him, do his laundry, cook his meals and sleep with him. After the first year, I realized that I was wrong. I had grown into a woman with responsibilities, and he was still the same "boy" that I had dated when I was 13!
Dorothy, 29, California corporate mgr.

He didn't ever realize that I was the best fuck he'd ever had!
Nora, 27, Illinois waitress

I base my divorce on immaturity on both our parts. I was married a month after my 19th birthday. He was black and I am oriental. He was a year older. We didn't have any financial difficulties because we both had good jobs. But he did commit adultery. When our marriage started going downhill I didn't want to admit it, so when I did catch him with someone else all it did was make me realize that it was all over.
Pat, 25, California postal worker

Immaturity of husband. My horizons opened, while his remained inflexible and we grew apart. Our children had emotional problems and we couldn't get together on them.
Margaret, 58, California housewife

At first I blamed her infidelity, but on reflection I realize that it was our mutual immaturity, compounded by her long-standing emotional problems. She needed reassurance and guidance, but I just withdrew into myself
—anonymous, male

I (think) I "outgrew" our marriage. I need much more experience—people, ideas, places—and I find marriage too limiting. I like relating to things by choice, not because a law says you must.
Janet, 31, California teacher

I got married when I still wasn't fully able to realize my direction and that of my husband. I have far more drive and tendency to accept responsibility than he did. He claimed I was far too materialistic; I said he lacked direction. In the eight and a half years we were married and the three years we went together exclusively before our marriage, he held about a dozen different jobs. He went to two law schools, not finishing either, ran for political office, started his own business, and ran us into debts I never knew about. All this time he kept claiming "things are going to get better," but they never did. All this wound up costing me about $15,000, which he'd spend frivolously in ways he couldn't even account for. Strangely, we're still friends, which I guess is fairly uncommon. I maintain I couldn't give him 11½ years of my life and still not like the guy, and he's the father of our only child. I didn't want a child until I was 30, and our son was born on schedule, but his birth and our financial straits finally precipitated the whole thing.

Nancy, 32, California newspaperwoman

We got married to get into each other's pants. I agree with the comedian who said marriage is like sitting in a bathtub, because once you get used to it, it's not so hot.

Steve, 30, Illinois bartender

I had to work two jobs and I think my wife was alone too much of the time. I wasn't home enough to get to know her, and I was a bit immature, so I know we didn't have a very good sexual relationship. A combination of all that made her start going out on me. I found out about it, but we talked it over and tried to start all over again. Still, after three more years I didn't feel I could trust her. We fought all the time, whenever I felt she was cheating on me, and I slapped her around a lot.

Bill, 36, California sportsman

Difficulty with regional and family cultural differences. I was New York middle-class Catholic; he was a rural Kentucky poor-class with no formal religion. The regional differences are more important than most people might think. The term "male chauvinism" is more apparent in the lower classes of the southern states than in the middle classes of the northern states. The southern male definitely feels superior to women, except for those raised in the big city. The man who is a good husband is neither the type to refuse to allow a wife to work under any circumstances, or to take advantage of her when she does.

Ginny, 46, Kentucky bookkeeper

Insecurity when going into the marriage. I just wanted to get away from home, and getting married was "expected" anyway since we'd been going together for six years. Also, total ignorance of what living together would mean, because it had been taboo before marriage.

Nancy, 33, Maryland teacher

The reason was simply that it's a great financial advantage for a woman to divorce her husband.

Robert, 49, California (no occupation given)

Immaturity. My wife was only 15, and pregnant.

Charles, 32, Iowa assembler

Inability to discuss our difficulties, together with the fact that his business required entertaining many women, among whom the adultery rate with married men was very high.

Sharon, 31, California bookkeeper

My husband was immature. He was a high school teacher who adopted the life-style of his students—long hair, sloppy clothes, etc.—and shortly after a trial separation from me he began living with a 17-year-old former student. That was the end of the trial.

Betty, 38, California government worker

Immaturity, heightened by "another man." And she drank too much.

—anonymous male, 30

The chief underlying reason would have to be immaturity when married on my part and deep untreated emotional disturbance on his part. Adultery was a result of marital problems rather than a cause. I think too many women consider adultery as a direct attack upon themselves (a blow to their ego, a rejection of their love, a moral weakness, etc.) when actually it may be a result of their husband's insecurity or immaturity rather than the fact he is not satisfied at home.

I was young when I married (19) and more in love with the idea of being in love and having a family than with the man I married. I was pregnant and from a strict religious family. At 19, you simply do not grasp the idea of being married for the rest of your life. Sex and being married and having babies seems all important; day-to-day living together is a faint glimmer in the background. He was 27 and wanted to do the right thing by me; he wanted to raise his daughter. Abortion or adoption were never even discussed.

Birth control was a problem. I was Roman Catholic; he belonged to no church. There were no IUD's yet; he did not trust the pill or foam or condom or diaphram or jelly. I wanted more children and took my church very seriously. So he used prophylactics and we had sex not often enough. The second child came three and one-half years later only after I threatened to leave him unless he gave me another child. Because there was so much conflict and the church's position violated his conscience, my pastor told me to take the pill and receive the sacraments. It was about four years before I finally talked him into trusting the pill. By that time he was so used to ignoring me, it was too late to bring us closer together.

We just grew farther and farther apart. Communication was poor, there was no companionship, sexual interest and even later potency decreased. I am warm and affectionate by nature, I need to be with people not things, and I like peace and order. There was no one to love but the children, no world to be a part of but their world.

He was out to bars four to five nights a week while I sat home with the kids. He would tell me about all the young girls that talked to him about their problems (mainly, loving a married man) after he had made love to me. I was so tired of mothering and forgiving a self-centered, insecure little boy. I needed a husband (as in adult) to love and to love me not another child (problem child at that). Eventually, he met a gal he wanted to marry. He was 37, I was 30, she was 23. I am brunette, tall, and large-boned. She is blond, short, and tiny (Protestant too). I got the house and the girls and freedom. He paid the bills (including the lawyer) and married her four months after the divorce was final.

She is a sweet person. The children like her and she is good to them. I am grateful. They have been married one year now. I *really hope it will work, but I have my doubts. He was shocked to hear her voicing the same complaints I made. They are fighting more often and longer. She is on the pill because she wants to be sure before they have children. I hoped she could reach him; for all his denials, he needs love so desperately. I still feel he must have professional help first.*

Kathleen, 31, Michigan secretary

Wow! It's difficult to take a marriage—a significant slice of my life which furnished the environment for my beautiful children—and say it failed because of "choose one." I feel it was our basic unreadiness for marriage—for the style and depth of commitment necessary to make a marriage work. We were totally unprepared and ignorant of what it would be like—not really in the absolute sense. As we grew older, the complications arose, alcoholism and infidelity, to name two landmarks. Neither of these in themselves is important—it was our unrealistic, self-damaging reaction to them!

Jim, 40, California salesman

Emotional immaturity on my part because of the way I was brought up. I was idealistic and unsophisticated and made a poor choice. My husband was a sheltered, only child reared by doting parents, particularly a domineering mother. He grew up with much sex guilt and over-developed feelings of self-importance. As a result, he preferred masturbation to intercourse (I was a virgin when we were married). He felt that sex was strictly a means of conceiving children and disliked it. He refused to get help from a psychiatrist to deal with the problem.

Elizabeth, 32, Tennessee C.P.A.

Adultery committed with my best friend and my boss! I had no knowledge of what was going on, until my wife just took off with the kids and left me the empty house.

Jerry, 44, New York sales mgr.

Over-expectation of the role of a husband on the part of the wife. She simply expected too much—money, devotion, etc.

Dan, 35, Illinois engineer

My ex-husband was only 23 when we married (I was 30), and I think he thought of me as his mother. He came from a divorced family and had a chip on his shoulder.

Natalie, 52, New Hampshire homemaker

Many factors were involved. I think the main problem was our immaturity at the time of marriage. My wife seemed to mature suddenly at about age 27, and underwent a complete personality change in the space of a few months. She started wondering how much she had missed by being married. As a result, we started a round of parties and nightclubbing which ended in a divorce. I grew tired of night life, and she seemed to blossom from it.

Frank, 33, California warehouseman

Immaturity. I was afraid of being an "old maid" so I married a man I had only known one month (at 21).

—anonymous female, 29

Adultery on the part of my husband. We had a very close relationship until the children arrived. It was then he began to "stray," when he knew I'd be home involved with the kids. Having children didn't enhance the marriage and I feel now he never wanted the responsibility of children to begin with. On the other hand, I strongly wanted children and have never regretted having them.

Harriet, 44, Maryland secretary

I had to get married. I was pregnant and only seventeen. I just wasn't enthused about staying with him after the baby came

L., 35, California housewife

She was ill and unstable; she didn't know what or who she really wanted; and never straightened out her priorities.

Jack, 36, California hotel exec

We had a handicapped child, who took all my time away from my husband. Another married woman gave him the attention he sought and built up his ego.

Muriel, 61, California (no occupation given)

It was his idea. The deciding factor was his utter lack of interest in lovemaking. We both thought this had a psychiatric cause and he sought counseling—which determined that he was OK psychologically, but just not in love or attracted to his wife. We separated for two years, during which time he became attracted to, and lived with, a psychologist, whom he later married. I suspect he's still undemonstrative and unaffectionate. I thought originally, when we were going together, that his lack of (sexual affection) reflected a strong moral fiber.

Margery, 42, Massachusetts R.N.

Children. Raising a family is a severe test of a relationship. It's nothing like an affair.

G., 59, New York housewife

My wife couldn't handle finances. She was always feeling sorry for herself. She got herself a girl friend and always put herself first over the family and me. She couldn't admit her errors. (married 24 years)

Lawrence, 50, Nebraska dispatcher

I guess we really did grow apart and matured in different ways in the 10 years of our marriage. At 21 we did love each other and had similar needs and interests. Ten years later, I was politically liberal, people-oriented and socially outgoing, and I had much more confidence in myself. I no longer felt at ease with my husband's values in the business world where money was the goal for which he worked. He became a "workaholic" and I couldn't accept it. He became politically conservative, developed a mistrust of groups of people by profession and race, and he expected me to do likewise. We were surprised to discover we had little in common with each other; in fact, we didn't like each other anymore!

Linda, 32, California teacher-counselor

Financial difficulties and adultery. I knew I was just an interim partner who stood in the way of his love for a former lover who was now free. The expense of maintaining two women totally depleted his income and I finally lost out. You should hear the whole story. I'll call him Hank. A marriage is doomed from the start when, unknowingly, one partner is a "last ditch" choice after many rejections. I married a man 11 years my senior only to learn later that years do not mean "maturity." In 1946 Hank fell in love with the wife of an Army buddy. Brief affair, but she didn't divorce her husband so Hank moved away and married wife #1. While married to wife #1, Army buddy and wife divorce. She writes letter to Hank for continuing the affair. Hank and Wife #1 divorce, but it takes a long time in that particular state. Meanwhile, she finds new love at closer proximity and marries. Hank now out in cold; Wife #1 won't reconcile. Hank moves 1,700 miles away and years pass. He's lonely. Correspondence with ex-lover, but no encouragement. He seeks new life and new love. Hank marries Wife #2 after nine months' courtship (that's me). Tells little of past life, which he claims he wishes to forget completely. Soon discovers he's unhappy with Wife #2. Spends excessive time at work and gambles heavily (to the tune of $52,000). Makes frequent trips back East to visit ex-lover. Buys her expensive gifts, neglects family. Her husband dies. He goes East to console her and take care of arrangements for her family. Brief affair again, but no suggestion of marriage during the funeral. It would look improper, they say. So Hank returns to Wife #2. The widow remarries again—to ex-brother-in-law, because he was "close-at-hand." More years pass. Hank still unhappy, but reluctant to sever ties with present family, etc., because of credit, social status, etc. He hangs on. Visits ex-lover whenever possible. Her third marriage shaky. She divorces finally and Hank drops everything—quits job, deserts family, leaves state and is reunited with now-free lover. They change identity and disappear forever. Wife #2 granted divorce on grounds of abandonment.

> Elizabeth, "over 30," Nevada (no occupation given)

Immaturity and different races. He became very involved in the Indian movement—and I'm not an Indian. And he drank.

> —anonymous female, 28

Lack of communication. We weren't in financial trouble; there was no third party. We were both in our mid-twenties and quite mature when married. But evidently there were things about both of us that bugged the other. Aren't there always? I can distinctly remember pointing these out to my wife, but nothing improved. I suppose the same thing happened the other way around. It's strange, but the one most important thing in life is communication. We can't exist without it. Yet I know of no school where communication with other people is taught. We are not educated for life, unfortunately.

> J., 43, Delaware marketing man

My mother-in-law.

> Anthony, 57, New York (no occupation given)

The reason for my divorce was my wife, her mother and her uncle realized how easy it would be to "get" me while we were separated.

> Bill, 50, New York stockbroker

We were not enough alike—we had very few common interests and grew farther apart in interests and viewpoints and values over the years.

> Ferne, 52, Michigan

Fundamental values different, financial problems.

> Dan, 45, New Jersey industrial mgr.

The more I wanted a good, close relationship, the more he wanted out. He got the divorce.

> Elaine, 33, California homemaker

My husband's immaturity, lack of stability, lack of money sense, and complete selfishness. His family was just a sideline.

> Alice, 48, Illinois hospital worker

My husband was too insecure, and it led him very close to alcoholism: His wife wasn't too understanding, either.

> Cheryl, 33, New Jersey teacher

Immaturity of my partner, possible sociopathic traits. Also, our growing inability to communicate about our feelings and to make important decisions together.

> Emily, 38, Maryland librarian

Failure of the female to leave the authority of her mother.

> Ralph, 44, Maryland publishing exec

My ex-husband was raised in an orphanage from infancy and could not form a deep or lasting relationship.

> —anonymous female, 49

He only dated one other girl before me and consequently had to have his flings periodically during our marriage. His conscience bothered him because of these flings and he started drinking. His drinking caused arguments, which caused more flings, and so on. He had one fling too many, and she convinced him to marry her.

Harriet, 46, Illinois

Failure to cope with present day problems. Immaturity, lack of understanding.

Barbara, 41, California postal worker

Society in general caused our divorce. The fast tempo of living. I've been divorced for five years and have gone over this millions of times in my mind. Maybe people live longer and learn more through television and the news media, more leisure time to idle away thinking. But I truly believe that if we had stayed in our small ranch town in Northern Wyoming, where kinfolk are near and divorce almost unheard of, instead of coming to Denver, we'd have weathered the marriage. I look back in my mind at old marriages, people living together after 50 years, etc. They are not happy acting. But would they be happier with a different partner? We were made to want a mate. The minute we lose one we hurry and find another, and then there is something wrong with the new one.

John, 36, Colorado truck driver

My husband's job and his immaturity. He met a woman who sympathized with the lies he told her.

V. (female), 50, Illinois factory worker

My ex-wife's immaturity when we were married (she was only 17 at the time), and my own inability to cope with the necessary adjustments.

David, 39, Virginia (no occupation given)

My husband's mother and sister created situations within a few months of the marriage which caused a lasting problem because of his loyalty to his family. Perhaps my immaturity did not allow me to handle the situation as I would today.

A. (female), 48, Michigan accountant

Mental incompatibility. We have different values and standards, and even though we tried to meet each other's, the variation was too great.

Sylvia, 36, Connecticut secretary

When he was close to age 50, he wanted to run. We had problems with our oldest boy, and he just could not face up to it and wanted out. He was a very immature person!

Arlene, 52, Pennsylvania bookkeeper

Definitely, emotional immaturity. All of the other causes are a result of this one factor. I think 95% of all divorces are caused by emotional immaturity.

Barbara, 51, Illinois health tech.

Immaturity of both members; poor parental models for male-female roles. Even though we both knew better, in the crunch, either reverted to less-than-positive reactions witnessed in childhood.

Mary, 55, Washington professor

Immaturity when married led to financial difficulties, adultery on his part, suspicion and unforgiveness on my part.

Jeanne, 33, Connecticut rental agent

No trouble until husband decided to trade me in for a much younger (28) model (after 25 years of marriage).

Margaret, 53, Kansas librarian

Right from the beginning, our ideas of what constituted security differed. He seemed to view marriage, itself, as security; I could not feel that secure without (owning) a home. Therefore, I suppose, you could term our difficulties "financial." To accomplish this aim of financial security, I put him through college, thinking that after graduation he would attain the kind of job that would afford my idea of security. My little bubble burst when I discovered that the degree gave him no more ambition, career-wise, than he had exhibited before.

Judy, 34, California secretary

We had financial problems, he committed adultery, but the real thing was that he sexually molested our daughter.

Jan, 31, California keypunch operator

I feel one of the major causes was the inability to argue. We both kept our annoyances to ourselves, never cleared the air, and over the years many resentments were built-up. It became too difficult to go back. In our case, children didn't help the marriage, either. I felt cut off from the outside world, and from his world, and he didn't seem interested in the details of my life, which was small children.

Elizabeth, 32, Massachusetts secretary

My wife's immaturity and infidelity while I was overseas in the Korean War.

Richard, 43, Minnesota divorce counselor

Stupidity about how to prevent conception. I was pregnant going into both of my marriages! That, and the desire to be loved led me into them.

Joyce, 40, New York college professor

Even though our family backgrounds were similar and our religious feelings were the same, we seemed to look at life differently, and though I tried to understand how he felt about things, he didn't seem to feel I made the effort. And I felt the same way about him. We could not communicate our feelings well to each other, somehow.

Della, 49, California teacher

My dependent nature led me to marry a man who abused me mentally. It was neurotic of me, knowing what he was like before we were married. Engaged for nine months. He was an immature, spoiled, temperamental, degrading, vicious man. He still is. He hurt me mentally and physically. On my third try (for the divorce) I finally went through with it. It was extremely difficult for me as he had destroyed my ego by that time, and being dependent by nature, it was quite a job for me to fight his cries of suicide (phony), manipulation to keep me, and strike out on my own. I am so glad I did, though.

—anonymous Michigan woman, 37

I was immature, we had financial problems, and I had made the mistake of marrying a girl from Germany.

Thomas, (no age), Pennsylvania painter

My wife refused to take care of me when I went into the hospital for my third spinal operation.

Russ, 65, Pennsylvania retired builder

He wanted to go into racing and decided to give up his family instead of exploring other marriage arrangements and to keep himself better off financially.

Sonya, 30, California teacher

Basic emotional immaturity, with severe emotional problems on his part. He refused to let me grow and become a "person."

Amy, 39, California (no occupation given)

I just got married to get away from parents who fought constantly.

Lillian, 44, Pennsylvania (no occupation given)

Drinking, jealousy, immaturity.

Sarah, 53, California clerk

It is my contention that failure to mature is the contributing factor that leads to financial difficulties, adultery, of which all three problems did exist.

Howard, 42, Utah contractor

My first marriage ended because of immaturity when first married—I was only 25—and my second because the marriage was only my wife's way of finding a meal ticket and a way out of her own divorce loneliness.

Raymond, 51, Pennsylvania ad exec

Lack of communication. We were unable to express our feelings to one another.

Billie, 30, California secretary

One marriage ended because it was a marriage without love—just a blundering adventure. My third marriage ended because we had only known each other for three months and only thought we knew and understood each other. My husband's age and insecurity from his evil past produced much guilt, and after major surgery he flipped out to be a swinger.

Ruby, 51, California teacher

Sexual incompatibility.

Neil, 34, New York (no occupation given)

My wife's inability to say "no" to over-demanding and possessive parents.

Nate, 40, Pennsylvania meat-cutter

Immaturity of wife and also outside pressure from her family, primarily her brother-in-law, who is also her attorney.

Julian, 46, Georgia (no occupation given)

She volunteered this information: "After a girl is out of her 20's she is no longer interested in sex, is glad when her husband's out of town, and wishes he'd go elsewhere for it when he's home."

R., 51, Michigan writer

Each case has its own merits. This marriage was calculated by an "intelligent" woman, i.e., one who was convinced of female superiority, to end in separation. Only purpose: to obtain a lifelong pension from a member of the hated opposite sex and to have children in order to back up this demand.

Henry, 66, Canada retired photographer

My husband's adultery was a symptom of his inability to adjust to aging, changing, accepting life in the middle years. Financial difficulties were always there, but just as the children were older and the burdens easing, he took on another wife and three step-children, and had two babies! At 56, I wonder if it's all that great.

Gwen, 54, Texas investigator

Adultery, financial difficulties, dishonesty.

W. (male), 67, Ohio physician

Immaturity when married. But since April, 1963, I have been living an unnatural life. Neither married nor single. My wife got a legal separation from me in 1963 but would not give me a divorce. Aside from the financial hardships, I have endured many other indignities. I feel as if I had the legal rights of a slave. I feel like an outcast.

Charles, 43, New Jersey (no occupation given)

First Marriage: *Complete incompatability of temperament; she wanted status quo, I wanted change.*

Second marriage: *Immaturity.*

Third marriage: *Spouse became an alcoholic.*

Chuck, 44, Connecticut writer

Immaturity. We had children too soon after marriage.

Dale, 31, Illinois roofer

My wife became interested in someone else, feeling my profession came first to me.

Ron, 37, Florida psychotherapist/marriage counselor

Variance in backgrounds, upbringing, ambitions.

Sondra, 38, California (no occupation given)

She had an operation, an aneurism, a brain operation. Her first husband committed suicide by jumping off a ferry boat. She had three children and the daughter tells me now that "Mother has never—and will never—admit that she was wrong." She married me for my money and then suddenly wanted to take off with all of it. She was a slob, anyway. I had to teach her how to wash the dishes and to wash clothes. I asked her to distribute the clothes around the spindle in the dryer, but she wouldn't and two bearings burnt out in six months. She never closed up the dishwasher, either. Left it open at all times, and never put the clean ones in the closet. My nephew told me he stopped eating at her house as a boarder because he never knew whether he was eating off dirty or clean dishes. She cleaned my white porcelain sink only twice in four months, and then testified in court that the enamel was off it and even water caused it to rust. My cleaning woman testified under oath that she has worked for me for fifteen years, once a week, and that the enamel was not worn off. My wife's bed was full of Kleenex, too. I have pictures of it with over 15 wads of Kleenex strewn from top to bottom.

Walter, 77, West Virginia retired exec

Psychological problems stemming from my ex's childhood. Her mother has been married at least eight times. My wife still gets treatment, still has the problem.

Bill, 33, Wisconsin minister

I think the divorce started with financial difficulties. We were fixing up an old converted building in _____ and after spending much time and money on repairs and upgrading, we found ourselves in a zoning problem with the city. We lost the building and all we had put into it, and were badly in debt. There were medical bills for the boys and we were almost to the point of filing for bankruptcy. My income was only enough to meet out day-to-day expenses and we were making no headway against the bills. I believe I went into a deep depression and withdrew from my family by closing myself off from them when I was at home. I also started drinking too much. I was going to take a second job, but my wife said she preferred to go back to work herself, so that the children would have a father around, as was their "right." So I worked nights and she worked days. Anyway, communication broke down to the point where we were just about out of debt, and I thought things were going well and were going to get better when I came home from work one day and she had left. I had no idea that this was coming and was quite shocked.

Frank, 39, Minnesota compositor

Personality conflict   Philip, 48, Pennsylvania clergyman

Almost all those things, plus lack of honesty and unreasonable expectations. He wanted me to do sexual things which shocked me. I'm certain no one else has ever done them.

Doris, 51, Louisiana secretary

My wife was always competing with me, and couldn't quite make it. Derogatory remarks, etc. whenever we were with other people.

H. (male), 57, Massachusetts merchant

I was married and had two children when my first wife died. I married a second time, and after about six years problems developed which should have been corrected. But after time went by, "friends" got involved and pushed her to file for divorce instead of working things out. I was cleaned out. I found that attorneys were so bad in these cases that I enrolled in law school and am now a lawyer myself. I get many people back together and I try to be 100% fair with my clients on both sides. I favor counseling as an answer—a must!

J., California lawyer

Certainly "immaturity when married" was a factor, at least in making a poor choice, but ultimately it was "incompatability of needs"—that's the nicest objective generality I can give. Yes, that includes sexual problems.

June, 42, Connecticut clerk

Bad judgment about character.

> Norman, 58, Texas (no occupation given)

She thought she was getting younger instead of older; she started running around with younger men.

> Mark, 38, New Jersey (no occupation given)

Husband's inability to function as a responsible adult. Married too young (at 19).

> Denise, 31, Indiana (no occupation given)

The profit the pimp lawyers promise tramps.

> Arthur, 44, Illinois (no occupation given)

I feel that I grew emotionally, while he didn't at all. Therefore, our ideas on almost everything changed. I was very young when we married (19).

> Carol, 29, New York (no occupation given)

Sex. My husband would treat me like a person with an incurable, contagious disease all day long, but when we got in bed at night he would roll over and grab my breast like it was a piece of lunch meat or something. No feeling, no nothing. I'd tell him he avoided me all day long, and not to expect any favors, and he'd say, "I want what I want when I want it." He then started going out on me, and when he'd come home at five o'clock in the morning he'd explain by saying he was working hard selling vacuum cleaners as an extra job. He accused me of cheating on him. When I found out for sure about all his cheating, I asked him to leave.

> Bonnie, 30, Illinois (no occupation given)

Immaturity of wife; too much involvement with the house, and (my) involvement with work. Adultery on her part, and I tried to be too understanding.

> Patrick, 32, New Jersey programmer

We were much too young to realize the seriousness of marriage. I had no idea of how to cope with a drinking husband or one that chased all the girls. Perhaps had I been older and more mature I could have handled (it) differently. Considering the fact that he has been married four more times since our divorce, I can't in all honesty say that divorce was the answer. A good marriage doesn't *just happen. It takes a true commitment, a great deal of true love, maturity, understanding, communication, acceptance, and the ability to forgive and forget.*

Rose, 53, California (no occupation given)

My husband drank quite a bit and was running around, never coming home some nights. We were fighting and doing nothing but hurting each other and the children.

Judith, 35, Colorado waitress

I don't know. My wife never gave me any clear answers. One time she did say that she didn't love me.

Tony, 38, New Jersey (no occupation given)

Inability to recognize incompatabilities beforehand. An incomplete value system.

Dolores, 44, New York (no occupation given)

My mother-in-law!

Stanley, 48, Connecticut (no occupation given)

Immaturity. My wife started using drugs.

George, 34, Illinois truck driver

We never could agree on the problem of child discipline.

Bill, 49, Texas mechanic

She didn't want to be a minister's wife, was going through the "change," and then fell in love with another man.

Lawson, 62, Illinois minister

My wife had trouble breaking away from her family. At first we lived with her mother, father and brother, because apartments were in short supply and my work required that I be close, but finally I couldn't stand the noise and the constant butting in, so we moved. She kept visiting her mother, though, and even ignored the house and kids, until finally she had a nervous breakdown. Eventually I was both mother and father to my sons anyway, so I divorced her.

Stewart, 56, New Jersey stock clerk

An intractable wife. First she refused to get up in the morning and feed our child, then she harassed my parents out of their own house so she could move in. She was too selfish and greedy to live with any longer.

Gary, 41, Delaware pharmacist

I guess everything. Financial arguments led to his adultery, which led to fierce guilt feelings on his part because he was immature.

Beverly, 30, Illinois (no occupation given)

I think we both changed over the years, and in different ways. I grew up on a farm in the Midwest and learned to enjoy new things and new places, attending classes to improve myself, working outside the home or doing volunteer work transcribing Braille, etc. He seemed to settle into a rut with no interests beyond his job and the television set. I felt that I had only lived half of my life and the best part was still to come, while he acted old before his time.

Vivian, 40, California secretary

My husband was "very unhappy." He wanted "to be free and on his own." He felt he was "too dependent on me." He wanted "to learn to stand on his own two feet." (The quotes are all his words.) I think he really felt tied down—restricted by a wife and children. He wanted relationships with other women, and I wasn't too happy about it.

Elsie, 51, California (no occupation given)

Immaturity, irresponsibility. I was only 19.

Marie, 22, Florida (no occupation given)

My first marriage failed because of immaturity when married (at 18). My second failed because of financial problems, adultery, problems with children from a previous marriage, and he was an alcoholic.

Martha, 35, California industrial clerk

Some degree of immaturity, but more importantly, not knowing what should go into a relationship. I also chose a partner who didn't know how to communicate. Communications and trust are the underlying causes for any breakdown in a relationship. Anything can be worked out if you care enough and talk about it.

Kathy, 35, Minnesota medical asst.

My wife was and is money-mad, crooked and vile. Just a plain thief and viper, etc. She is and always will be insecure from the depression of the thirties.

Larry, 48, Michigan (no occupation given)

She was jealous of the children. After the divorce, she was classified as having an emotional age of seven or eight.

Robert, 52, Illinois farmer

Several factors applied. We were very different types of people, and I didn't become what she wanted me to be. I never could furnish the life-style she wanted. She stopped all sex activity. Now it develops that she's a lesbian.

John, 47, Pennsylvania insurance exec

We were unable to compromise. Neither one of us lived up to the other's expectations of the "ideal" spouse.

Robert, 34, Missouri contract analyst

My husband simply asked for a divorce so he could marry someone else. He said he didn't love me any more.

Jane, 48, New York R.N.

She had two abortions without my consent.

Dave, 30, Kentucky civil servant

Totally different backgrounds, so we had different views of what was expected in marriage. Also, he had no love when he was a child, so I think he was incapable of loving another person. The private humiliation went for years, but adultery at the end caused me to decide I couldn't live that way anymore.

Mary, 31, California student

Everything, as well as no appreciation of the wife on the part of the husband. He could see that he was working hard, but not that I was, too. He had an outside job, and a business at home, and spent long hours. And we had four children, too.

Peg, 46, New York cosmetician

There are many underlying causes of my marriage breakup. They started two years after my marriage. Up until five and one-half years ago, my husband was a sleeper. Work, eat, drink and sleep. We had no friends, as my husband didn't like anyone I brought into the home. I raised our four children alone. This I never regretted, as I wanted my children very much, and planned them the best I could with a husband who rationed out sex. Five and one-half years ago my husband started drinking heavy. He was involved in homosexual activities, child-molesting, sat in topless bars nightly drunk, ran to parties alone, and came home all hours of the night drunk, sometimes staying away the entire weekend. He ended up in a solid drunk for eight months before he deserted our 14-year-old daughter and I. During this time he came home only once a week to change his filthy clothes. He had lived with a man one month, and a woman who was 48 and had three children three months before deserting us. The woman said she brought him home, when he said he had no clothes, no money, no home or food. Between his job, when he worked, and my nursing jobs, we made $20,000 or more a year. He demanded, and got, hundreds of dollars at a time so he could run and drink. He lied to get this money. Said he had repairs on the truck or needed money for tools. Nearly a year before he left, he hardly worked, and the full responsibility of the house and family was on me. Although, I was quite ill. He told people I made enough money to support the family and he could take a job when he wanted. The final blow was the fact that I was unable to work any longer because of my poor health, so he found another woman who worked and could supply his expensive habits.

Sex was a big problem. My husband refused my advances all but the first 2 years of our marriage. He offered sex only when he felt like it, which was rare. During the last year of the marriage I finally realized I was paying for my sex. Whenever he wanted large sums of money he would go to bed with me several nights, then ask for the money. When I finally realized what was happening, I refused to give him the money and the sex ended. The final decision that a legal separation was necessary was after adultery. This is hard for a woman to take when she has had to beg for just about all the sex in her married life.

Evelyn, 53, California nurse

A combination of everything, especially adultery. But on both sides, not just him.

Alice, 37, Kansas housewife

Complete disagreement on every aspect of life, except intellectual considerations of art. There was no amity of thought from the beginning

Norman, 41, Pennsylvania (no occupation given)

Children! I consider them very important to a marriage, and he thought I loved them more than him and was quite jealous of the attention they required from me. Our last child came when the other two were 11 and 8, and so maybe the long time span contributed. In looking back, I think the one big goof I made was nursing the baby. I think he resented it. In all honesty I love them because they're part him!

Patsy, 37, California R.N.

Immaturity on my part contributed to a polarity of outlooks. We were both college graduates (she's a social worker) but I was hung up on personal insecurity and used intellectualism as a shield. I tended to get frustrated . . . she had a stronger grasp on her own version of practical reality. Family (pressure), moving to the suburbs, etc., increased the interpersonal strain which reflected itself in money arguments and other oblique outlets.

Roland, 48, Connecticut engineer

Financial difficulty, adultery, immaturity when married.

Stan, 29, Florida author

I got tired of being treated like Minnie Mouse. The mouse finally roared and he moved out.

Jean, 45, Illinois secretary

Immaturity when married . . . the romantic notion of love as a standard excuse for marriage.

T., 44, Pennsylvania minister

I believe my divorce resulted from a combination of many reasons. First, I think there was immaturity on both of our parts when we first were married. For my part, I had no business getting married in the first place. I did not like being cooped up in a house all day, and I absolutely despised housework. Secondly, I sincerely believe that I let myself think I had fallen in love with my husband, when in fact, I really had not. I substantiate this fact on the grounds that in 1966 I had lost a man who I still think about to this day, and in my own estimation, my husband's apparent love for me gave me someone to cling to. Sometimes it just seemed better to be loved than to love, although my mind did not comprehend that at the time. Also immaturity became apparent with the difference of religion. Two grown people did not even tell their parents they were getting married. We just eloped. And, last but not least, I knew he had been in trouble before, although I did not really know the full extent of that trouble until after we were married. I should have dated him for a much longer period of time before deciding to take such a big step in life.

Immaturity on his part was there from the beginning to the end of our marriage. He had been an only child. In fact, both he and his mother had almost died when he was born; his mother was then told that she could never have another child. His family was well-to-do and had given him anything he wanted, even to the point of buying him a bar when just a little over 21, with him and his father as owners and managers. The police would never touch him if he went tearing down the street in his hot-rod because he was the————kid. He thought he could get away with anything and that the world owed him a living.

Alice, 29, Minnesota factory worker

Utter dependency on roles we couldn't play. Emotional growth led to increasing incompatibility.

Mary, 26, California student

The whole bag, believe it or not. Financial difficulty, immaturity when married, which in turn led to drinking problems on the part of my husband, which in turn led to adultery.

Wendie, 33, New York (no occupation given)

Immaturity—one can be too old to be rational, as well as too young. I felt life was passing me by and that I'd better grab this "last chance." He was very immature.

Linda, 34, California secretary

We lost interest in each other.

Sandra, 32, Missouri college professor

My husband didn't want to continue in the role of husband and father.

Dianne, 32, California homemaker

Lack of communication. Whenever I tried to express my feelings he would change the subject and make me feel foolish. It's pretty hard to talk when the other person doesn't respond. I didn't realize the pattern was developing.

Margaret, 55, New York (no occupation given)

I was married four months after our son was born, because my fiancé was in jail from the time I was one month pregnant. After four months of marriage, he moved out to his girl friend's apartment, leaving me and my eight-month-old son without money or food. Subsequently, his parents, who were also our landlords, forced my son and I to move out because my husband hadn't paid the rent. Two months after my husband abandoned us, he commited bigamy, for which he was arrested, convicted and put on probation. He left the state in 1971 and for quite a while his whereabouts were unknown. I'd say that his lies and adultery and his refusal to talk about our problems were the cause of our marriage collapsing.

Sandi, 23, New York homemaker

We got married too young. For the first four years it was fine, but when our baby was born and I had to stay home, I became very dissatisfied. I began to develop my own interests—politics, population control, the women's movement—and he found his own hobbies: bowling and bar-hopping. My myth collapsed and I got hysterical at having to make my own life.

Barbara, 28, New York bank teller

There were several reasons, any one of which, I think, could have been tolerated, were it not for the others. But put them all together, and you have the formula for disaster. I will begin with your suggested reasons:

a) Financial difficulties; this was sort of the "last straw"; at the time we finally decided to give up, I was and had been out of a job and had no prospects for one. Throughout the marriage, I had earned a "respectable" living and one of my ex's few virtues was her ability to manage money. She was a good shopper and if anything, was somewhat penurious. I tended to be a little loose with money. (I have since become much tighter!)

b) Adultery: several counselors told me that if anyone ever had a reason to be unfaithful, it was I. Two things kept me from it: (1) although the marriage was in trouble more often than not during its six-year duration, we were seeing counselors and hopefully, moving in a positive direction; I didn't want extramarital flings on my conscience if we ever did get things worked out; and (2) even if I had been so inclined, there just wasn't any opportunity for it; we lived in small towns throughout the marriage and I as a teacher (which I no longer am), was in the "public eye" all the time. I worked many evenings, and there really wasn't that much time. As for my wife, I doubt very much that she would have had an affair. She could hardly tolerate marital sex, much less going for the other kind.

c) Immaturity when married; well, if (a) and (b) are quite specific situations, (c) is something of an abstraction and therefore subject to interpretation. What qualities distinguish "maturity" from "immaturity?" At what age does one cease being "immature" and become "mature"? Or does the process even depend on chronological age? Is it possible to be both simultaneously? I had just turned 28 when we were married and was academically mature (I began to study for my doctorate in education during our first summer of marriage), but socially (i.e., in terms of interpersonal relationships) I was quite naive and immature. The sad truth of the matter is that I married my wife because no one else would accept my proposal and I was getting desperate. She was 21, very unsophisticated, and marriage to an "up-and-coming-teacher" was a better alternative than returning to an intolerable home situation or clerking for $1.60 an hour when the college money ran out. I guess it might be said that we chose each other because no one else would have either of us. And that's a hell of a way to begin a marriage.

d) Basic differences in personality: too late, we discovered that I am an "obsessive compulsive," my wife, a "passive aggressive." I am very methodical, schedule-oriented, a "plotter and a planner," neat, prompt, dinner-at-six kind of person. She is very impulsive, disorganized, "happy-go-lucky," chronically late, always a day behind (or more). In the jargon of Transactional Analysis, I was forced into the role of super-Parent, and she functioned as a Child. I tried to get her into an Adult role, so we could interact Adult-Adult, but it just didn't work. She finally "graduated" after we separated. Then she had no choice.

e) Sexual incompatibility: maybe this should be #1. The old saying is: if you can make it in bed, then everything else either falls into place by itself or else just doesn't make that much difference; if you can't, then everything else can be OK, but the marriage will still fail. When sex and everything else turns sour, then I guess you might as well just forget it. For a variety of reasons (church and parental influence, primarily), I had had sex relations only once before I met my wife. She and I had relations perhaps 4 or 5 times during our engagement period (5 months) and while the experiences were never successful, there were always "good reasons" for the failures: wrong atmosphere, she was too tired, I was in too big a hurry, perhaps most of all, fear of pregnancy (she didn't start on the pill until a month before we were married), you name it. We kept telling ourselves that once we were married, everything would straighten out. But they didn't; I have a very strong sex drive and I'm sure that for the first several months of our marriage, I was considerably less than a considerate and understanding lover. When I was finally able to calm down a little, the die had pretty well been cast. My wife, who was 21, had been raised in an extremely prudish, religiously-fundamentalist home and really had it drummed into her that sex was a duty and at that, one to be performed as little as your husband would tolerate. She suffered from chronic vaginismus, and each month, dysmenorrhea and menostaxis, during all of which she refused to have sex relations. In our six years together, she never once had an orgasm.

f) Differences in values and interests: I am basically an indoor person; I have a graduate degree in music and was a music teacher throughout our marriage. I am a reader and a writer, and I have also done a great deal of work in photography (uncounted hundreds of hours in lab work). I enjoy the theatre and I have always been active in church work. She loves gardening, horses, hiking, and art, yes, and she was a very competent cook, too, when she took the time to be. She enjoys music, but given the choice of a horse show or a concert, she would prefer the horses. Now the above differences would not be incompatible if they were handled appropriately. But time after time, she would leave a dirty house and dishes in the sink to go out and "piddle with the posies" for the afternoon. (Her excuse: "I might as well take advantage of the sunshine to work outdoors, then I'll do the housework after it gets dark.")

Lee, 37, Iowa civil servant

We had to get married. She got pregnant just as I was going to Korea. When I got back she said she wanted to run things herself.

Weldon, 40, Ohio (no occupation given)

One of our biggest difficulties was money. My husband was always buying something and then not paying for it. My credit cards and my parents' help got me through that, but after I left him I couldn't get any credit. This after paying off all his bills and never missing a payment.

Lynn, 21, Illinois (no occupation given)

Immaturity, plus progressive alcoholism on his part.

Terese, 40, Michigan secretary

First time, immaturity and incompatibility of cultures and intellect. Second time, sexual incompatibility. Third time, financial difficulties, symptomatic of noncommunication and sex identity problems of husband.

Jan, 35, medical secretary (no location given)

Although my husband made good money, he wouldn't supply me with the necessities. We lived in a roach-infested apartment in a poor neighborhood. Our furniture consisted of a bed with no mattress, two dressers, a sagging couch, a stereo, a TV and a table (but no chairs). All except the TV were left over from his previous marriage. We had no drapes, no rugs, no pictures for the walls, no lamps, etc. Money was a big source of irritation. He would come home on payday with $2 in his pocket and announce it was all we had to live on all week. To my knowledge he didn't drink or gamble and I've never been able to figure out what he did with the money. There were many times when there was no food in the house and I went hungry. The final problem was our child. My husband wanted a child but when I became pregnant he decided babies were too expensive . . . when the baby was born my husband told me not to come home. I did go back but he wouldn't touch the baby or me and wouldn't give me any money to buy formula or baby food and I was forced to leave.

Dawn, 23, Maryland homemaker

The underlying reason for my divorce was incompatibility; she had certain habits and ideas that I found intolerable. She was very undisciplined, kept a dirty house, never had meals on time, was a slovenly hostess, laid around in bed all day. Her reading was of cowboy and Indian stories, never of anything that I liked or wanted to discuss. She was emotionally unstable, given to tantrums, fits of anger that would last for months; one time she actually went into the hospital with intractable asthma because she was so upset over something her sister-in-law did. She was fear-ridden; everything and everybody in our lives was a threat and a danger; there was never a time that I could relax with her and think or accomplish anything. I see now this was her mode of keeping me in line, if the intellect is constantly attacked by the woman's emotions, the man becomes timid and can't get away from her. Mothers use this all the time to unman their sons and keep them at home. Adultery is not a cause of divorce, but it's a symptom of trouble. A happily married man is not looking for another woman. He just does not want her and becomes upset when another woman offers herself to him. Financial difficulties are in the same category. If these are a consideration then the woman is using this as an excuse to beat the man with his inadequacy and his inadequacy will be in the bed and not in the world of commerce. A couple that really enjoys sex together can stand a lot of poverty.

R., 45, North Dakota M.D.

Did you make a determined effort to "save" your marriage?

I went through three and a half years of personal counseling before making the decision to go through with it.

Jane, 34, California writer

We tried everything—marriage counselors, psychiatric help, group therapy, even swinging. We tried it all.

Bill, 34, California bartender

We tried to con ourselves into thinking we were staying together "for the sake of the kids" and that "things would work themselves out." What we were really saying was "it's a sin to get divorced so let's bear this cross." Never let religion enter into any effort to "save" the marriage.

Don, 36, Missouri commercial pilot

Sometimes things aren't really the way they seem. It takes time before things sink in during the whole divorce process. We had a bunch of things go wrong with our marriage, and even as long as ten years ago we tried a semi-separation thing. I was in the Army in Germany and went to school in Paris and we'd see each other on the weekends. At the time, we put it together fairly well and it lasted for a while. The last time, neither of us tried very hard to keep it together, probably because we realized a lot of things had gotten away from us.

Gerry, 41, California engineer

No. When I realized that it was no longer a positive relationship and that neither of us was going to change, I asked him to leave before I began to dislike him and the new negative relationship started hurting our child.

Jill, 31, California journalist

We tried therapy together, but the communication barriers were (too) strong. Ultimately I kept up the therapy, but he didn't. Then I took a separate apartment, and he lived in the house, but I kept looking more and more forward to dissolving the marriage to achieve total freedom.

Sue, 29, California teacher

We had one experience with counseling, but the "Family Service" counselor was so cold and impersonal that it discouraged us from trying anything else.

—anonymous male

I sought counseling and continued it for three years, but my husband only went for a short time.

Jane, 57, California housewife

We didn't seek counseling because we both wanted the divorce and wanted to go our separate ways. The marriage was a failure, but the divorce was a success, because we're good friends and see each other often, but there's no sex.

Mary, 24, California postal worker

I had several trial separations from him, but it was always the same thing. We'd go back together and after a day or two, he was back to pushing me around, degrading me in front of others and staying out all night. I remember our last "trial" separation—we went back together just long enough for him to "relieve" himself and have dinner! Then he told me he wasn't ready to go back together yet. I was humiliated and refused to leave or separate, but for the next four months he (wore) me down until I was hardly a human being at all. When I somehow knew a nervous breakdown was coming on I filed for my dissolution.

Carmen, 28, California corporate mgr.

*Yeah, she left me and then asked to come back, so I accepted her.
This happened twice. We talked to our priest a lot.*
                                       David, 25, California student

No chance. He wouldn't try any counseling, etc.
                                       Ann, 37, California homemaker

*None except a brief counseling session a few years before the
divorce.*
                                       Dan, 36, California teacher

Extensive counseling and individual marriage counseling.
                                Nora, 49, law student (no address given)

*I sure was determined, even after he tried to coerce me into wife-
swapping. I tried to help and support him as he went through
therapy in every way I could. He was under psychiatric care for
months. I begged him for joint counseling especially after periods
of very intense (domestic strife). He refused, saying it wasn't my
problem, just his. After a year of this, in desperation, we tried a
trial separation and it was a disaster to say the least. It was torturous for me particularly, because I desperately wanted the marriage to work. I clung to the hope that he would see that our
"straight" life had been much better, even after I moved with our
18-month-old baby to a small house on a beach (in a nearby
state). Suddenly, though, I was thrown into the "singles" life myself, and after I unsuccessfully tried to convince him that I was
worth coming back to, we made the ultimate decision to divorce.*
                                       Linda, 29, North Dakota homemaker

Several years of counseling for myself, but my husband refused it.
                                       Ann, 63, New York R.N.

I underwent counseling, but he would have none of it.
                                       Dolores, 47, California journalist

*Yes, I sure did, without any cooperation from him. I counseled
with attorneys, his doctor, my doctor, a few different psychiatrists
and a lot of friends. Nothing worked.*
                                Pat, 36, California (no occupation given)

I offered only to "save" the marriage if he'd repay all or part of the funds he took out of my bank account and replace some of the sentimental, personal belongings of mine that he sold. He didn't.

Mary, 62, New York legal secretary

My husband refused to work out any problems whatsoever although he claimed he still wanted to be friends with me. I tried to show as much interest as possible in his activities, but he was convinced our so-called life-styles were too diverse to attempt reconciliation.

Helen, 29, Michigan graduate student

Let's face it. I don't know what your survey is going to turn up, but it's mostly the guys who won't go to counseling or psychiatry or some such, because that's admitting to themselves that they're either "failing" or somehow in the wrong. It breaks a guy's masculinity to admit that there's something he can do to save the marriage. It's a shame that I can only admit that now.

Stan, 37, Arizona carpenter

No effort whatsoever, once the polarization became obvious to us.

Don, 29, California (no occupation given)

Yes, five years of psychoanalysis. My husband would have no part of it.

Carol, 45, New York teacher

By the time I had decided on divorce, there would have been little to change my mind, although six months into the marriage I did ask to have some outside counseling (married almost three years). I didn't feel that things were as they should be, but he convinced me things would work themselves out.

Joan, 27, California medical secretary

I went to counseling, but he refused. I think men refuse to count themselves in on such measures because they subconsciously or otherwise don't want to be married anymore in the first place. Saving it would be a defeat, actually.

Kate, 31, Idaho waitress

Trial separation, several visits to psychologists, endless discussions, advice from close friends—all in vain!

John, 45, California artist

First marriage: *No, she wanted no part of it. She became heavily involved in a job and Women's Lib, and no longer worried about raising kids, etc.*

Second marriage: *Yes, but it was offset by the problem of mental illness. Eventually the doctors themselves advised divorce for the children's sake.*

Tim, 47, California ad exec

Yes, I tried both counseling and trial separation. I also tried being a doormat.

Sue, 38, California teacher

No. Well, yes. But I was losing too much weight and becoming neurotic. You can't save a marriage to a nymphomaniac.

Arthur, 32, New Jersey fireman

He refused help through church, marriage counselor or Alcoholics Anonymous, because he felt he didn't need it. He said it was all my fault.

Pat, 32, North Dakota R.N.

No, not after he stated flat out that he wanted the divorce. Up until then, yes, but only on my part. I even offered him his choice of alternatives to divorce, such as change jobs, change cities, have an affair . . . . No, all he wanted was to divorce me.

Patricia, 38, California teacher

I sought counseling and the advice of friends, but my wife didn't because she said she "liked me but didn't love me."

Joe, 31, California teacher

Yes, I went to counseling for four months, but my wife was unwilling. I finally gave it up.

Dave, 33, North Dakota exec

The idea of counseling enraged him; it went downhill from there.

Ruth, 30, California (no occupation given)

First marriage: *No, I just wanted to undo the mistake I made.*

Second marriage: *Yes, I tried to get him to see a counselor with me, but he didn't think it would be worthwhile.*

June, 27, California sales representative

Yes, and even though we're now divorced, strangely, we're still trying to "save" it by individual counseling and therapy. He's a psychiatrist himself, but had an immaturity problem.

Carol, 36, Illinois secretary

Yes, we went through counseling for more than three years. It was a disastrous waste of time.

Larry, 42, New York film producer

Are you kidding? Name me a man who'll admit that he needs some of the help!

Ellen, 32, Texas actress

Yes, but we realized too late it was a mental problem.

James, 43, California credit mgr.

We tried a trial separation twice.

Sheila, 38, California housewife

She went to therapy, but I only went to two meetings. I guess I didn't have my heart in it, because I loved the practice of law more than her. (His wife: He didn't think he needed any help, the son of a bitch!)

Jim, 36, California lawyer

I went to counseling, but he wouldn't have any of it. I finally realized I was really only going to get up the psychological nerve to leave him.

Sylvia, 32, California real estate woman

Counseling, three years of separation.

Barbara, 45, New Jersey researcher

Yes. He wouldn't go, but I saw a marriage counselor and a psychiatrist, but only for five visits or so. He even refused to pay the bills, so you can guess how much of chance we had!

Joanne, 54, New York housewife

I had psychotherapy. The doctor strongly urged that he attend also, but he refused to do so.

Joan, 43, housewife (no address given)

It was too late. Counseling is needed before marriage, much more than after!

Matt, 54, New York insurance broker

Several years of psychotherapy and joint counseling for months.

Jean, 35, California librarian

Family Service help one year, but he wouldn't cooperate. Then my husband was psychiatrically confined to a hospital, and I was involved also. It only helped temporarily.

Veronica, 44, New York secretary

We tried to counsel ourselves, without "outside" help, but things had deteriorated beyond repair.

Emily, 33, New York R.N.

I tried to bend to her rules and regulations as long as I could and hoped she would gradually adjust. I finally gave up.

Charles, 37, North Dakota engineer

We went through counseling to try to spare the child any anguish.

Gordon, 44, Toronto salesman

We separated after three years, and after three months went back together again. The second separation didn't involve any effort to get back together, and we finally divorced.

Denise, 29, California secretary

No, we simply parted, citing religious reasons, and admitted we just didn't want to be married.

Marilyn, 38, California housewife

No, it was obvious.

Don, 44, New York restaurateur

Several trial separations. I actually filed for divorce once, but we got back together. The next time it all fell apart.

Linda, 31, California (no occupation given)

Yes, because symptoms of the bad relationship started to become evident in our children. An effort to help them led to extensive counseling for us, but it didn't help the marriage as much as the kids.

Aileen, 43, Illinois teacher

We tried a trial separation, but that hardly ever works. The under-lying problems are too great to be solved simply by moving apart. If one person wants the divorce, no amount of separating and counseling is going to help. Of course, it depends on what that reason for wanting the divorce is, but most of the time you're beating a dead horse. If a guy wants to screw around, he's going to do it married or no. If a woman wants to screw around, ditto. Each of them can go to counseling, repent, go back to being happily married, except that he or she will start being a little more dis-creet about stepping out on the other. And if a person simply no longer wants to be married, because he's got a girl friend who's bugging him or she just can't stand his guts, trying to "save" it is a complete waste of time and money.

R., 35, Pennsylvania (no occupation given)

Yes, but counseling didn't work, so he suggested a trial separa-tion, because he wanted to play around some more. Then we read a lot of books on the subject, and I tried making myself more attractive so he'd stay home once in a while. I worked hard at it.

Margery, 47, California realtor

I went to a licensed marriage counselor, but my husband wouldn't go.

Nancy, 33, Maryland teacher

I tried every kind of counseling available. My pastor, United Fund family service agencies, prayer, books, all of it. I begged and pleaded but there was no problem for him (until about the last year when the emptiness of our relationship finally struck him); he had everything his way. You must work together, you must both care and want to save the marriage.

Kathleen, 31, Michigan secretary

No, she wouldn't go. She said it wouldn't help. I offered her a trial freedom on her own but she declined.

Charles, 32, Iowa assembler

He didn't want counseling so we didn't seek it. I did attempt to have his parents and friends talk to him. After we did decide to separate, in March, we remained together until September to give me time to accept it and prepare for it by working out our ar-rangements. At first I thought he might change his mind, but I soon realized a separation was inevitable. The final date of separation was my choice.

Betty, 38, California government worker

Yes, we tried counseling, but my husband refused to take the advice given us. I got into therapy, and only through intensive therapy came to grips with the realization that my only salvation was to leave my husband and build a life of my own.

Elizabeth, 32, Tennessee C.P.A.

My wife refused it; she refused anything but the divorce.

Jerry, 44, New York sales mgr.

I did. He didn't.

Elsa, 31, New York secretary

No, I made no effort whatsoever. My wife attempted to persuade me that we should do something, but I couldn't see the point. These little things that bugged me had done so for so long that my affection and love for her had completely disappeared. The process is insidious. You first note the little things, which were formerly quite acceptable, also begin to grate on the nerves. Undoubtedly they wouldn't if the atmosphere had not already been provided by the situation caused by the other little bugs. And so things begin to deteriorate without you realizing it. Suddenly, before you know what's happening, everything has gone. There is no love left. And I'm quite sure that you can't make yourself love someone whom you do not love. Or perhaps I'm wrong. Anyway, no effort was made towards reconciliation.

J., 43, Delaware marketing man

In my first marriage we tried counseling and a trial separation. In my second we tried just counseling. And in my third we didn't try anything.

Penny, 34, Texas travel agent

If we'd seen a marriage counselor together we might have saved our marriage. Though I doubt we would have been happy even if we'd learned to "adjust" to our personality differences. We never really communicated. I was too embarrassed and emotional to talk rationally, and I guess he was too confused as to exactly what was wrong.

Margery, 42, Massachusetts R.N.

We went to a marriage counselor who told us it was impossible for us to live together. And we thought at the time that we were happily married. Stay away from counseling.

G., 59, New York housewife

No. Why fight a battle you can't win and in which the stakes aren't worth it?

Elizabeth, "over 30," Nevada (no occupation given)

I wanted to, but he said he could solve his own problems. My brother tried to talk to him but he walked out. The woman my husband was going with went to a psychologist, with her husband, and the psychologist told [them that] what she and my husband were doing "was nothing wrong."

Natalie, 52, New Hampshire homemaker

There wasn't time to "save" the marriage. When I found out about the affair (his girl friend came to the house, which was my first inkling of it), the other woman was pregnant and I didn't choose to be a part of the situation. I sought an immediate divorce.

Harriet, 44, Maryland secretary

I arranged for us to see a counselor, but she refused to go. Then I contacted a minister, but she refused to see him, too. Then I proposed a trial separation, and she accepted. A week later, without my knowledge, she filed for divorce.

Frank, 33, California warehouseman

I saw a priest, and a psychologist. She went by herself, and then we even tried seeing a psychiatrist together. I asked her a total of eight times to try to get together and work it out, but she refused. I hung on there for two years trying to save it. Now I've learned my lesson.

Jack, 36, California hotel exec

I tried to save it by trying to be and do whatever he wanted. But he finally just confessed that the "fun" of cheating was what he wanted.

Muriel, 61, California (no occupation given)

Yes, counseling with church leaders, a psychiatrist, a Transactional Analysis group, Alanon, and a conciliation court.

Elaine, 33, California homemaker

For eight months I went to a counselor who was also a psychiatrist and was on antidepressants, but my ex-husband refused to go. He didn't want to save the marriage.
Alice, 48, Illinois hospital worker

Trial separation, counseling, Alcoholics Anonymous. Too late.
Cheryl, 33, New Jersey teacher

We agreed to relocate, but her mother wouldn't let her go. We moved once to the West Coast but her mother came after her.
Ralph, 44, Maryland publishing exec

I visited a counselor several times. My wife visited him once or twice.
W., (male), 47, Delaware (no occupation given)

I couldn't save it. When I refused to see a lawyer for a divorce, he did and filed for a divorce on grounds of desertion! He still came home late every night and slept in the same bed with me! This continued until the day I went to court. While I was downtown, he moved out. Anyway, I couldn't let him charge me with desertion so I had to see a lawyer who convinced me it was useless to fight it, because nobody needs a husband who doesn't want her, so we had his suit thrown out of court and I got the divorce myself.
Harriet, 46, Illinois (no occupation given)

I tried a trial separation, and then marriage counseling, and then self-improvement to try and be the person he wanted me to be.
Barbara, 41, California postal worker

Yes, we both went to counseling, but in vain. I believe by the time you know there is something wrong, it's too late for counseling or anything else.
John, 46, Colorado truck driver

I consulted two doctors and a psychologist, but he wouldn't go for counseling and refused to talk to anyone about our marriage failing.
V., (female), 50, Illinois factory worker

Yes, but my wife wouldn't go.
Lawrence, 40, Wisconsin (no occupation given)

A trial separation, and I tried to convince her to go for counseling together, but without success.

David, 39, Virginia (no occupation given)

Yes, family counseling services were used for a number of years. My husband went one time and then no more.

A. (female), 48, Michigan accountant

Yes, the Family Service, but I feel she did more harm than good.

Olive, 52, Pennsylvania bookkeeper

Yes, I did, through counseling and by constantly trying to save it for seven years. I'm convinced a man (or a woman) is a very sick person if they do or say something to harm or destroy their family.

Barbara, 51, Illinois health tech.

Yes, a very determined effort was made to "save" it. Starting probably two or three years before the break, I began counseling with clergymen; two by myself, later with others along with my husband, though admittedly the interviews were brief since he didn't see any value in them. The last year before the divorce we did, at the suggestion of my lawyer, consult with a Family Service counselor. His (my husband's) participation was with the greatest reluctance, unfortunately. You might even say he was "black-mailed" into it.

Frances, 45, Massachusetts L.P.N.

I had counseling on and off for eight years. My partner asserted that there were no problems that couldn't be solved "if you'd straighten up and fly right."

Mary, 55, Washington professor

Yes, we tried counseling to save our marriage, but the counselor suggested that maybe we weren't right for each other. Our neuroses fed on each other, he said. We were both insecure, he said.

Jeanne, 33, Connecticut rental agent

After about three years I asked him to go with me to a marriage counselor. His answer was, "You go—you need it." After five years, I asked him for a trial separation. His answer was, "Make up your mind whether you want me or not." After six years I told him I wanted a divorce, and he said, "How about marriage counseling?" My answer was, "I was ready for that three years ago when I asked you." Then he said, "How about a trial separation?" I told him it was too late.

Judith, 34, California secretary

I talked to a psychiatrist several times. Most 45-year-old males are reluctant to go for counseling. Mine was sure he was in the right!

Margaret, 53, Kansas librarian

Yes, we went to a marriage counselor once at my urging, but my husband had already made up his mind to separate and didn't feel additional visits would do any good.

Elizabeth, 32, Massachusetts secretary

Yes, but I finally gave up. I tried everything from pleading to a punch.

Richard, 43, Minnesota divorce counselor

My husband decided he wanted "another wife" and went out looking, found one, and proposed before he even left me. From the time he started looking, until he found one was about six weeks. Since I didn't want the divorce, I told him to go get it if he wanted it. He went to Reno, leaving our home in the middle of July, got the divorce and remarried in Reno the same day.

Della, 49, California teacher

I saw the family doctor, and the minister three times, went to psychology classes to understand him better, and saw a psychologist, and then we had counseling for more than a year. To no avail; our love was destroyed already.

—anonymous Michigan woman, 37

He went to one session of the reconciliation court, but he was so negative and angry that the counselor dismissed him.

Sonya, 36, California teacher

We separated for six months, but it didn't work. I had counseling, even after the separation.

Billie, 30, California secretary

My third husband—who left me and was the only one I loved—would not allow any help to register with him. I even submitted to, and passed, a lie-detector test!

Ruby, 51, California teacher

No. Once we agreed to the divorce we just went ahead and did it.

Neil, 34, New York (no occupation given)

Yes, the intercession of a priest for arbitration and reconciliation, but she refused to continue meeting with him or to adhere to his suggestions.

Nate, 40, Pennsylvania meat-cutter

At first he refused to admit that something was wrong with the marriage. Then after a year he agreed to marriage counseling, but it was too late. . . . too much damage had been done.

Carol, 30, Maryland secretary

Yes, I tried to get her to enter some kind of dialogue. Marriage counseling for a year before filing; then a half-year before the summons, and another half-year during the proceedings. Nothing worked.

R., 51, Michigan writer

I tried, through counseling, but was unable to get my husband to admit the need for professional help.

Gwen, 54, Texas investigator

We tried a trial separation. She tried playing around. In the end, she wanted out . . . and so did I!

Charles, 55, Connecticut writer

I tried but got no cooperation from my wife. I tried through the pastor of our church with little or no results. Also, tried through Catholic Church, as she was a Catholic, but the church didn't want to get involved. Went to a mental health clinic and discussed the problem with a marriage counselor. I think this helped me, but the wife wouldn't attend the meetings. This was during a temporary departure.

Dale, 31, Illinois roofer

I had known that she was interested in someone else for some time, but I tried to anticipate the lack. I reduced my work hours, went out more socially, etc. I have counselled many couples and individuals who have marriages in trouble. My own marriage was considered by friends to be near ideal, because I worked hard at eliminating problems before they could start. As I grew professionally and received some national recognition, my wife began to feel that I was "outgrowing" her. She was employed, and developed an interest in a fellow employee, much older than I, somewhat religious, very much involved in a sedate, secure life—quite the opposite of my routine with dinners, speeches, occasional late hours, etc. (Although she was included in most activities, she confessed that it bothered her to remain in the background while everyone gathered around me.) I suspected her interest in someone else, but tried to counter it, as I said, by cutting down my hours, etc. When we married, we promised that if either of us developed an interest in a third party, we would let the other know. I was extremely disappointed that she would totally disregard this promise and I considered her actions quite selfish. She admitted being in love with this man, eventually, and I simply accepted this and filed for divorce. (Incidentally, I don't know exactly who this person is even today, and in counseling we try to get others to totally disregard the temptation to follow and check-up, etc.) Following a three-day separation, she became ill, quit her job and asked that we start all over again. I stayed with her, but found it most difficult to resume a normal relationship. My feelings weren't the same, but I quit my practice and relocated elsewhere in the state, thinking the change would help. I lost a lot financially, and when my new practice didn't start up as quickly as I had hoped, I blamed our situation and called it quits.

Florida psychotherapist and marriage counselor, 37

Yes! Marriage counseling through Family Service of (major city), plus another minister, plus a psychologist. She had too big a problem.

Bill, 33, Wisconsin minister

I did everything I could think of to try to save the marriage but she was in no mood to cooperate on anything, and when I asked her to sit down and discuss it with me, she replied, "What is there to discuss?" About a month after she left, I began to suspect from some of the things my boys told me that there was another man in the picture, and after the divorce this proved to be the case. I consulted with a psychologist, a social worker, and my wife's attorney, who was sympathetic and who did his best to stall her action in the hope that time would help. I wrote to her family and begged their assistance and got no reply. She wasn't in the least interested in saving the marriage, and told me so. To this day we haven't discussed the matter, and our communication is only about visitation rights and when she'll get her money.

Frank, 39, Minnesota compositor

Since it was a bigamous marriage, things got too bad too soon.

Doris, 51, Louisiana secretary

Feeling utterly hopeless about my marriage and acutely depressed, I went to a psychologist. I asked my husband also to get some professional help. Despite acknowledging that he had some serious problems in maintaining a close relationship, he flatly refused. Later I asked for a trial separation of a year's duration.

June, 42, Connecticut clerk

I stayed with the children, and would have continued happily were it not for the child-molesting pimp shysters and judges.

Arthur, 54, Illinois (no occupation given)

We tried marriage counseling, but it was a one-sided effort.

Carol, 29, New York (no occupation given)

Yes, we went to a marriage counselor, but my ex said he was talking about me and not him, and that he'd do what he damned well pleased and that I'd have to change my ways and give him sex every night. The counselor didn't help.

Bonnie, 30, Illinois (no occupation given)

I've been married twice to the same person. The first time we were going to get a divorce we did go see the doctor and a marriage counselor. But my husband couldn't be fully honest with them and it was a waste of time. The second time there was no effort made at all to save it.

Judy, 35, Colorado (no occupation given)

Counseling, begging, threatening, anything.

Tony, 38, New Jersey (no occupation given)

I tried marriage counseling, psychiatry, religious leaders, everything. But when a marriage is dead, there's no point in living with a corpse.

Dolores, 44, New York (no occupation given)

I tried, but he refused, so we separated for six months and got back together for four more years. Then it started all over again. He just couldn't keep it in his pants.

Beth, 30, Illinois secretary

My ex-husband, through his guilt, came back once and went through the motions of one therapy session. The communication was gone many years prior to our separating. This is true of most divorces, I think.

Kathy, 35, Minnesota medical asst.

We went to a psychologist for a year and a half, and to a second one for six months, then tried group therapy and our pastor. We just weren't suited for each other.

Robert, 34, Missouri contract analyst

A forced trial separation and counseling. She had me arrested and placed under a peace bond, and then got mad when the counselor said I was okay.

David, 30, Kentucky civil servant

I tried for years to get him to go for professional help, but he refused. Then near the end he went to a counselor because his girl friend told him to go, but I think by then the marriage was dead.

Mary, 31, California student

We went to a psychologist for six months, a psychiatrist for six months and a marriage counselor for a year. They were all divorced people. Even our minister was divorced, both lawyers were divorced, and I wouldn't be surprised if the judge had a mistress under his bench.

Louis, 35, New York businessman

Nine years ago after my husband had rejected me for nine months, our marriage was saved by counseling with the family doctor. My husband decided to go to him on his own, as I was ready to quit the marriage. We had another one and half years of a good thing, but then he started (homosexuality, adultery, drinking) and he even turned to pornography. Sex was offered in lust, not for my needs. This is definitely when I should have divorced him, but all he did was cry and beg me not to leave him. He accused me of having boyfriends, but because he knew I wanted and enjoyed sex, there was nothing else for him to do but accuse me, since he wasn't giving out sex that much. Counseling would have helped, together with moving as far away from his drunken friends as we could get. But he refused all reasoning.

Evelyn, 53, California R.N.

We sought help through Catholic Charities at my request. I went several times and he went three or four times, and quit. We had a 60-day separation before the final divorce.

Alice, 37, Kansas housewife

We tried individual therapy, counseling together, and family counseling along with trial separation.

Amy, 39, California (no occupation given)

After a brief separation, we reconciled for 18 months. During this time I tried very hard to do everything to please him, but I just didn't love him. I decided I had to be free to find someone to care for. He never thought there was anything wrong with our marriage.

Lillian, 44, Pennsylvania (no occupation given)

Yes, I attempted every means on my own, read extensively, and then—with my mate—tried to solve our differences. We went on a marriage encounter weekend, talked, spent a great deal of time together and apart without any long-range effect. Finally we sought professional help. At this point, the idea of divorce hadn't even entered my mind. I just thought we had some problems and was sure we could work them out. I went to our minister, and we went to him together, then separately over a period of several months. After that we went to a marriage counselor, a psychologist, and then two psychiatrists. He went to a group. We tried two short periods of separation, and then after two years of trying to make it work, we separated permanently.

Elizabeth, 34, New Jersey R.N.

I saw a priest, a rabbi, a doctor and a lawyer. My husband admitted he needed psychiatric help, but refused it whenever I suggested it was either that or divorce. Whenever we tried to reconcile, he was tearing me down after 48 hours.

Linda, 33, Arizona bookkeeper

We made some effort. I had had some private therapy during the marriage, but it didn't seem to help practically. The last few years before the separation were a growing strain. She seemed to spend more time at her work. Six months before the breakup we joined a marital counseling couples' group of about five couples, and I vented a lot of my frustration. So did she. The irony is that after six months in the group she told me to get out, that she'd found enough strength (insight) to say so.

Roland, 48, Connecticut engineer

Yes, in several ways. By often seeking a new basis for mutual commitment. Openly discussing problems with a professional counselor. By trying to get at the root cause of dependency on the wife's part. Wife consistently refused professional counseling.

T. (male), 44, Pennsylvania minister

Dozens of counselors, new contracts, fidelity, mate-swapping, teeth-gritting, trial separation.

Mary, 26, California student

I went to marriage counseling at Family Service. Husband refused to go. We were separated three times and reconciled before final separation and divorce.

Wendie, 33, New York (no occupation given)

I entered an attorney's office in the spring of 1973 asking for a divorce. However, I did not state definitely that I needed one. Instead I said, "I think I should get a divorce. I don't know, but I think so." Being more of a corporation attorney than a divorce attorney, he talked me into giving the marriage a good try before going for a divorce; with the idea, I believe, of possibly getting more money for himself. The attorney talked a lot of incorporating my husband's business with him, while at the same time, writing to all our creditors and stalling for time on payments. So, partly to really give the marriage another try, and partly because I

was on the verge of a nervous breakdown, and just had to get
away from everything, I went with my husband on the road to
help him in his business. This lasted from May of 1973 to
November of 1973.

Alice, 29, Minnesota factory worker

No. I had already been trying to save the marriage for at least six
years. His finally choosing another sexual partner without my
knowledge finally let me know it wouldn't last.

Sandra, 32, Missouri professor

Counseling just once. He wouldn't continue with it. I tried discussing various aspects with which I wasn't happy, but communication was always difficult.

Diane, 32, California homemaker

She refused all attempts at counseling. She was suspicious of
professionals.

Jack, 52, Colorado exec

Yes, as soon as I could locate a good counselor, I started seeing
him. But my husband wouldn't attend with me, stating that since
he decided to stay with his family and break off his relationship
with another woman, it wasn't necessary. About four weeks later I
asked him again to go, and he did. I had hoped we could get some
things out in the open and discuss them, but he wouldn't talk and
the whole thing was a waste of time. Finally the counselor suggested that we separate for a while. In the mean time, I heard that
the other woman had started divorce proceedings. Then my husband said he wanted to "leave," and I assumed that it meant he
wasn't going to stay with us.

Margaret, 55, New York (no occupation given)

Yes, separation, to determine whether we could be independent
of each other. But the children were very much involved in our
dependence, and they were the victims.

Irene, 39, New York (no occupation given)

No. I felt I had no choice. My husband wanted no reconciliation
and had cut off all contact with me. There was no alternative.

Sandi, 23, New York lab tech.

We went to a marriage counselor, a psychiatrist, tried a second honeymoon, and then I spent six months trying whatever he wanted to try, whenever he wanted to try it. Nothing.

Barbara, 28, New York bank teller

Good Lord, we tried everything in the book to save our marriage! Four or five counselors, including a professional psychotherapist with whom we spent well over a year; reading books; talking about our problems, and even a trial separation, too. The marriage just wasn't meant to be. I think the best things to come out of our counseling experiences, even if the marriage couldn't be saved, were the personal insights we developed. I cannot cure my compulsiveness, but now that I know what I am, I can learn to control it. She will never be an organized business executive, but she functions well as a mother and she has a rapport with animals and flowers that I really kind of envy. Each of us has done well by ourselves; together we were annihilating each other.

Lee, 37, Iowa city employee

I tried counseling, but my husband wasn't willing to try anything. I simply worked as hard as I could to keep the marriage alive, because I couldn't stand the word "divorce" or the thought of failure. Another woman came along and I tried until the night before the separation to make it work.

Joan, 48, Kansas receptionist

We did counseling, doctors, Family Service, ministers, a year of separation and two years of divorce during which we dated quite often. Still nothing worked. She would go to the same counselors as me just to tell her side of the story.

Weldon, 40, Ohio (no occupation given)

No, neither one—(married twice: once, seven years; once, six years). I was just not happy with married life and stayed around too long thinking I didn't want to hurt anyone.

Marilyn, 49, New York (self-employed)

He wouldn't go to anything I suggested, and I must admit that I hated him so much toward the end that I quit trying to suggest things.

Lynn, 21, Illinois (no occupation given)

We both went to counseling and tried a trial separation but I knew in my heart I wanted out all the while and didn't have my heart in it.

Terese, 40, Michigan secretary

When we separated the first time we went to a marriage counselor. We only had a few sessions and then stopped. The effort appeared to be one-sided although it was his idea to go back together with some concessions on my part. I had enrolled in night school and was working full time. He wanted me to quit both work and school. Which I did, but I missed it terribly. My husband didn't want me to have any outside interests or friends. I became a doormat.

Sandra, 28, California (no occupation given)

I went to a marriage counselor but my husband made me stop going. We had two separations before our final parting. With only one person trying to solve a problem, there's no way it can be worked out.

Dawn, 23, Maryland homemaker

I made a very determined effort to keep it together. I gave up my folks because my wife did not like them. A big blow up and told them that was the last time I would see them, and it almost was. I moved twenty times thinking the place we lived was the cause of our trouble; every place we went we found people that upset her and made her uneasy and that she just couldn't stand. But, even at the end, six months before I moved out, I went to a counselor and tried through him to find out what could be done to save the bankrupt thing.

R., 45, North Dakota M.D.

Did you experience any unanticipated financial, social or emotional calamity as a result of your divorce?

The misery of loneliness. Divorce is a terribly emotional experience and don't let anyone kid you that it isn't. I'd bet anyone that chances are better than two-to-one you're going to need psychiatric help before it's over. When you finally end up sleeping in an empty bed, making Wheaties three times a day for yourself and your children in school, having to find a job and work every day—which means new clothes, etc.—and then having to live with the stigma itself of being a divorcée! Well, be darned sure a divorce is what you want, instead of changing a few attitudes and outlooks and making a go of it. I'd rather have stuck with a lousy marriage than be as miserable as I am now.

Nancy, 34, California bank teller

The realization that suddenly it's everyone for himself.

Mel, 38, Texas stockbroker

I wouldn't exactly call it a "calamity," but one unanticipated feeling is that I'm beginning to like it. I may never get married again.

Janice, 33, Oregon storekeeper

What was really unanticipated in my case was that the hostilities and suspicions built up tremendously fast. We thought it would be one of those nice, quick, amicable things you read about in the newspaper—no chance! There's always one or the other attorney who will try for more than what's fair, and botch things up between the two parties.

Ross, 38, California plumber

You learn a lot of things about the whole process of human relations which you didn't know before. After 14 years, I thought I knew him, but you'd be surprised how people change when they're trying to get as much—or as little—as possible out of you.

Carol, 34, Maryland R.N.

I discovered nothing was predictable in the divorce process. You get things moving, and then you hit a point of no return and practically lose control over the entire proceedings. You've done it with your eyes open, sure, but lots of things can happen that you'd never expect going in. I didn't expect the way it got dragged out, because her attorney kept trying to get more from me. There suddenly was take, but no give.

Gerry, 41, California engineer

When he decided to get the divorce I took his word for what my taxes and costs would be, because he was a lawyer himself and a tax expert. They turned out to be double what he said.

Virginia, 62, New York housewife

Our married friends couldn't include me in their plans as they had before, because I was this "single woman" all of a sudden. And it was heartbreaking, actually, to have my little daughter see me dating other men after so many years.

Helen, 29, Ohio housewife

Yes, the fact that I seriously considered suicide.

Harvey, 35, Arizona innkeeper

Actually all I felt was extreme relief because he was no longer a financial burden.

Karen, 31, California newspaperwoman

Finding out that he was a fraud all along—the wrong name, occupation and even where he originally was supposed to have come from!

Maryanne, 42, New Jersey secretary

The realization that he was renegging on his financial obligation and only gave us barely enough to eat.. The realization that it was necessary to get a job in order not to be dependent on anyone.

Carol, 29, Michigan student

My ex-wife suddenly sent me repair bills for car damage and other indebtedness, claiming it was my responsibility, even though we'd been divorced for quite some time before they happened. Lawyers threatened me that I was still liable, although I've since found that I really wasn't. They were after their share of whatever more she could get out of me.

Bill, 39, Pennsylvania pharmacist

Social, yes. My married friends, most of them, have excluded me from all their social gatherings. Invitations come only for "lunch" now.

Beverly, 45, New York teacher

I'm not getting laid as often as I thought I would.

Pete, 38, Idaho engineer

Financially, I soon had to learn how to do without the two checks coming in that I was used to, but I learned how to budget and make ends meet. Emotionally, the shock was that I had actually done such a thing; I missed him very much and I missed the security that a married woman has. The majority of the men I dated turned out to be newly divorced themselves and we'd wind up telling each other our "sad" stories!

Barbara, 27, California medical secretary

Trying to accept the way people reacted toward me at a social gathering. I had expected people to show pity, or to be standoffish, and I felt men wouldn't be as interested in me once they knew I was divorced with children. I found this to be entirely untrue.

Peggy, 24, California cashier

I was shocked at the behavior of the lawyers. They were like ravenous animals, each trying to get as much "food" as he could.

Norman, 41, Nevada banker

Emotional upset far more than the financial or social aspects—a sense of failure and frustration even though we seemed to have tried everything.

John, 45, California artist

I thought it would be much easier. I started drinking much more, because I couldn't cope, and I finally joined AA.

Tom, 35, Illinois advertising man

Total financial disaster.

Marvin, 41, New York editor

The emotional depression because of the sudden social isolation. And that was fed by the financial difficulties.

Barbara, 37, California teacher

The fact that he refused to pay a single debt, leaving me with all financial obligations. He was making a good wage at the time, too. The fact that the courts awarded me child support far below a realistic sum.

Mary, 33, North Dakota R.N.

After the papers were filed and things seemed pleasant he apparently resented the fact that the children and I were doing well without his supervision. He had stated previously that he would pay all my bills until a certain date, but he suddenly cut all the payments, leaving me with the obligations, simply because I wouldn't let him come live in the house in a separate bedroom. He continually harasses me, prying and meddling in my private [life].

Patricia, 38, California teacher

Old friends took sides and turned their backs on me.

Barbara, 28, California teacher

The fact that we're better friends now than during our marriage.

Carol, 36, Illinois secretary

The fact that even though we accomplished a split down the middle, financially, I still had so much to pay out. I also paid the lawyers' fees and for the complete divorce! And I feel guilty, still, about the whole thing. It was quite a while before I felt highly of myself again.

Yvonne, 29, California (no occupation given)

I was severely depressed for months. It's not easy to start a new life after so long with one woman. I thought it would be.

Hank, 47, Texas salesman

I was taken to the cleaners!

J., 39, California (no occupation given)

I was shunned by neighbors and his family, castigated by my own relatives; the heavy financial burdens and the feeling of worthlessness.

Barbara, 45, New Jersey researcher

I got no credit for being fair. The lawyers just used my fair appraisals and offers as a wedge to try for more and more.

Jerry, 40, New Jersey accountant

I didn't expect the severity of everything. I lost 25 pounds because of the financial, emotional and social difficulties. Only two or three couples stayed in touch and showed some concern, even though I stayed home in the neighborhood for a whole year.

Joanne, 54, New York housewife

It bothers me sometimes when I think that my present wife and I can give our children a better home life and freedom than they had a chance of before. I'm not sure why—it just bothers me sometimes.

Aaron, 37, Kansas policeman

The legal fees and weekly payments were much higher than I had anticipated, and the continuing alimony payments were a shock. And I suffered an extreme guilt complex where my children were concerned. But it seems ludicrous to me to continue to make alimony payments to an able-bodied woman who refuses to seek gainful employment, especially where there are no longer minor children involved. I felt no hesitation to pay for the maintenance of my ex-wife and a minor child, but when the child reached maturity two years ago I was still required to keep paying $60 a week to a woman who could certainly earn enough to take care of her needs. She currently resides in another state, some 1200 miles away, and for all I know does have a good job and salary, yet I have to keep paying. It's a continual source of amazement to me.

Max, 54, New York insurance broker

I'm having a great deal of trouble financially, because even though I've got three children, I'm not getting much child support. It seems to be a typical pattern where after the first year of child support it seems to trickle off into almost nothing, and of course he usually gets away with it. He was going to keep one of the (three) children living with him, but none of them liked his new wife. Now, my family pays my rent, I get a minimum of child support, and it's all very denigrating and embarrassing. There is no dignity in dependence.

Pat, 34, California writer

° I had never been financially independent before, and the full-time work, the Blue Cross, car insurance, and all that was monumental. Even the lawyer's fees were a shock. Emotionally, the after-effects were beyond all imagination. Guilt, isolation, feelings of inadequacy, inferiority complex, and all this compounded by added responsibilities toward the children!

Emily, 33, New York R.N.

Because of the deeply rooted religious training, I somehow felt I could never remarry, and this was depressing. I had to come to grips with the moral problems involved, and make up my own mind that a second marriage would not be eternally condemning.

Marilyn, 38, California school administrator

I was shocked at the cost of divorce. Why do they make divorce so difficult and marriage so easy?

Don, 40, Colorado businessman

Society is geared to married couples. I felt I had been downgraded in status in my neighborhood, office and among my relatives. There was also a great shock in finding that my husband had two secret bank accounts and had cancelled all our life insurance, etc.

Margery, 47, California real estate broker

° I couldn't shake the feeling of deep regret that I had been a failure. It was some time before I could realize that it was the marriage that failed, not me, not her. I think too many people brood about how they've "failed" when in reality there was a third entity working, and it was that entity which failed, not either of the two parties.

Bob, 26, Nebraska repairman

I rushed in full speed ahead with my eyes closed, and so the enormous expenses were totally unexpected. I had to take a second job for a while to handle it. I started dating almost immediately, however, and socially felt quite liberated.

Robert, 24, California electronics tech.

Social calamity—I experienced both isolation by my neighbors and in the community activities in which I had been actively engaged.

Gert, 57, California housewife

My husband took the car and all the furniture, yet he didn't pay the bills and they started coming to me. I didn't pay them, so my credit rating went bad and to this day (three years later) I still can't get good credit from most stores. (A large bank) gave me a Master Charge Card with an $800 limit, but (two major department stores) will not give me credit.

Marsha, 24, California postal employee

The loneliness and uncertainty were the biggest problems. I went back home to my parents for two weeks, and it was just unbearable. I had no one whom I could tell what happened to me; my parents wouldn't understand because I had always pretended to them that my marriage was working out fine. I was very bitter, too. I thought I would never let a man beat me emotionally like that again. It took me a long time to become able again to relate to them. My second husband gave me back my faith in the human race.

Carmen, 28, California corporate mgr.

No calamity. I just cried a lot.

Dave, 25, California student

The finality of it all didn't hit me until I started to talk reconciliation and she would have none of it.

Ron, 36, California teacher

My ex-husband married the wife of a mutual friend within the same social circle, and then I was ostracized.

Milly, 49, law student (no address given)

I thought he would keep in closer touch with his son, and maintain that important father-son relationship. But he was "too busy." I guess all women try to remain "friends," somehow cherishing this notion makes it all more acceptable. Men feed on this feeling to make it less painful and to make it easier for them in the financial arrangements. My ex-husband assured me he would care for me and the children and blah, blah, blah, and to keep it all "friendly" we used the same attorney, our family attorney. I soon realized that in all litigations an attorney can only represent one party, so in essence I suddenly had no attorney! But I didn't wish to fight and we reached a mutually agreeable settlement. Less than a year later he tried to break the agreement, and now I'm about to go into court and all I hear is "I only earn $48,000 and I'm entitled to live a good life." Disillusionment is the name of the game.

Doris, 47, California newspaper reporter

The loneliness, the worrying about my son because he and his father were so close. I felt more for him than for myself, and I felt very guilty about their pain.

Nancy, 33, Maryland teacher

Because of the divorce, a going business had to be dissolved. I'll be lucky if I can amortize after the property settlement has been achieved.

Francis, 54, Wisconsin salesman

I had a well-paying job, so I was more fortunate than most, but I did have considerable other financial difficulties, during the first year, because I took over all the debts and taxes rather than hassle about who owed what to whom. My main concern was that he provide monthly child support I could depend upon, because I was afraid he might lose his job or drop out completely (if the debts killed him). I also was quite apprehensive since I never expected to be separated or divorced and was extremely embarassed about telling friends. Fortunately, I began to participate in a social group for people like myself and it helped enormously. Bad as my situation was, it was far better than some of the women I got to know.

Berry, 38, California government worker

Adjusting to the single world was quite an emotional experience. I had been very family-oriented, and now I had to reorient my values.

—anonymous male, 30

Loneliness and fear came to me in a measure totally unexpected. Loneliness because of the emptiness of my life, and fear because I was afraid to do the things I saw as being necessary to mitigate the loneliness. It was a vicious circle and one which I broke only with a very great effort.

Jim, 40, California salesman

The greatest emotional turmoil was learning to become independent of my ex-husband and breaking all ties.

Margaret, 37, Texas secretary

The large alimony award was a shock, especially since it didn't diminish in subsequent years when my earnings dropped to half of what they had been.

Bill, 50, New York stockbroker

Yes, it was a financial, emotional and social calamity. Period.

G., 59, New York housewife

Yes, my wife won't let me visit the children and she finally moved away to Indianapolis to be with her girl friend.

Lawrence, 50, Nebraska dispatcher

The emotional calamity was almost devastating for me and the children. We came out to California from Minnesota at the end of July, '72. At that time, my husband was depressed, which is all I knew because he closed up completely the previous winter and we no longer communicated. Three weeks after we moved here, he moved out. The 2,000-mile move, no friends at all, and abrupt exit of the male figure left the children and I frantic with fear, rejection and guilt. The confusion and uproar was almost unbelievable. Financially it was frightening for me because I had no residency and didn't know whether (he) was going to pay the rent, car payments, food bills, etc. So as soon as I had three months' residency, I filed for legal separation to preserve my financial security.

Linda, 32, California teacher-counselor

Nothing unanticipated. All I could do was brace myself.

> Elizabeth, "over 30," Nevada (no occupation given)

Legal fees of $3,500 were at least double what they had told me they'd be.

> Dan, 35, Illinois engineer

I suddenly found myself under a doctor's care. I went from 110 pounds to 90 pounds in three days until I got hold of myself and brought my weight back up. He hadn't paid the bills and the house was attached before the divorce went through, and I've got to make all the retribution. They cut off the phone and the utilities. Luckily, the kids had some money in the bank, which helped, but they were only eight and ten and it didn't amount to much. My lawyer insists I sell the house and move back to Florida. That's all the help I get from him.

> Natalie, 52, New Hampshire homemaker

I have a wonderful feeling of freedom, but the disappointment of being back in the dating game, with all its evils, is kind of sad.

> —anonymous female, 29

The attendant problems of "starting over" were unanticipated. It was extremely difficult returning to the job market after a seven-year absence, but it was necessary due to the lack of support from my husband. Adequate child care was almost impossible to find while I worked, and it took a large portion of my paycheck. Little social life, because of the limitations of children obligations and small income. Even now, when they've reached their teens, there aren't many places an unattached woman can go to meet decent men. I was unprepared for the attitude society has toward divorced women and how difficult it would be for a divorced woman to get credit.

> Harriet, 44, Maryland secretary

The unanticipated financial problems were staggering. In a continuing effort to salvage my marriage, I didn't contest the divorce proceedings, but allowed her to draw the agreements on her own terms. As a result, I was awarded all outstanding debts, I lost the house, both cars, etc. I left with only the clothes to show for my 11-year marriage.

> Frank, 33, California warehouseman

I was surprised that men suddenly looked at me as "experienced" and thought I was an easy lay. Some of them younger ones, even wanted me to go to a motel with them and "teach" them what they had to know as college boys.

L., 35, California housewife

Not getting the kids crushed me. I had hoped to get them.

Jack, 36, California hotel exec

Only social—I found a single woman was a "threat" to all other women, married or single.

Muriel, 61, California (no occupation given)

Marriage Number One: *I was emotionally unprepared for the life of an adult in the dating line again after the first marriage was ended. I suffered tremendous guilt complexes over sex during this period of life.*

Marriage Number Two: *No unanticipated financial or emotional problems with second divorce. I cannot regret the divorce, although we do not have the security we had with him. Life was dull and uninteresting. . . . he wanted to watch TV every night. A whole new world has opened up for the three of us since the divorce and I wouldn't have missed the experiences I've had that marriage to him prevented. He was very jealous and dictatorial and I'm enjoying my freedom.*

Marriage Number Three: *My children went through a great emotional upheaval at the end of this very short marriage. My youngest, 12 at the time, very much wanted a father and loved this man very much. She has a problem relating to men (which is no surprise, considering what she has been through with me) and she and this man did get along beautifully. . . . but not to her benefit. They loved each other, but I cannot say he was a good influence on her in so far as character, honesty, etc. was concerned. We are about on an even keel again. . . . after counseling for her . . . and I would not risk marriage again for anything until they are grown. . . . even though they both want me to remarry very much. They have never seen a really bad marriage because I got out of them before hate set in. Probably the third marriage would have lasted and both of us would have been very, very happy together except that we had children to whom I felt a* stronger responsibility than he did. I'd have loved to "bum" through life with him. . . . except for the children.

The second marriage, too, could have been saved. But all you would have had would have been a "saved" marriage. Neither me nor my children would have been as happy as we are now. Although this husband was very, very good for the children insofar as discipline was concerned. I was too understanding and I suppose guilt-ridden and they have a better chance to adjust as adults because of the six years I was married to him. I'd rather be married 19 times and have them end in divorce than to live 19 years in a marriage that did not make both parties happy. I can be happy without a husband and see no reason to be miserable just to have one. I give a lot to a marriage, my problem has not been not pleasing my husbands, on the contrary, they do not please me. I am a successful woman in many respects. One thing I learned in the last marriage. You can't give yourself away to one lesser than you.

Penny, 34, Texas travel agent

I was not able to find a satisfactory job, as I had hoped, even though I took special training. . . . I also found I was extremely upset emotionally when my husband remarried immediately after obtaining his divorce. I then realized he had been seeing this girl for a number of years, and I hadn't taken his relationship with her seriously. She was the secretary where he worked and so he'd known her for quite a few years. I trusted him.

Ferne, 52, Michigan (no occupation given)

I lost my job and was out of work for five months, so I had to take a much lower paying position. Also, the legal fees were excessive.

Dan, 45, New Jersey industrial mgr.

Yes, I had a spontaneous abortion. I wanted the child.

Elaine, 33, California homemaker

I am yet experiencing emotional calamity. I have been seeking love and companionship, seeking it in bars, etc., and ending up with potential alcoholics, men looking for sex, one-night stands, promises of phone calls which never happened—none of the things I really wanted.

Alice, 48, Illinois hospital worker

Mainly financial. I received none of the property of the marriage, even though the lawyer said I would. It was very difficult to start all over again. Also social—it's a couples' world!

Cheryl, 33, New Jersey teacher

I did not realize at the time the cumulative effect so many years of heavy responsibility would have, or how tired and overextended I would come to feel as a result.

Emily, 38, Maryland librarian

My ex-husband, living out of town, was asked to pay only $30.00 for the support of our two children. I was also plagued by feelings of guilt—"Where did I go wrong?" kind of thinking.

—anonymous female, 49

Financial. My wife had complete control as to how much I would get of our assets, for no other reason than she was a woman and I wanted the divorce. I don't think it would have diminished her power if she had been the one wanting the divorce.

W., 47, Delaware (no occupation given)

Emotional is what killed me, still does. It sure seems like I have to have a female in my corner. There are lots of single ladies, but a fellow wants only one. To do for, to fight with, to look after, to worry about. I sure have learned that sex without love is meaning-less. You think, wow, she looks nice, but then in bed a few times and I think, God Damn, how am I going to get rid of her!

John, 46, Colorado truck driver

My emotional reaction to getting the divorce, a few days before the court date, was unanticipated, since we'd had a legal separa-tion for the previous two years, and I was used to handling the house and children. I guess finalizing the end of a 12-year rela-tionship is difficult, even when both parties know it is for the best and have adjusted to the situation. I had anticipated some social negative reactions as a "divorcée," but I'm happy to say these never materialized. It was probably my own upbringing that had put negative connotations on divorce.

Sylvia, 36, Connecticut secretary

Social. I expected more support from my church but did not even receive a visit. I didn't realize that the world is almost one hundred percent geared for couples and families, and a single person is an outsider. Your scale of living has to go downward.

A. (female), 48, Michigan accountant

I have experienced every kind of calamity there is, as a result of my husband's abnormal behavior and his abnormal ability to influence and control other people for my destruction, and the lives of my family.

Barbara, 51, Illinois health tech.

I was not prepared for the fact that a "devoted" father could go to extreme lengths to avoid parental responsibilities both before and after the fact of the divorce. Also, I was completely and almost childishly naive in the faith I put in our system of court "justice" in dealing with the welfare of minor children.

Frances, 45, Massachusetts L.P.N.

The loneliness. The lack of bisexual relationship. I felt I was always pretty independent and confronted with more sex than I needed in marriage.

Mary, 55, Washington professor

Desperate loneliness.

Margaret, 53, Kansas librarian

Social, yes, because I didn't date much before marriage. Dating as a divorcée is completely different than a single teenager! Most singles' clubs or social clubs are mainly for swingers. It is a lot harder to be decent. If you are divorced and moral, you are almost an outcast!

Judy, 31, California keypunch operator

I did not expect that my husband would miss the children so much, to the point of a threatened custody suit. Almost overnight he turned into the model father, which has benefitted them tremendously in adjusting to their new situation, but has made me quite bitter—because I feel if he had taken as much interest in previous years our marriage would have been better.

Elizabeth, 32, Massachusetts secretary

Yes, the children were literally destroyed by an incredibly bad maternal environment.

Richard, 43, Minnesota divorce counselor

I was physically cruel to the child of my first husband, and I was physically lonely for male companionship.

Joyce, 40, New York college professor

Became mentally unstable, hospitalized for seven weeks, still suffering. No steady employment.

Neil, 34, New York (no occupation given)

Yes, the emotional upset was terrific and devastating. Immediate adjustment is difficult, and you find out pretty fast who your friends are.

Nate, 49, Pennsylvania meat-cutter

Financially, the judge gave my ex-wife 100% of my income. I was in court five or six times in one year for contempt. After 16 years of being divorced, my ex-wife remarried, and both of my children are married. My ex-wife went into a clerk of courts office and swore that I owed her $55,000 back support and alimony. On the strength of her affidavit the judge issued a garnishment of my checking and savings account, my salary, and everything I owned. In Georgia the court can issue a garnishment for alimony and support that is 100% of a husband's income, no exceptions!

Julian, 46, Georgia (no occupation given)

Grave financial losses, through loss of home, furnishings, appliances in excess of $20,000. Also the loss of a long-range savings plan and insurance benefits. I was forced by the courts to relinquish some (treasury) certificates. Emotional problems caused a nervous breakdown, and then I had to pay a total of $75 a week for child support and alimony.

Dale, 31, Illinois roofer

How could any fair judge have believed her perjury? My lawyer told me that her lawyer told him that he had never seen a judge treat my lawyer with such disrespect, uncouthness and rudeness. I am thoroughly disgusted with our judicial system on matrimonial cases. I don't think crooked judges should be allowed to settle these cases.

Walter (no age given), West Virginia retired exec

God, yes! As a direct result of a very vindictive lawyer, and every conceivable rotten trick in the book, I lost a damned good-paying job. I have had to battle to stay above water financially, as a result of the divorce, by filing bankruptcy.

Bill, 33, Wisconsin minister

Yes, I experienced an emotional calamity. I suppose it was something like shock. I had no desire for food. What little I ate was forced and there were times when I didn't eat anything for four days and still wasn't hungry. When I did get hungry, and I had to eat in five minutes and read a paper while I was doing it because after five minutes I would be overwhelmed with grief again and start crying.

Frank, 39, Minnesota compositor

Not really unanticipated. My marriage was an "emotional calamity" and the decision to separate and divorce was the most difficult resolution I've ever had to make, so I didn't expect joy and tranquility to follow in its wake. The unexpected was in the amount of time it took us to negotiate an agreement.

June, 42, Connecticut clerk

Yes, I had a good job and a promising career, stationed in Italy, but the conduct of a bitch spouse made me ask to come home and protect the good name of my company and country. It was the asking to come back that hurt my career.

Norman, 58, Texas (no occupation given)

Yes! She stole everything I owned and then some!

Mark, 38, New Jersey fireman

I had a hard time adjusting to the "single" role again. I still had feelings for my ex and had to make new friends. Also, I had to learn to do for myself and get involved in extra activities.

Carol, 29, New York teacher

Yes, financial. He left my father and me with all his bills to pay and skipped town. I had to go on public aid to support myself. Emotionally, I was fine because I was rid of him, and socially, I gained more friends without him than with him.

Bonnie, 30, Illinois (no occupation given)

Extremely bad emotional times, but it was expected. The financial aspects were horrendous; near bankruptcy.

Pat, 32, New Jersey programmer

To say I experienced emotional and financial problems is a mild statement. It was like a nightmare. I was young with no means of support and two children to care for. I finally got a job by lying about experience and a friend's phony reference.

Rose, 53, California (no occupation given)

Not too bad. It was kind of nice not having to wonder whether he was ever coming home.

Judy, 35, Colorado waitress

My wife promised to help support me and never ask for alimony, but three months after she left I was in court to support her when I couldn't even support myself. I almost starved.

Tony, 38, New Jersey (no occupation given)

All of it. I became an angry, bitter alcoholic who got into serious trouble, and finally had to join AA to save my present marriage and my sanity.

Robert, 35, New Jersey machinist

I worried a lot about the children, and about getting a job, but after a while I was just glad to be rid of her.

George, 34, Illinois truck driver

It was a year before I had regained my self-respect.

William, 51, Texas mechanic

The emotion a man goes through when a wife is trying to divorce him is hard to describe. A woman will put him through hell on earth. It's a wonder there aren't more women shot. My wife tried to ruin my business and my ministry. She tried in every way to get me to hit her so she would have grounds for divorce. I was lucky—I had the Lord with me and I prayed. That's what kept me going.

Lawson, 62, Illinois minister

My husband spread malicious rumors about my character, and I had a tough time of it socially. I didn't realize I'd be on partial public aid, with food stamps and medical help. Socially, things got a little better, but raising the kids alone is no fun.

Beverly, 30, Illinois (no occupation given)

Most of the unexpected difficulties are emotional. While I enjoy my independence, I don't like the feeling of aloneness. Hours on the telephone are a poor substitute for a mate! I thought I had all the responsibility of child-rearing and taking care of the house before the divorce, but now they are tiring, thankless chores after working all day! The eldest is graduating from high school and entering college, and the other had medical problems and had surgery last summer, so I miss having someone to share these things with. It's discouraging to attend activities and never meet anyone interesting. I've dated quite a bit and have seen one man for three years now, but there are no prospects for marriage. I'm still anxious for that. . . . when my 17-year-old came home unexpectedly and found a man in my bed one Sunday morning, it didn't seem to upset him. In fact, I got the impression that he was glad "Mom had a man."

Vivian, 40, California bookkeeper

I found I was constantly "put down" by even my closest friends for giving my child out to foster care, when, all things considered, I did what was best for her.

Marie, 22, Florida (no occupation given)

So-called friends have dropped me socially. They often think you're interested in their husbands. Your whole life, especially socially, is an object for discussion. Who you date, where you go. You are automatically assumed to be sleeping with whomever you date, and I resent this very much. Emotionally, I was in a state of shock when my husband walked out telling my children how he loved me, two days after he insisted I have an abortion.

Kathy, 35, Minnesota medical asst.

The divorce proceedings led to estrangement from my father, with whom I had always been close. I felt he was unfair in his testimony as an outside witness, and I was finally disinherited by him.

John, 47, New Hampshire bank exec

The emotional failure feelings were unanticipated. I felt totally worthless and a failure. After six months I happened on Parents Without Partners, and found that these feelings weren't unusual.

Then I began to come out of it and started back to college to finish my degree. This has given me a great new outlook on life.

Mary, 31, California student

I had practically become a single person ever since reentering the work world ten years ago, which was ten years before the divorce. Even today, few people link up except in a negative way, like calling him "the skirt chaser," or asking "How did you ever put up with it?" and that kind of thing. Financially, it's hard. It's impossible to live on a department store's minimal wages.

Peg, 46, New York cosmetician

Financial. I found that the $500 a month child support my husband offered me was generous and sufficient at the time, but with rising food and energy costs, etc. it isn't going to be sufficient. I'm sure he simply didn't want me to have to work, but there's nothing in this small town (pop. 600) for me to do, and I'm thinking of moving away to make a better life for myself and my four girls.

Alice, 37, Kansas housewife

I was wiped out financially, even though I was entitled to considerable assets. My property settlement was discriminatory against me. He became vicious and uncooperative and we are still battling legal conflicts. I never expected him to be so horrendous and selfish.

Amy, 39, California (no occupation given)

The five o'clock blues—when everyone has someone coming home for dinner, and you don't. It also was obvious my lawyer had some agreement with my husband's lawyer, as later developments proved.

Lillian, 44, Pennsylvania (no occupation given)

Some financial, to establish credit. Emotional trouble over visitation rights and custody battles.

Sarah, 53, California clerk

I found no social ostracism; in fact, I regained many old and former associates after the divorce. The emotional problems were calamitous prior to the divorce, but were under control by the time the divorce was granted. Financially, it has been a pain in the neck, especially when the I.R.S. troops jump in. What was unanticipated was how well everything went. It was as if a cloud had been lifted for myself, and subsequently for the girls. I lost 25 pounds and 10 years.

Elizabeth, 34, New Jersey R.N.

It was very difficult financially. In the beginning he was very generous with his offer but it was quite a while before he started paying. And, of course, after all these years he still owes me a lot, and I have never asked for an increase, but every birthday and every anniversary, he is really late. My mother says it's coincidence. For nine years? Socially, I had to fight the divorce image but I soon learned to handle that, no big problem. I set my standards and lived by them. Emotionally I was against marriage until perhaps a year ago. I dated and partied a lot, but I ran whenever it got serious. It took me five years to accept the fact that he's a sick man and . . . that I did what I could. I wasn't (perfect) but I was a decent wife to the best of my young ability. I got very down sometimes at the thought that I was the only breadwinner, as well as mother, father, housekeeper, laundress, etc., ad infinitum. Now that I'm older I can handle it better. I had a near-fatal illness four years back and became almost suicidal under the pressure—the inability to stay home in bed or be in the hospital where the doctors wanted me. I was petrified at the thought of being without that paycheck. That still haunts me, sometimes, because everything depends on me. But I can make it better than most, and I'm not trapped in a miserable marriage. When my old boyfriend came back and asked me to marry him, I even ran from him! I'm overly cautious now. Yet I want to remarry.

Linda, 33, Arizona bookkeeper

Everything goes wrong. It's almost a comedy of errors. It's a joke among the girls, now. We laugh about an imaginary list of those people who harass us! Butchers, bakers, candle-stick maker. Unfortunately, problems don't come one at a time; if they did I could handle them. They come in droves. I began to set a frantic pace for myself and was more or less avoiding facing any of them. My physical health began to fade, but it was all mental. Eventually, after many medical bills, I admitted it and was on tranquilizers for a while.

Sandra, 28, California (no occupation given)

Financially, I was clipped for everything I had. I got picked up on drunken driving and lost my license for a year.

Martin, 54, Pennsylvania production worker

Against my lawyer's advice and because of guilt feelings and a fervent emotional wish to win myself back into the house, I paid my wife in temporary support more than I really could afford. This eventually put me under great strain and we had to go to court to petition for a reduction (which we finally got). I actually felt exhilarated for the first two months of the separation, but then the whole radical situation closed in on me for a considerable number of months. Living in a furnished room, having practically no new friends, hanging onto some of the former couples I was close to—it was a whole new scene I wasn't prepared for.

Roland, 48, Connecticut engineer

Six months after the divorce it was discovered that I had severely high blood pressure. I should have had a thorough physical check-up before the divorce—I hadn't seen a doctor in three years.

Jean, 45, Illinois secretary

I found I had to double my financial cash flow to afford the support payments.

T. (male), 44, Pennsylvania minister

I discovered an unexpected defensiveness toward my ex-husband, and anger that something I worked so hard at could have failed. My immediate reaction to my first day in court was this poem:

A marriage begun in a church
ends in a courtroom.
Lawyer words measured in dollars,
dreams dissolved on paper.
The Reverend with trembling fingers is replaced
by a judge yawning behind his hand.
The bride and groom are sullen strangers
grabbing for community property.
The only similarity of start and finish
is the shit . . . of pigeons on the roof.

Mary, 26, California student

Financial problems were present, of course, but the greatest calamity for me was the emotional aspect. After being treated with little or no respect and love for eight years, I felt like less than a human being for quite some time. Also, the social aspect was difficult. My husband was the one who had the drinking problem and who committed adultery, but I was embarrassed to appear in social circles for a while. Our marriage was in a terrible mess and we should have called it quits before we did. Four years after the divorce, the children are happy and well-adjusted, and I'm happier than I've been in years. Maybe other couples who are living in constant turmoil can realize it just may not be worth it. Especially if they are staying together for the children.

Wendie, 33, New York (no occupation given)

No, it has all been just as dreadful as I anticipated. Especially with the responsibility of a five-year-old child who was only a year old at the time.

Linda, 34, California legal secretary

Terribly great overall emotional distress. The sense of grief. The loss of idealism, as in "the-great-American-marriage-partner," was stupifying.

Sandra, 32, Missouri college professor

Severe physical effects of the traumatic separation; stomach disorders, severe weight loss, etc.

Diane, 32, California homemaker

An inability to enter into an emotional or sexual relationship with another woman.

Jacob, 52, Colorado exec

I didn't realize it would be so difficult for a single woman to establish credit. Even though I have a checking account and an automobile loan with the same bank, they suddenly refused to issue me a charge card.

Margaret, 55, New York (no occupation given)

I guess all my problems were unanticipated, since I never expected my husband to walk out on us as he did. Having to go on welfare, having to raise my son fatherless, having my ex owe me

$4,000 in support payments without the courts helping me. And to top it off, his parents thinking I was the one who corrupted him and now refusing even to see their grandson. I guess that's a blessing in disguise, though.

Sandi, 23, New York lab tech.

I was surprised to find out that all our friends were his friends and felt they had to take sides. The neighbors act a little standoffish and suspicious, as though I were the plague of (name of community).

Barbara (no age given), New York bank teller

After spending six years with a frigid woman, I found I was nearly emasculated. But I found out quickly that more women now are sexually responsive. I guess, though, the predominant response I've noticed in myself and other divorcées is manic depression. But if it is only a passing problem with most, it is an everyday reality for a few. I have done a fair amount of "wee hours" phone counseling with friends who got off the deep end on one extreme or the other over the past few years. Quite an experience.

Lee, 37, Iowa city worker

I found I was suddenly free and was very happy, even with the low spots. He got a quick divorce and it was over fast. I'm lucky.

Joan, 48, Kansas receptionist

Very rough financial period, but nothing unanticipated.

Marilyn, 49, New York (self-employed)

Yes, my husband won't pay child support even though I am unable to work for health reasons. I had him put in jail once. My little girl is five-months-old and he's never even called to see how she is. I have found that society will accept a divorced man but that a woman is an outcast. Her girl friends think she is a threat, and men think she's an easy mark. The propositions I've had would make you sick!

Lynn, 21, Illinois (no occupation given)

I had been living away from (my home town), and when I returned as a divorced woman, my friends shyed away from me. This was mostly because as a Catholic, divorce was a real stigma.

Terese, 40, Michigan secretary

The first time I could bring myself to sleep with a man after my divorce, he was gone when I woke up! It took me a while to get back to normal after that. I can see why lesbians make the decision.

Maryann, 31, New Jersey secretary

My lawyer's fee alone was $2,850, plus $6,000 medical expenses for my wife; $6,000 loss of equity in our home and the expense of requiring a full time housekeeper. Socially, I was suddenly an outcast, a failure, a fifth-wheel. The only thing I had in common with my married friends was having children. Husbands always thought I was trying to steal their wives.

Donald, 39, Ohio physicist

Living on state aid is like living in absolute poverty. I can't work because of a near-fatal childbirth, so I've become dependent on family and friends which is totally degrading. My social life is nil because girls think I'm another rival, married women think I'm a threat, and men, all of them, think I'm just an easy lay. They think I "need" sex. But I'll take this loneliness any day to the fighting and hurting and crying.

Dawn, 23, Maryland homemaker

I was amazed to find that my practice fell off and my net income for that year fell by $4000. Even more, that my partner's income fell by the same amount. Of course this is a small town and I was rather severely judged. I lost no friends as I had none, my wife had seen to that, and I am strong enough to go my way in spite of the town and was able to function in spite of being less busy.

R., 45, North Dakota M.D.

What would you do differently having once made the decision to get a divorce?

Nothing except do it a lot sooner.
Gary, 35, New Mexico farmer

I've got a good piece of advice for women going through a divorce: forswear honesty as a means of dealing with the legal apparatus!
Jean, 45, California librarian

I'd shoot the son of a bitch!
Margie, 28, Pennsylvania secretary

Watch out for the money angle. Her lawyer will make her try to get everything she can.
Tom, 29, Colorado lawyer

I'd lie a lot on all the paperwork.
Myra, 33, Illinois secretary

I wouldn't let him get horny and con me into bed. It only makes it hurt twice as much later on.
Helen, 30, California receptionist

Nothing differently. Just sooner.
Ed, 34, New York fireman

I wouldn't be so fair. The lawyers are going to take you for all your worth, so forget about that amicability crap and start right out trying to save everything you've got.

Stan, 40, Florida engineer

I wouldn't believe a word my husband said about how simple and cheap it was going to be.

Ginny, 55, Massachusetts housewife

I would decide not to formally marry ever again. I'm looking forward to intimate relationships, but not with legal ties.

Patricia, 30, California teacher

I would have separated immediately. We didn't. Immediate separation lets you decide on what you're going to retrieve from the shambles. It lets you think without being bugged.

Bob, 24, Ohio tech.

I would have divorced earlier in the marriage, instead of waiting it out. I stayed because I had the mistaken notion from former parental training that I was benefitting the children. That was my biggest mistake.

Janet, 57, California housewife

I wouldn't have let him assume payment of bills without some sort of bond, or something. Once he stops paying them, you're stuck with a black mark after your name, not only his.

Monica, 24, Georgia government worker

I'd try to have some say in how she would allocate the child support funds.

Charles, 37, North Dakota engineer

I wouldn't be naive enough to depend on my spouse to pay the divorce costs. I wouldn't trust my lawyer at his word, either. It's impossible for him to act impartially when the other side is supposed to be paying his fees. I hear this happens a lot.

Vera, 60, New York housewife

I would have boned up a little more on what other divorced people had to say; get myself more prepared for it intellectually.

Gordon, 44, Canada salesman

I'd make more of an effort to save the marriage. I'd go to a counselor and see whether it could be saved, instead of giving up so easily.

> Denise, 29, California secretary

I would have gone to a marriage counselor before marriage!

> Max, 54, New York insurance broker

At the first sign of trouble, I would have taken pains to expose the whole consequence of separation and divorce to both parties. I think this would "get their attention" and prevent the thing from deteriorating past the point of no return.

> Ed, 43, California architect

Separation should have been sooner, and I shouldn't have let some medical and clerical influences have any effect on my "responsibilities" to the husband.

> Veronica, 44, New York secretary

I would have divorced immediately, rather than waste two more years of my life with trial separations, etc.

> Linda, 31, California (no occupation given)

I would "lose" a lot more money, i.e., hide more assets so the courts and lawyers don't break you.

> —anonymous I.R.S. tax adjuster

First marriage: I wouldn't have run as far away so fast. I would have made a greater effort to be less emotional and more calculating; the more methodical you are, the more financial sense you'll make in the long run. My "escape" was too rushed and disorganized, because I left everything behind to be sold.

Second marriage: I would have divorced her much earlier. You can't "duel" with a swinging young chick.

> Tom, 46, California ad exec

I'd get all the small parts of the final agreement in writing; get all the money and property separated before agreeing to "do it later." I say this because it's very difficult to deal with someone who is irrational, tends to forget and has no intention whatsoever of keeping his promises.

> Marilyn, 37, California teacher

I'd try a "trial divorce." Not a separation, a trial divorce. I'd split up everything, all the property, etc., and one of us move out, let the woman try to work, I'd cat around, etc. and we'd be "unlegally" divorced. That's the best possible way to find out if divorce is really what both parties want!

Larry, 42, New York film producer

I wouldn't have acted so immature and wouldn't have discussed the divorce with friends. In fact, I'd move away to a totally new area right away and start all over again without even waiting for the final papers.

Lillian, 26, Ohio stewardess

I'd do it earlier. Period!

Carol, 36, Illinois secretary

I'd get him to move out sooner after deciding on it.

Karen, 31, California newspaperwoman

I'd be more cautious—I wouldn't make decisions with my heart, but with my head.

Mary, 62, New York legal secretary

I'd postpone it long enough to get more thorough training for work. Probably either a secretarial course or a beautician course, and then go into business when the divorce was completed.

Gloria, 46, Kentucky bookkeeper

Move away immediately, because too many people suddenly decide to interfere, especially mothers-in-law. I'd also get a job faster.

Carol, 29, Michigan student

Study the law and file my own paperwork, thereby saving money in every aspect of the ordeal.

Galen, 37, California teacher

I'd do everything I possibly could to have her thrown in jail and kept from poisoning the rest of society in the future.

Nate, 44, Montana rancher

I found it very difficult to communicate, for fear of hurting him, so I would have sought outside counseling myself in order to al-

leviate that inhibition. I should have communicated more, because then the final shock would have been less.

Barbara, 27, California secretary

*Make more of an effort to maintain myself financially, in order to
have that "I can make it" psychological boost.*

Emily, 33, New York R.N.

I would have done it sooner, but once having made the decision I
would have tried for a cleaner break than the way I handled it.
Maybe leaving the county would have helped.

Peggy, 24, California cashier

Go to a counselor quick to help me see life more clearly and to
make the marriage (work).

Clara, 30, California artist

I wouldn't be so agreeable about things.

Yvonne, 29, California (no occupation given)

Not much—just look a bit more carefully into it.

Jim, 43, California credit mgr.

I'd move out of the state. He still harasses me because the woman
he ran off with left him. Now I'm remarried and he's jealous of my
new husband.

Sheila, 38, California housewife

Permanent separation would be a lot cheaper, if it's possible.
Maybe I'd look into that a little more thoroughly before deciding
that divorce was the best way out. It would depend on whether
each party thought he'd get married again, though.

Joe, 39, Nebraska policeman

I would live a more (quiet) life so my husband would have been
more aware of what he was doing to me and the children. I put on
airs of cheerfulness and was too convincing, so he had no guilt
feelings as a result.

Barbara, 45, New Jersey researcher

The decision itself was the most painful. The need to separate
was obvious for such a long time, but the length of time it took
until the actual divorce took a far greater toll on all members of

the family than it should have. I'd try to make the time of decision to the time of divorce as short as possible, for everyone's sake.

Jennifer, 43, Michigan housewife

I didn't make the decision!

Jeanne, 45, California writer

I'd take all the time I needed to get an experienced divorce attorney, and have him as the mediator. With two attorneys the hostility and suspicion builds up too much. I'd look for the best man available.

Gerry, 41, California engineer

I'd keep very good records in order not to be cheated by her attorney and taken advantage of, and I wouldn't treat the damn thing so lightly. When you decide to divorce, it's all-out war, between four people, not two!

Gary, 44, Texas engineer

Nothing. I thought everything out quite thoroughly.

Pat, 36, California (no occupation given)

I'd have sought counsel regarding legal services which might be alternatives to expensive "specialists."

Aileen, 43, Illinois teacher

Maybe a more determined effort to solve the problem, rather than run away from it.

C., 31, Illinois personnel mgr.

Found a better lawyer. I would have been more selective in my choice of dates, but I was 46 and very lonely! I finally did settle down and become more selective and made a good choice on a second husband.

Margery, 47, California real estate broker

If I could do it over, I'd get divorced before the first year was over. I knew it wasn't going to get any better, but I didn't want to disappoint my parents with having a marriage fail.

Camille, 28, California corporate mgr.

I'd get some kind of clause in the agreement to allow for cost of living rises, emergencies, etc.

Ann, 37, California homemaker

I'd save up the money as far in advance as possible and then find some Mafia guy to murder him!

Merla, 44, New York seamstress

I wished to discharge my responsibilities as a parent so I decided to wait until the children were grown. Now, I question the advisability of that.

Agnes, 63, New York R.N.

I'd learn how to recognize the "penis-pause" when it happens to a man, and be especially careful when it did. I'd make all agreements as binding as possible and leave nothing to promises.

Doris, 47, California newspaper reporter

Give away as little as possible. The name of the game seems to be "fuck the man."

Murray, 34, Oregon architect

I wouldn't trust the proceedings to lawyers, because their job is to promote bitterness and make as much as they can off their clients. Quick settlements aren't as profitable as drawn out ones. I'd get some sort of professional mediator, and after we agreed on everything, then get a lawyer to draw up the proper documents—for a set fee!

Marty, 37, Illinois maître d'

I would have eliminated the father's visits to his son earlier than I did. It was very painful for each of them, so much so that the visits were more harmful than good.

Nancy, 33, Maryland teacher

I have little faith left in our court system, so I don't know what could be done differently.

Robert, 49, California (no occupation given)

I'd make more sure I had a partner I could communicate with. My wife couldn't talk things out with any reason.

Charles, 32, Iowa assembler

I'd have made sure I got a college degree before the divorce was begun.

Sharon, 31, California bookkeeper

I'd find a lawyer who agreed to place the matter before a court immediately and have it over with. After a year of friendly visits between my lawyer and my wife's lawyer at a cost of $1,800, I fired my first lawyer and hired another, who placed the matter before trial and finally received the divorce decree at an additional cost of $1,000. The property settlement is still not resolved.

Francis, 54, Wisconsin salesman

If you honestly feel there is no hope for saving the marriage, don't stay. You'll only destroy your own personality. Don't be afraid; make the move. It's not as bad as you think. Living with someone you don't love is the emptiest life in the world, because there is no hope. I personally would have left after one year instead of ten. I was afraid to raise a baby alone. I didn't want my child raised by sitters. I wanted to enjoy my baby. It nearly cost me my sanity. Then I realized I had been so unhappy I was living on radar—one day at a time, one day so painful it must be totally blacked out of my memory when it ceased. Prayer, a strong faith, and the promise of another child I so deeply wanted brought me out of that depression. I realized I had been mentally ill and I was scared.

I was sick one more time about six months before we filed for divorce or about one year before it was final. I never had any intention of not going through with the divorce so I always consider I ceased to be his wife when we filed. It just took the courts awhile to recognize what was already real. When it happened, it was as if the world (which was real and alive) became a stage. Everything was literally squared off and I was not a part of the real world. It is like the scene in the play Our Town where the girl tries to come back home from the grave and no one can see her. I could hear and see everything, I could talk back or do my housework but I was not real. I would keep struggling to come back to a sense of reality. I was frightened. What if one day I woke up and never came back? Surely this was insanity—the never coming back. Sometimes the feeling lasted for two or three days. I knew I had to be free or be destroyed. The new divorce law to eliminate grounds and witnesses had been in effect since January. I knew it was the only answer. I would lose the love of my Dad and be alienated from my church, but I could not be his wife any longer no matter what the cost. On my youngest daughter's sixth birth-

day about an hour before his parents were coming over, —————
*told me he wanted to change himself and his whole life. I told him
there was another woman and that he wanted a divorce. He
couldn't believe I knew. I had hope again; it was over. At last we
could stop fighting and agree on something.*

Sue, 30, California secretary

*I wouldn't have accepted all the debts and taxes I did. I'm still
paying off a loan I had to take from my brother to pay taxes.*

Betty, 38, California government worker

I would have contested her getting custody of one of the children.

—anonymous male, 30

*It was all out of my hands. One of the "wives" involved gave me
love letters as evidence, which saved my neck.*

Jerry, 44, New york sales mgr.

*I would have done more "research" on it before getting the di-
vorce. I would have sought some others my age and divorced, and
talked at length with them.*

Elisa, 31, New York secretary

*I would have made us seek more "professional help." My hus-
band wouldn't take counseling seriously.*

—anonymous female, 28

*Because I didn't see it coming, it happened suddenly and I didn't
have time to make plans. The next time, however, I'll do my
damndest to seek counseling to either try to save it or ease the
separation.*

Howard, 46, California engineer

*The only change I'd make would be not to rush it. Rush into the
separation, by all means. But then take your time to think out all
the little—and big—details. By the time we actually made the
break we both wanted to get out from under everything as soon as
possible. As a result, we sold the house at a loss, when the market
was just beginning a meteoric rise. But even the loss on a house is
minor compared with the trauma of separation, so I wouldn't
change very much, I suppose, if I could do it again.*

J. (male), 43, California marketing specialist

I wouldn't be as easy on the man in the settlement. I'd demand more financial help.

Margaret, 37, Texas secretary

I would have sued her first and been the plaintiff, not the defendant.

Bill, 50, New York stockbroker

I wish now that I'd been more decisive and made more demands for action, instead of letting things drag on as they have.

John, 32, California tech.

Move out of the house and out of town. I still live in the house, three bedrooms, that we brought ten years ago. Also, I'd set up a new will immediately and give a copy to the wife and kids.

Jim, 50, Arizona retired U.S.A.F. navigator

I really had no trouble, once the decision was made. We are financially comfortable and there was no malice on either side. The charge was simple desertion.

Margery, 42, Massachusetts R.N.

I would have stayed home and worked out the solutions. I know now that if anything would have worked, that was it.

Lawrence, 50, Nebraska dispatcher

I wouldn't do too much differently. I definitely would not start dating any sooner, as I needed that breather to see who I was, what my needs were, what to do about living conditions, and my children had to adjust, also. I did wait and try to save my marriage: I would have tried again if it were at all possible. Mentally, there are some things I wish I could have done differently, but maybe my feelings simply had to have time to work through. The anger and bitterness I felt at (husband) for having uprooted us was tremendous and very physically and mentally exhausting . . . . like others, I became insomniac, lost 20 pounds, etc. The anger really was at myself for being so obtuse as not to have seen the danger signs earlier—and read them correctly. The job depression and withdrawal from his family—we were too close and intimate—he was uncomfortable. He also didn't love his children—and it took me a long time to accept that. As I look back, I think all that guilt I piled up on myself for not being what he wanted me to be was extremely self-destructive and unwarranted. I would definitely hope others could accept what I didn't for many months—when one partner needs and refuses therapy and insists the other partner must do it all, the marriage is dead. Stop killing yourself over it and start that new life!

Linda, 32, California teacher-counselor

I would have separated for a trial period. I gave her an ultimatum to settle our differences or get a divorce. Now that we're divorced, she wants me back.

Dan, 35, Illinois engineer

I was bitter at first, but now I think (the divorce) was the best thing to ever happen to me, except for the children. I'd have my lawyer talk only to his lawyer and get it over with quickly. I'd sell the house after I got it and then move as far away as possible, forfeiting, if necessary, any support money.

Natalie, 52, New Hampshire homemaker

I'd get a better lawyer.

—anonymous male, 29

I'd try to establish a credit rating in my own name, not my husband's, and be employed before making the break. I'd insist on some cash settlement of some kind at the time of divorce to help during the transition. This could help eliminate the financial worries, but little can be done to prepare one's self for the emotional problems and lack of social opportunities. A large measure of resignation and a sense of humor are helpful.

Harriet, 44, Maryland secretary

If I were to do this over, I'd take a more realistic and less emotional approach to the divorce. I'd make a stronger effort to work out a more practical agreement, so I could at least live without the constant threat of being sued or jailed for a late support payment. I lived for two years on $35.00 a week, after payments.

Frank, 33, California warehouseman

I never should have gotten married in the first place.

L., 35, California housewife

The guy's dealing from weakness and is usually willing to give anything. "Just let me out" is what he says, as I did. I wouldn't *make as many "deals" to get it over with fast. I'd try to save everything I could for myself.*

Jack, 36, California hotel exec

Husband #1: *I would not have continued to see him after the divorce; until he remarried there was always the hope in the back of my mind that maybe he'd grow up and we could raise our children together. He still calls me and tells me he loves me —although he's been remarried over seven years. See? He still hasn't grown up!*

Husband #2: *There are times—when we're so broke—that I think I was crazy to have left him and that maybe I should go back to him. But all that I have to do is remember a little harder and recall some of the wonderful personalities that have come to us since the divorce, male and female, and I can't regret it.*

Husband #3: *I wish this one could have worked out. I adored the man, in spite of his faults. If only the children's welfare had not been so much at stake. He was worth all the pain and misery that his faults brought about, but I couldn't ask the children to go through it all, too. My oldest daughter, who was 14 at the time, would most certainly have left home one way or the other to get away from him if I'd stayed married another six months. That's not to say it was all his fault—she was wrong, too (and me, of course), but when a child's future is at stake it doesn't matter too much who is to blame; you just have to find an immediate solution.*

Penny, 34, Texas travel agent

I'd find out as much as possible beforehand about the process of divorce, the state of the divorce laws, etc. My attorney was very little help to me.

Ferne, 52, Michigan (no occupation given)

Recognize that it will be a brutal, no-holds-barred fight, and then get a lawyer who'll help you plan and execute an attack.

Dan, 45, New Jersey industrial mgr.

It looks like maybe I spent too much (time and effort) in trying to save the marriage.

Elaine, 33, California homemaker

I would have become involved in something to occupy my lonely hours such as a night school course, singing group, league bowling, crafts class—anything to occupy my thoughts and energies in a more productive and worthwhile way instead of the demoralizing results I seem to have achieved.

Alice, 48, Illinois hospital worker

I'd find a lawyer who would explain to me every detail of the case, so I'd understand it. Perhaps fight harder. My divorce was contested by my husband.

Cheryl, 33, New Jersey teacher

I was so anxious to avoid hassles and get it over with that I accepted a very low level of support payments. Had I been able to hold out and obtain more, it might have made my own and the children's lives easier.

Emily, 38, Maryland librarian

Nothing, except leave sooner!

Ralph, 44, Maryland publishing exec

I would not have gone back to work before the divorce. Then they think you're self-sufficient and your husband gets away with financial murder.

—anonymous female, 49

I would try to secret away all the money I could lay my hands on, which wouldn't be missed and about which no one would be aware.

W., 47, Delaware (no occupation given)

I probably never would have gotten the divorce, no matter what.

Harriet, 46, Illinois (no occupation given)

The decision to divorce was very traumatic. If emotions would allow, I would be more understanding.

Barbara, 41, California postal worker

I'd do nothing different. She took one house, one car, two kids, one-half the money. I took one house, one car, one kid and one-half the money.

John, 46, Colorado truck driver

I don't believe I would have done anything differently. I guess I would ask for more alimony, so I would not have to work so hard now, although I've had difficulty paying my bills and keeping my standard of living as it was.

Verletta, 50, Illinois factory worker

I would think differently in the way of finances. Try to keep more for myself.

Lawrence, 40, Wisconsin (no occupation given)

I'd do it quicker and cleaner. Like, first see a lawyer, then pack up and move out, without further discussion. Discussion of settlement details, if necessary, would wait until I was out of the house.

David, 39, Virginia (no occupation given)

I'd reverse the decision (to divorce) and use other outlets to add fulfillment to my life instead of the dependency on a marriage partner.

A. (female), 48, Michigan accountant

I don't think anything. I got our home, a new car and a full-time job. I was lucky in finding a good job with a wonderful boss, and at this time I'm pretty well-adjusted in my life.

Olive, 52, Pennsylvania bookkeeper

If one does not believe a situation, one hesitates to take legal action against a person who is not able to control himself. If I had known what he would do by trickery and deceit, I would never have stayed with him one day!

Barbara, 51, Illinois health tech.

Given the gift of hindsight I believe I would be tempted (though perhaps with small success) to approach the matter with a more hard-boiled attitude. I certainly would be reluctant to believe that a fair-minded and civilized attitude could do anything but make me a loser, in the financial end, at least. Nevertheless, it no doubt made it easier for me to live with myself afterwards.

Frances, 45, Massachusetts L.P.N.

I was opposed to the whole idea and didn't confront the inevitability of it until I received the papers. Another time, I'd start *planning the first time he told me it would ultimately happen—like 15 to 20 years earlier!*

Mary, 55, Washington professor

I would go to court for a legal support order. We had a "gentleman's agreement" that he would send $54 a week support, but when he was operated on, I couldn't collect the legal support for my children because there were no legal orders and we weren't legally divorced yet.

Jeanne, 33, Connecticut rental agent

I would get a lawyer immediately and start into the social life a little more slowly. My reaction was to date right away—my ego needed that—but I should have gotten the legal arrangements out of the way first.

Elizabeth, 32, Massachusetts secretary

I would kill, if necessary, to get custody.

Richard, 43, Minnesota divorce counselor

In my first marriage, my husband left me and took our two-week-old baby, so I had to go to court to get the baby back. Six months later I told my attorney to go through with the divorce because my husband refused to show any interest in what had happened to us. This was an emotional decision, because I didn't want to be divorced from him, but being in a state of limbo was more upsetting. Given the decision again (which I had in Divorce #2) I would have suffered through the limbo period to arrive at a mutual divorce. As it was, my husband did not want the divorce, because he didn't respect the laws governing marriage and divorce, nor the money involved. My asking for a divorce put a real end to any good relationship we could have had as friends who "agree to disagree." So, haste not into a divorce, is the message. After my Husband #2 left (he was ill and moved to his home state and doctor), he tried to "win me back," but I maintained the separation. We agreed to divorce six months later, and it wasn't final for another year. This was a calmer decision; we are now friends and so are his new wife and me. I do resent their relationship periodically, because he is so much nicer a person now than he was then. Oh, well!

Joyce, 40, New York college professor

I would not have let him talk me out of temporary support, trusting him that he would give it to me directly. He did not, and laughed about it.

—anonymous Michigan woman, 37

Never get married again.

Thomas, (no age), Pennsylvania painter

I would leave (a certain Pennsylvania county) and its crooked judicial system.

Russ, 65, Pennsylvania retired builder

File for the divorce immediately.

Billie, 30, California secretary

My first marriage, I'd probably go back, because he loved me and we had a five-year-old and he promised to change his ways if I'd return to him. My second marriage, nothing, because we just weren't meant for each other. My third, was the man I loved and tried so hard to help. After signing the divorce papers, I wouldn't try to contact him, but instead let him rest his mind. If I'd let him get the "running wildness" out of his system I feel he would have come to me.

Ruby, 51, California teacher

I wouldn't let the lawyer continue his excessive hunt for "hidden" funds that I might have, thereby running up the expense excessively. I would have fought the excessive control my wife received to keep me away from the boys.

Alvin, 57, California (no occupation given)

I would hide every asset. I would either get a flat settlement or leave the state. I believe alimony is involuntary servitude and unconstitutional!

Julian, 46, Georgia (no occupation given)

If I had to do it all again, I would make sure that I had a job, a car and a place to live before even contemplating a separation. I would make sure that I had a good baby-sitter and a little money in the bank for emergencies!

Carol, 30, Maryland secretary

I would have stayed in the bed and let her move to the couch!

R., 51, Michigan writer

I probably would get the divorce much quicker, rather than waiting too long for things to get better. I was so exhausted from the emotional turmoil that I was nearly ill.

Gwen, 54, Texas investigator

I'd work out the details between both parties before ever going to the court hearing, and I'd represent myself, saving the cost of an attorney's fees.

Dale, 31, Illinois roofer

Frankly, nothing. It was just harder understanding that the kids would be "divided," and that I was talking them into staying with their mother.

Florida psychotherapist and marriage counselor, 37

I would not have tried to be so "fair," and would have looked out for my own and my children's best interests.

Sondra, 38, California (no occupation given)

I would never get the divorce or separate. I'd try to work things out.

Elizabeth, 45, Ohio medical assistant

Having no choice regarding a "decision," your question doesn't apply. However, if I had to go through it again, I would most certainly follow a different course of action. First, I would not go the marriage salvation bit. . . . I'd dig in and gear for total war. Had I gone that route in the first place, no doubt I'd have won.

Bill, 33, Wisconsin minister

Naturally, I still wish the divorce hadn't happened. But if I were going through it again, knowing what I know now, I would have pressed an attack to put her in the defensive and thereby salvaged more for myself. If I had not stalled the proceedings I could have gotten by with half the child support and eliminated other things she was able to get. I have a hunch her friends were telling her she was letting me off too easy by letting me have the house.

Frank, 39, Minnesota compositor

I would try to get involved in some relevant activities sooner. I'd start working out the arrangements as soon as possible, and spend less time in fruitless speculations as to why the marriage didn't work out.

June, 42, Connecticut clerk

I'd shop around for a lawyer, and get the best!

Norman, 49, Texas (no occupation given)

I wouldn't go to court with a lawyer, and wouldn't tell the full truth. It doesn't pay.

Mark, 38, New Jersey fireman

I don't dare say it in writing.

Arthur, 54, Illinois (no occupation given)

The only thing I would do different would be to take the legal action sooner; also, I'd shop around for a lawyer.

Carol, 29, New York teacher

I'd make sure he was legally obligated to pay his bills, and to inform the courts of his address and place of work at all times so any collectors who were looking for him would know where he was at all times and not call here looking for him or bugging me for the money.

Bonnie, 30, Illinois (no occupation given)

I'd never leave a joint house, or, if I did, I'd take everything of mine with me. And if I could keep my cool, I'd represent myself in all legal proceedings, and list a lawyer as a referee only.

Pat, 32, New Jersey programmer

If I had to do it all over again, the only thing I would say is to try harder to grow up and seek counseling for both of us. So many seem to think the divorced life is one of fun and freedom—not true! It is a life of one traumatic experience after another, a life of loneliness, panic when the baby-sitter can't show up, being desperate when you are too sick to go to work and wondering where the money will come from, lost when the car breaks down and you have to depend on strangers, having to leave your children with a sitter when they are sick, etc. Even Mother Nature works against you when (the weather) makes it impossible to get to work. I worked two jobs to make it, and had to leave my children alone a great deal.

Rose, 53, California (no occupation given)

I would try to make my husband understand so we could have parted on a friendly basis and not have the hard feelings.

Judith, 35, Colorado waitress

I would have left the state and tried to start a new life (away from) my ex-wife, children, and the courts under the present system.

Robert, 35, New Jersey machinist

Do it sooner!

Dolores, 44, New York (no occupation given)

I wouldn't let the lawyer make verbal commitments. I'd make sure any deals are in writing. I was ripped off.

George, 34, Illinois truck driver

Both husbands are back in the Midwest, where I came from. I think perhaps I would have adjusted better if I had stayed there, in a place I knew and where I had friends, and where I could have contact with my ex if for no other reason than a reminder. Absence does strange things to the memory.

Martha, 35, California clerk

First, I would plan the divorce down to the last detail. I'd visit the local court house and listen to cases that come up. I'd try to find the best judge to hear the case and shop around for a good attorney that will do as you ask and not sell you down the river. I'd reduce my earnings for a period of time and even quit my job, if I could. I'd run up a pile of bills for her to sweat over and get fat and lazy. I'd insult all her friends and relatives. I'd make her get a job and stay at it right up to the court action and then under Michigan law ask for custody of the kids and child support and alimony from her. I could go on and on, but the point is to fight fire with fire, and therefore I would also contact the first divorce reform group I could find and study the situation before making the first move. If I didn't have any children I would have moved 20 miles east into Canada and tell them all to drop dead. But first I would sell and steal everything that I could.

Larry, 43, Michigan (no occupation given)

I'd go to a place with fair divorce laws, and maybe get an even break.

Robert, 52, Illinois TV technician

I'd try for a divorce in another state. Pennsylvania law still requires adversary action, meaning someone has to be "injured" and someone has to be "innocent."

John, 47, Pennsylvania insurance exec

I would have gotten a woman attorney, who understood the feelings I went through. Then I probably would have lived out-of-state and got a divorce outside of California. The "no-fault divorce laws" are insane! The children have no rights at all. I'm still involved in court proceedings, since he abuses the children during his visitation, but the law protects him. The law disregards the children's right not to be abused!

Mary, 31, California student

There was plenty of warning along the way from psychiatrists, et al., but there is no easy way to leave a marriage. The emotional impact during the first year runs the gamut from tears to hysterical laughter and then depression. I would have legally divorced him two years before I did, but it took him that long to sign the agreement.

Peg, 46, New York cosmetician

Based on experience, I'd sell all community property except personal things, and not settle for legal separation but only for immediate divorce. I'd get a divorce lawyer, instead of the regular lawyer.

Evelyn, 53, California nurse

I'd try to obtain the divorce in a different state, such as my home state of Ohio—that way when the children needed the feeling of belonging to a family, my own family would be around. My husband's "friend" kept him on a short leash so he didn't have much time for the children.

Patsy, 37, California R.N.

Had I anticipated his viciousness, I would have hired the sharpest lawyer in town. I would not have separated first.

Amy, 39, California (no occupation given)

Hire a very good lawyer. Not a small-town lawyer to keep it quiet.

Lillian, 44, Pennsylvania (no occupation given)

I wouldn't return for trial reconciliation.

Sarah, 53, California clerk

If I knew then what I know now, I would study the divorce laws of my state, shop around for an efficient divorce attorney, gather all of the evidence possible to support my defense and to prove my wife an unfit person morally to get custody of the children, and I'd be mentally prepared to appeal any adverse decisions to the State Supreme Court and even on to the District Court of Appeals.

Howard, 42, Utah contractor

Certainly not delay, or be so afraid. Not hesitate because of the children. Move swiftly. Not wait another year and a half of separation before divorcing. Once the decision is made, finalize it as soon as possible.

Elizabeth, 34, New Jersey R.N.

There's nothing I could have done differently. I turned down part of the support money he offered—I wouldn't change that. I would though, get a better, more expensive lawyer, (even though, by decree, he still owes me on the other one) to prevent him from pulling me into court on every little thing to avenge himself on me.

Linda, 33, Arizona bookkeeper

Not tried to do everything myself. Accept the help of friends and family. Pride has a way of clouding things. One person cannot take on the whole world.

Sandra, 28, California (no occupation given)

Sell everything I had and take all my money out of the bank. If the car is in both names, I'd sell the motor, transmission, tires, windshield, doors, and leave her the shell with the title, and keep my cool. There are still a lot of nice people around.

Martin, 54, Pennsylvania production worker

I wouldn't have just taken a furnished room in a boarding house while hoping that I would "go home again." I would have moved into an "extended family" setting so that I would have had more supportive people around me, not just gloom.

Roland, 48, Connecticut engineer

I would have gone to Reno or somewhere and gotten a "quickie." I simply couldn't cut through the legal manipulations and biases held by the courts and exploited by the legal profession. The tendency is to get tired of the hassling and just give in, usually to your disadvantage.

T. (male), 44, Pennsylvania minister

I would have tried to understand that there is no shame in divorce, and got one quicker.

Alice, 29, Minnesota factory worker

Foregone the trial separation, and not had a baby on the strength of the reconciliation. I would have waited until I was sure I wanted to leave (that is, without precipitation by relatives) and then left and stayed gone. I would have saved two and a half years of my life that way.

Mary, 26, California student

What can you do? It would be lovely, of course, to make sure you're quite well-off at the time, have a guaranteed income and a live-in housekeeper who loves children. I only wish now that my ex could be civil, instead of defensive and unfriendly. He rarely visits his daughter.

Linda, 34, California legal secretary

I would have joined a divorced peoples' group sooner; I didn't know how to begin dating, etc.

Diane, 32, California homemaker

I wouldn't be such a pushover for my husband!

Sandi, 23, New York lab tech.

Nothing—we had a bad marriage but a good divorce.

Barbara, 28, New York bank teller

I think I would seek some post-divorce counseling to get back on the track. It's funny, but people get all kinds of counseling before their divorce, but not too many think about getting some personal help afterwards . . .

Lee, 37, Iowa city worker

Since I wanted the divorce and my husband didn't, I made all kinds of concessions to get it over with. Now, I'd be more patient and wait to get the best possible deal, financially. Other than that, I have no regrets, other than the six children and the financial hardship.

Terese, 40, Michigan secretary

I'd join a singles' organization right away.

Donald, 39, Ohio physicist

What advice would you give others about avoiding certain pitfalls or making the divorce situation easier, smoother, etc.?

Go to Reno or Mexico or someplace for a quickie. The anguish of waiting for the lawyers and the courts isn't hardly worth it.

> Alan, 32, Georgia engineer

Don't contest it. Come to some agreement on the settlement among yourselves, and nobody contest it. You'll only drag it out and wind up hating each other.

> Barry, 34, California bartender

Get every possible penny out of the guy every chance you get, because the way the laws are set up he could very easily get away with falling behind on child support and alimony and then finally never paying you anything.

> Myra, 33, Illinois secretary

Get a top-notch lawyer and don't see each other during the divorce process.

> Helen, 30, California receptionist

The problem with most divorce proceedings in the United States today seems to be that the laws and the lawyers themselves encourage open warfare instead of sensible, intelligent, rational discussion. I'd advise others to be willing to keep it friendly and amenable, and to share everything right down the middle, and

not let the lawyers get into the act and make you fight each other
for every cent.

Penny, 28, New York fashion designer

Be very careful to have a competent lawyer, because there's no
such thing as an amicable separation or a friendly divorce.

Mel, 38, Texas stockbroker

Before you announce that you want to get a divorce, start a plan
to get yourself prepared by either going to school and learning
something to earn your own living, or else start setting things
financially straight so you can take what's coming to you before
his lawyer steals it.

Lila, 31, Massachusetts artist

Hire an experienced divorce attorney, a specialist, or else agree to
a single lawyer to handle both parties, to act as a mediator or
negotiator, without taking sides. I know that's difficult in most
cases, so assuming you have two lawyers, I'd go after someone
who is known to have a good track record. Don't treat the divorce
settlement lightly, as is the temptation when you first start out.
Make no concessions in the beginning and start right out working
through your attorney and not through your wife.

Gerry, 41, California engineer

I wouldn't put too much trust in your lawyer; it's impossible for
him to act fairly on your behalf when your husband is paying his
fees. Realize from the start that the other party will lie and get
friends to support him, and by the time the real truth comes out it
will be too late to help you. Make sure there are provisions for
inflation in alimony payments, and if you've been married 10
years or more there should be an equal division of all property.
Otherwise, the unscrupulous spouse can leave you destitute.

Virginia, 62, New York housewife

If there are no children, move to another city and break off all ties.
If there are children, decide on a mutually agreeable visitation
schedule and stick to it religiously.

Robert, 24, California tech.

My advice would be this: your happiness is the most important
thing. Don't be concerned with whether your family or friends

approve. You are important, and your children will benefit much more from one happy parent, than with two miserable ones.

Janet, 57 California housewife

Remember what you once meant to each other. I know someone who was married 15 years, had three kids, and after they got divorced and to this day they still don't speak to each other, which is totally ridiculous because they had so much before. You have to have loved each other to be married so long and to have children. Never forget that.

Marsha, 24, California postal worker

Considerable thought should be given to who will have custody of the kids and what can be done afterward if the one who gets custody doesn't handle them properly.

Charles, 37, North Dakota engineer

Get a female lawyer!

Ginny, 40, New Jersey teacher

Realize that the other party is capable of lying and getting his friends to lie for him, even under oath. Be ready for it.

Cindy, 31, Kansas therapist

Keep your personal happiness foremost, and avoid "staying together" for extraneous reasons, like kids, society, etc.

Gordon, 44, Toronto salesman

I think the financial obligation on the man's side should be less, although he should still pay child support. I think also that both parties should have visiting rights with children, with no hitches.

Denise, 29, California secretary

In the first place, marry a person who is intelligent enough to accept a divorce if it becomes inevitable.

Max, 54, New York insurance broker

I'd keep attorneys out of it. They increase tension and give you the feeling that you're in a full-scale battle.

Ed, 43, California architect

Go more slowly in getting married. Be prepared from the start to face reversal.

Marilyn, 38, California school administrator

Seek help from professional sources, like counselors, lawyers, etc.
Try to accept the situation, but go on with rebuilding your life
slowly, step by step. Financial bitterness is your worst enemy,
and . . . don't be afraid or ashamed to seek Social Service Aid to
help you over the rough spots.

Veronica, 44, New York secretary

Search your Bible and compare those things that you have done
in your marriage against what is taught that you should have
done, and you will see the major cause of your difficulty. Everything that a man and woman hope for in a marriage can be
fulfilled providing you utilize the divine principles taught in your
Bible. Read it. Understand it. Follow it. It is your only true and
valid foundation upon which to place your trust. Nothing else can
supercede it. Never accept anyone's advice on marriage or human
relations until you've double-checked it with your Bible. Use the
intelligence God gave you and accept the teachings of Jesus and
you will never be alone, lonely or unhappy. He will give you
comfort and lift the burdens from your shoulders—seek Him and
you will find Him. Ask Him and you will receive your needs.

Warren, 41, Missouri (no occupation given)

Communicate and negotiate a lot more than you think you
should. Take tranquilizers at the same time. Really shop around
for a good lawyer, and don't rush! The paramount thing is to
complete the property settlement first.

—anonymous tax adjuster

First marriage: After-the-fact advice is easily given. The pitfalls
are often based on immaturity. In any case, the keeping up with
the Joneses was stupidity, along with the big house in Connecticut, etc. when I was transferred to New York. None of it's important. What would have made more sense would have been some
cautious investments in real estate or sensible stocks, etc.

Second marriage: Give up early when you have to, instead of
saying to yourself, "Oh, she'll grow up and understand." If you're
living differently-paced lives, discuss things more freely before
it's too late.

Tom, 46, California advertising exec

Break down all your debts evenly, because they're debts of both parties, and avoid any placing of "blame" in court. Try to make the court appearance the final act—there shouldn't be any "waiting period," as most states have.

Patricia, 32, North Dakota R.N.

I don't know how to avoid "pitfalls" when I'm constantly on the receiving end. I didn't want this in the first place and now I'm finally getting some good advice from a sympathetic lawyer friend who isn't a divorce mill chiseler. I'd advise everyone to have a good attorney before any trouble starts.

Marilyn, 37, California teacher

I'd take pains to find a good, honest lawyer, if there are any left.

Mike, 28, Arizona merchant

Live together for a while and discuss important issues and get to know each other as well as possible before taking a step as "permanent" as marriage.

Barbara, 26, California sales rep.

Do it earlier.

Carol, 36, Illinois secretary

The sooner you realize that life still goes on and you've got to concentrate on the future, the better off you'll be mentally.

William, 30, California teacher

See a marriage counselor before marriage, not after!

Mary, 62, New York secretary

No couple should divorce without fully discussing it first, because if they're in agreement about child support, visitation rights, etc, it could prevent attorneys from "taking" either party. Kentucky has a new law that says either party can request a court order for marriage counseling, and I think it is a good law. No attorney is going to push for reconciliation if his fees are at stake, and many of them will even hide the existence of the new law.

Gloria, 46, Kentucky bookkeeper

The woman should train herself at something so she can make a living immediately.

Carol, 29, Michigan student

Remember that a woman in America is fundamentally an exploitative factor that acts to the detriment of man; that, though blessed with greater rationality than man, she chooses to undermine his position rather than affirm it in the universe; that the man should be sure he has a separate domicile to which to retreat.

Galen, 37, California teacher

Be aggressive in attacking the loneliness and despair! Get out and meet people, take an art class or a gourmet cooking class; play volleyball at the beach—just get out! Those new people you meet will restore your confidence and self-worth. After you've definitely decided on divorce, see your "ex" as little as possible, and avoid any "heavy" discussions at all costs.

Lillian, 29, North Dakota homemaker

Avoid lawyers. Their shingle is a license to practice greed!

Bob, 35, Idaho physician

Don't procrastinate once you've determined you've got an unhappy marriage. Get out into the world and make a new life for yourself.

Beverly, 45, New York teacher

Communicate despite the courts, which only make a bad situation worse. Get a lawyer in whom you can confide and talk to easily. My greatest relief was when I turned everything over to my attorney.

Emily, 33, New York R.N.

Make sure you're secure within yourself before you try to find security in someone else. Realize that the world is half-male and half-female, and that everyone is going to meet people he admires or respects, and this should be accepted by both partners.

Peggy, 24, California cashier

Definitely seek professional help, a psychiatrist or someone else to talk to.

Yvonne, 29, California (no occupation given)

Avoid counselors; they thrive on disputes!

James, 43, California credit mgr.

Change your life-style rapidly so as not to dwell on past associations.

Sheila, 38, California (no occupation given)

Forget marriage to start with!

J., 39, California (no occupation given)

I would go to his family and close friends and seek help in getting through to him, if that's the problem.

Barbara, 45, New Jersey researcher

Don't let your husband's ambition take top priority in your lives; instead seek mutual interests, rather than the interests of only one party.

Jo Ann, 43, housewife (no state given)

Settle everything in advance, and then get a single attorney.

Elaine, 53, New York housewife

Don't rely on the opinions of family and friends.

Aileen, 43, Illinois teacher

Get yourself familiar with a courtroom and the procedures involved, so they won't be so alien and frightening to you when you confront them.

Margery, 47, California realtor

I think it would help, once having reached the decision to divorce, if you just got away from everything for a while. It's a very depressing thing, because you end up talking about it and never solving anything. It would also be nice if you could do it like grown-ups. My ex-husband didn't want me but he couldn't stand to be divorced, so I had to get a restraining order to keep him from harming me or the children.

Camille, 28, California corporate mgr.

Believe in yourself.   Pat, 34, California writer

Don't get married.   Dave, 25, California student

Once the fact of "irreconcilable differences" is established don't prolong the inevitable; it only makes it harder on the children and yourself.

Ann, 37, California homemaker

Ask yourself if you've truly exhausted all the alternatives, such as counseling, trial separation, etc. Realize what a sudden change in your life you are going to cause, and understand fully the finality of it.

Ron, 36, California teacher

Don't permit remarriage for two years.

Milly, 48, law student (no address given)

If you're going to get divorced, get divorced; don't go around whining or crying or bitching to others about how miserable or sad or victimized you are. Get the goddam divorce and shut up and start living again!

Art, 35, Missouri disc jockey

Take plenty of time to think through the seriousness of it all and its implications. Make your points succinctly and with balanced emotional control. Try to find a lawyer with whom you have some rapport.

Agnes, 63, New York R.N.

My advice to women who are "dumped" is to face it, dearies, when a man is through, he is through! No matter how sweet the parting, how tender the words, how sincere the promises, no man likes to make payments on a used car after it's sent to the city dump. Therefore, whatever agreement is made, make sure it's binding as possible, and know that soon—very soon!—he will be tired of it all and go to court to change it. In the agreement, make it specific on which date the payment is to be in your hands. Most women feel that the man drags it out often, as an aggravation, and often the women have to belittle themselves by begging for their legal payment. And whatever a woman had when she got married, she should keep. Everything else should be split, because everything else was acquired mutually. But not what she had going in.

Doris, 47, California newspaperwoman

Live with a person for at least a year before marriage. If you decide to marry, a legal definitive statement as to responsibilities in the partnership should be a prerequisite. A new edition of the contract of responsibilities would be required annually.

Barbara, 37, California teacher

For a man, my advice would be to try to hold on to everything you can, because she'll try to screw you out of everything since the whole breaking down of the marriage was probably your own adulterous fault anyway. For the woman, I would advise to steel yourself for the realization that, from husband to lawyers to court, you will be dealing with nothing but bastards.

—anonymous male, 42, Ohio politician

None at all. A person has to experience the hell for himself.

Nancy, 33, Maryland teacher

Make sure you're getting a fair deal financially. Be very explicit about getting your own wishes into the decree.

Charles, 32, Iowa assembler

Be sure your attorney is on your own and your childrens' sides. I have always believed mine was bought off by my husband and his attorney.

Sharon, 31, California bookkeeper

I would recommend that if their state doesn't have a no-fault divorce law with an absolute time limit of, say, six months, for a decree, then go to Reno or Mexico for a real quickie divorce. Divorce litigation under present Wisconsin laws merely gives one or the other, or both, a big club to continue clobbering his or her former mate. And if that's not the case, then the lawyers promulgate for higher fees.

Francis, 54, Wisconsin salesman

Nobody gets everything he wants in any divorce. Be fair, be reasonable, be ready to compromise. This isn't the time to try to punish each other. Don't use children as levers or pawns or spies. When you start thinking you want to get married in the first place, be friends first and foremost; you'll spend a lot of time together. You must like each other. If you want to be lovers before marriage use birth control. Getting married because of pregnancy may be the biggest mistake you'll ever make. If you can't accept someone the way he is, keep looking—don't try to change someone into what you want.

Kathleen, 31, Michigan secretary

Immediately seek out others with the same plight. Make new friends, male and female, and take on new activities that interest you and which you may have neglected while married.

Betty, 38, California government worker

I would recommend concentrating on the attitudes of the children, particularly their feelings of being involved and/or responsible for the marriage's end.

Jim, 40, California salesman

Use counseling before and after to help you get the (moral and psychological) support you need and to gain suggestions for problems as they arise.

Elizabeth, 32, Tennessee C.P.A.

Don't let the lawyers play chess with you and your spouse. They try to make you fight so their work seems more complex and lengthy, just so their fees will be higher. You'll both lose out, anyway.

Tom, 34, Oregon teacher

Hire the most experienced attorney, no matter what! Smooth things out. Also, hire a man attorney. Especially, find out whether your attorney favors men or women in the first place. Some do, regardless of their own client's sex.

Jerry, 44, New York mgr.

Don't let her use your children as hostages!

Barry, 41, Illinois artist

Get a good, rational lawyer.

Elsa, 31, New York secretary

First, seek professional therapy. If, as a result, you "save" the marriage, okay. If not, you'll go into the divorce with your eyes open wider and you'll be better able to cope with the emotional (burden). Undertake some good financial planning, certainly. It costs more to keep two households going.

Howard, 46, California engineer

Communicate better in marriage. If there is something you feel important about your relationship, then say it and make sure the *spouse understands and is aware of what you said. If you haven't got that assurance, then you're asking for trouble.*

J. (male), 43, Delaware marketing man

Break completely, but remain friends. Try to understand why and how it happened, instead of hating each other.

Margaret, 37, Texas secretary

Anticipate the high-priced "esquires" who feed off the husband, and the other financial costs.

Bill, 50, New York stockbroker

I would advise having the property settlement, child custody, visitation rights, etc, settled out of court before the actual trial. I would also advise not to put anything in writing, at least not without your attorney's knowledge and consent.

John, 32, California tech.

Talk to divorced people. Invite representatives of Parents Without Partners or some similiar group to talk to you about the single life and family programs. Attend reconciliation court for three months. Get complete property assets in black and white, including the income tax situation.

Jim, 50, Arizona retired U.S.A.F. navigator

Avoid interracial marriage even after you've extensively studied its ramifications. Keep the muddling mother-in-law away from her daughter.

Tony, 57, New York (no occupation given)

Make up your mind as early as possible, to avoid prolonging the agony.

Margery, 42, Massachusetts R.N.

Do everything possible to keep hatred, recriminations, accusations, etc. to a minimum. Try to regard the divorce not as the end of something, but as a new starting place for the rest of your life and forget all that went before.

Lawrence, 50, Nebraska dispatcher

Don't hang on for the sake of the children. Don't put the children in the middle and make them suffer; they love both parents. Be true to yourself—know who you are and changes you could make and want to make—and know when a compromise really means you'd be selling your very soul and being. Get a good lawyer and be fair about your financial expectations—in a divorce your living style will have to change, but isn't it worth it to get that precious second chance at life? You can't make a divorce easier, but it isn't necessarily true to look on it as a failure symbol.

Linda, 32, California teacher-counselor

Make certain positive, irrevocable legal commitments are made on paying existing financial debts. I was left holding the bag for $7,000 in charges when he pulled a disappearing act. I was a cosigner.

Elizabeth, "over 30," Nevada (no occupation given)

Try to work out a property settlement prior to seeing an attorney. Write a marriage contract before marriage. Examine how much you have—rather than what you don't have—prior to the divorce.

Dan, 35, Illinois engineer

Don't sign a thing. Don't sign a single, goddamned thing!

Ira, 46, New York salesman

Once the woman asks for a divorce, or makes any move at all in that direction, run for the hills and get all the help you can.

Jack, 36, California hotel exec

Go right to work and keep busy. Do all the things you couldn't do before, and do them as soon as you can.

Muriel, 61, California (no occupation given)

I'd recommend always getting counseling and end the marriage when you know it's hopeless, before too much hurt is inflicted. I think it's important for all of us to learn that we have to be happy alone before we can be happy with a mate. Don't expect a marriage to suddenly make you happy.

Penny, 34, Texas travel agent

Counseling is always helpful, especially in regards to trying to help the children adjust to the situation.

Ferne, 52, Michigan (no occupation given)

Realize that lawyers are basically out for what they can get and that the two parties should work out details as much as possible. If not, fight hard for everything.

Dan, 45, New Jersey industrial mgr.

I have a theory. Some people don't suffer over divorce—they just celebrate their freedom! Others do suffer. Maybe those who do need it, for a period of change in which to grow later on.

Elaine, 33, California homemaker

Don't try to desperately find love and companionship immediately. Get involved in something you enjoy, and don't get wound up emotionally or sexually with the opposite sex too soon, because after a divorce there is a strong tendency and a strong susceptibility to get involved, and it's much too soon for a meaningful relationship.

Alice, 48, Illinois hospital worker

Get a lawyer who can communicate.

Cheryl, 33, New Jersey teacher

The more you can talk over rationally all the aspects of the situation and any settlement details with your spouse, the better. Understanding friends are a godsend at this time, but avoid those aquaintances who put you down for "not trying hard enough."

Emily, 38, Maryland librarian

When divorce is the only way out, don't extend the marriage for the sake of the children, because I believe the children suffer more from the daily exposure to an insecure marriage.

Ralph, 44, Maryland publishing exec

Don't ever have so much faith in your spouse that you're positive he would never be unfaithful. If your marriage does hit a snag, instead of being angry or hurt, and jumping into a divorce, I would recommend a good hard fight to save the marriage. Perhaps a period of separation should be mandatory before a court date can be set. Give each mate a taste of what's in store for them.

Harriet, 46, Illinois (no occupation given)

Do not compromise yourself in order to make it easier or smoother; there is no substitute for integrity.

> Barbara, 41, California postal worker

Don't feel as though it was all your fault if your husband finds another woman.

> Verlette, 50, Illinois factory worker

See a lawyer immediately. Avoid "adversary" type legalities wherever possible, Better yet, discuss the divorce before you get married.

> David, 39, Virginia (no occupation given)

Counseling with an objective third person you both respect is a good idea. One argument which kept us together longer than we would have stayed was that we should stay together for the sake of the children. Children do need two parents, and there is a risk when the parents separate. But we both came to realize that the children need a home with love and no tension, even if it means only one parent in it. How will they know how to make a loving marriage if they don't grow up in one?

> Sylvia, 36, Connecticut secretary

I always made a point to let the father have first choice on visitation privileges, and then I made my plans for that particular day around his visit, be it Christmas or whatever.

> A., 48, Michigan accountant

The best way to make a divorce easier is to make damn sure you want to marry him in the first place. Know your partner well, even if you have to create crises and arguments just to see how he reacts.

> Brian, 29, Ohio stockbroker

If a husband and wife really love each other, really care about each other, there is nothing they cannot solve if they both try.

> Barbara, 51, Illinois health tech.

Advice? I wouldn't presume. Except, maybe, to say don't count on or be disillusioned or surprised at anything that happens.

> Frances, 45, Massachusetts L.P.N.

Don't ever become totally wrapped up in the children or in your role as a homemaker and mother. Do cultivate the role of wife, companion, and sweetheart. Always retain something of your own individuality.

Mary, 55, Washington professor

Do everything legally, even though you are having a "friendly" divorce. The legality is what holds up. Don't knock the other party. He's still the children's parent and they need to have a Dad to look up to, no matter how you think they don't deserve him.

Jeanne, 33, Connecticut rental agent

Every woman needs to be able to support herself. Then death or divorce is easier. Inexpensive counseling should be encouraged, especially where children are concerned. Somehow counseling should be made more acceptable to men.

Margaret, 53, Kansas librarian

Don't use the children to hurt each other; never stay together "just" for the children; respect each other as human beings and try to communicate with each other.

Judy, 31, keypunch operator

Speaking from the point of view of one who didn't want the divorce, I feel acceptance is the most important factor. If one person wants out, for whatever reason, accepting the situation is the first step to making a new life for yourself. Your own acceptance makes it easier for children to accept also.

Elizabeth, 32, Massachusetts secretary

Obtain competent divorce counseling. The Men's Rights Association is the only source I know of.

Richard, 43, Minnesota divorce counselor

Do not rush into a divorce without counseling for your own emotional stability. A trial separation, a chance to cool down and gain your emotional footing is essential. It is a big step!

Joyce, 40, New York college professor

Get out with people. Join groups, singles' clubs; have good times! Enjoy hobbies, and things you like to do.

Della, 49, California teacher

If you can stand her, let her file for the divorce. It's against the law to kill her!

Thomas, (no age), Pennsylvania painter

Do not believe any lawyer, and leave the state of Pennsylvania.

Russ, 65, Pennsylvania retired builder

A woman is supposed to be stronger in all ways except physical strength. I would advise her to look at her husband like a little boy when she suspects he has a problem—don't nag, but open up the way for him to pour out his hidden problems. Never tell your man your experiences with men before you were married. Confessions don't clear the slate!

Ruby, 51, California teacher

One of three avenues of approach: First, set up a pre-nuptial agreement, setting forth a settlement in advance of any problems. Second, and this isn't revolutionary, organize a National Divorce Insurance system, financed (underwritten) by the insurance companies and just like auto insurance. Different rates for different people—alimony and support. The couple would have to have the insurance to get a marriage license. It would be paid monthly. Third, where there are no children, have a no-fault divorce with no alimony. Where there are children, try to force compulsory arbitration.

Julian, 46, Georgia (no occupation given)

Try to save the marriage if there is any love there for each other. However, if one or the other absolutely does not love the other, then it should be broken off. But I personally feel that you can not and should not hate someone just because they no longer love you. You can hate the fact that they don't love you, but you shouldn't hate the person. After all, you do not love everyone. I loved my husband, but how could I hate him for not loving me. Love is something that has to be freely given—it cannot be demanded. Unless one loves you, you cannot make them. Because of the love you have shared, you should respect one another and try to help each other help the children adjust.

1. Reassure the children that although you no longer love each other, you both love them and always will.

2. Explain that when brothers and sisters fight, they are sometimes sent to different rooms and separated until they stop fighting. Mommy and Daddy are fighting too much and we are to be separated until we learn to stop fighting. This will give the children a better understanding of the situation. If problems can be resolved, then reuniting might be possible, if not, then by that time the children will have adjusted to the situation better.

3. Tell the children that although you do not love each other you still respect and like each other.

4. Remember that your prime concern is your children. Do not try to destroy the other parent in front of the children. The children need both of you and love both of you and want to believe in both of you. If you try to destroy, then you are leaving yourself wide open for rebuttal from your spouse.

5. Do not deliberately try to hurt the spouse! You cannot hurt someone else deliberately unless you hurt yourself also and who needs any more hurt. Stop and think about it. When your child does something wrong, you punish him; but, aren't you also hurt by the fact that you had to hurt him. No one likes to do things to hurt other people; it tends to depress your natural desire for life, liberty and the pursuit. Hurting someone is a very negative attitude in life, helping someone is a very positive attitude. Establish a positive attitude with your ex-spouse and try to work out your differences. When my husband and I separated, we agreed to leave the house in both names. We would each pay half of the mortgage and we would each claim half of the interest at tax time. By doing this I retained a roof over our heads for half of the going rate of rent and he maintained the investment in our home. We agreed that I may live in the house as long as I do not remarry. At such time, we will either sell the house and split the profit, or we will rent the house out and keep our investment going. Also, I could not afford a baby-sitter and on several occasions he would baby-sit for me so that I could date. In turn, I would have him over for dinner or bake a favorite dessert for him. I continued to do his laundry in exchange for his repair work on the house. By working together we helped the children believe in what we were telling them. Not only that, but it gave the children a more secure feeling of being loved and accepted by us both. We worked together a lot

better after our separation than we ever did during our marriage. I guess this was due to the tremendous amount of pressure which we were no longer laboring under. We couldn't make it as husband and wife, but we sure made damn good friends!

Carol, 30, Maryland secretary

Don't try to be nice to a vicious spouse.

R., 51, Michigan writer

Don't talk about all your problems before and after to anyone who'll listen. I suppose it can be therapeutic, but action is needed more than words.

Gwen, 54, Texas investigator

Know the divorce laws previous to marriage, to avoid certain legal problems in regard to property settlement and child custody.

Dale, 31, Illinois roofer

Counseling first. A good counselor keeps either party from feeling inadequate or like a failure.

Florida psychotherapist and marriage counselor, 37

Get a recommended attorney. The amount paid makes no difference—my attorney didn't look out for my interests at all. Don't try to be fair.

Sondra, 38, California (no occupation given)

I urge that no man marry anyone without knowing her for at least a year. See how they act, live and get along with their friends. See if they like housework, the duty of all wives. See if they are clean.

Walter, West Virginia retired exec

Don't do it.

Elizabeth, 45, Ohio medical asst.

For a man, I think if he's faced with the prospect of divorce, he should prepare for the battle and look at the wife as if she were a stranger who is going to try to rob him of his ability to create a new life for himself if she goes through with it. She only wants to divorce the man, not his wallet.

Frank, 39, Minnesota compositor

Seek to work out a financial and child custody agreement with a concerned mediator, rather than in an adversary process of law and courts.

Philip, 48, Pennsylvania clergyman

If you are in no rush to remarry, wait . . . wait until a suitable financial and social adjustment is made. Suitable for the man, that is, who is always wrong.

H. (male), 57, Massachusetts merchant

Get an honest and upstanding lawyer, which may take a while to find.

Ron, 32, Nevada musician

Liquidate all your monies as soon as possible, and then lie like hell.

Mark, 38, New Jersey fireman

Go pro se and tell the truth in writing, calling the judges and lawyers exactly what they are and demanding your constitutional rights such as the right to a jury trial . . . and refuse to obey illegal and unconstitutional orders from crooked judges and lawyers—only orders from a Court of the People.

Arthur, 54, Illinois (no occupation given)

If children are involved, let them make up their own minds about the other parent. Don't preach to them about your bad experiences!

Carol, 29, New York teacher

Divorce is never easy, but to make it more pleasant I'd say don't try to cut your mate's throat. After all, during your married life you shared, and the same should go for the divorce. Sure, the husband has worked hard to buy material goods, but the wife has also done her share of the work, so don't be a hog. Share and share alike—it makes for much better feelings.

Bonnie, 30, Illinois (no occupation given)

Full disclosure of all conditions before getting married, and have it on file with the state so that there can be no alterations.

Tony, 38, New Jersey (no occupation given)

Don't get married until the present system is changed. There is no way to make it any easier or smoother.

Robert, 35, New Jersey machinist

Refuse to become a participant in the emotional hysteria and histrionics of the other party.

Dolores, 44, New York (no occupation given)

Make sure everything is in writing and signed by both parties. Know your lawyer and his reputation.

George, 34, Illinois truck driver

Don't give your wife a divorce, just separate. If she does get a divorce, divide everything equally and sell it, splitting the profits 50-50. If you don't, you're going to lose everything you've got, because if you give her the house she'll get married again and you'll be supporting another man. Also, go into court as your own lawyer—you can lose very easily without paying out $1,000. Whether you believe it or not, the Bar Association runs the country.

Lawson, 62, Illinois minister

Be very careful in selecting a lawyer. Get the best. Be aware that this is a lawyer's game at his client's emotional expense. I would advise a woman to take a division of estate as opposed to alimony. It frees you emotionally, job-wise, and lets her spend money the way she wants to. Most men stop paying alimony after a while and get away with it, and this keeps the woman in a dependent position.

Kathy, 35, Minnesota medical asst.

Very simple: take a cooling-off period and back away and think the problem over. Stay away from head shrinkers, judges and lawyers, and from church people. They all serve a definite need in our society, but in divorce cases they are a joke, and completely devoid of any understanding of the situation as it exists in the U.S. today. Stop fighting (with your mate) and recognize what a real racket the attorneys make of divorce.

Larry, 48, Michigan (no occupation given)

Check all the angles and don't hang on trying to "make it work."

Robert, 52, Illinois TV tech.

For women, avoid the temptation to "take" your husband or to "get revenge." For the man, get good financial planning advice to avoid a raid on your assets.

Raymond, 51, Pennsylvania ad exec

If you're the man, don't bother getting a lawyer. Get it over with as quickly as possible.

Robert, 34, Missouri contract analyst

Be certain to keep the children's welfare in mind at all times. Never talk the other party down in public. Be brave.

Joyce, 48, New York R.N.

Have a valid agreement drawn up upon getting married, have no children, and move far, far away from your in-laws.

David, 30, Kentucky civil servant

Make an agreement with the spouse to divorce and to cut off all communication and ties. It is too difficult to have to do business with a person who is abusing the children and not become upset. The only way to handle it is to cut off all contact between the divorced persons and to lead totally separate lives.

Mary, 31, California student

A good lawyer, priest or minister for support. Most of my support came from Parents Without Partners and my family. Also, oddly enough, I got money from my husband when I needed it.

Peg, 46, New York cosmetician

I don't know what I would have done differently, but if he had just sat down and told me there was another woman instead of lying incessantly to me and to the judge, things would have gone much smoother.

Evelyn, 53, California nurse

Open your eyes to a bad situation, no matter what it may be, and get professional help no matter what he does. Don't ignore it and hope it will go away, because it won't.

Alice, 37, Kansas housewife

Be sure you have a competent lawyer. Get professional supportive therapy, if necessary. Work out details you can agree on. Don't be afraid to rely on your friends. Get involved in a new social circle.

Amy, 39, California (no occupation given)

Make a clean break—never continue past arguments, especially in front of the children. Permit visiting in the home with the children, which I did. He came on Sundays when I worked, and cooked their dinner at my house. This way he could rest, enjoy the children and not have to spend money which he didn't have to take them places.

Sarah, 53, California clerk

I'm not sure that there is a way to make a divorce any easier, but if there are children involved I would recommend that you make sure you don't get involved immediately with any one of the opposite gender, that you instead give your children as much of your time and efforts as you can muster. It will give you a chance to regain your emotional strength and increase your child's image of you.

Howard, 42, Utah contractor

Have more confidence—once you've made the move, look ahead, not back. Stop yourself from the "if I had only done this or that . . . . " or " . . . it could have been . . . . " Stop trying to figure out why. Accept it. Don't do the "for the sake of the children" bit. Children are much happier in a good relationship between their happily divorced parents. The time that's difficult for all and is destructive to the children is when the parents are unhappily married. And start a new life immediately. I meet so many divorcées who are legally divorced, but emotionally still intertwined with the other person. Money seems to be a hassle, too. It all boils down to finances that day in court. It becomes the outlet for all the hurts.

Elizabeth, 34, New Jersey R.N.

I don't think anything can make divorce easier except for finding a lawyer to really protect your emotional interests. Any loopholes in the decree give the other party chances to cause trouble. My ex never won a case but he found many loopholes to work on, and it was pretty miserable. He even bought out my lawyer, finally.

Linda, 33, Arizona bookkeeper

Join Parents Without Partners or a like organization geared to the single parent—and to the children.

Sandra, 28, California (no occupation given)

Get rid of the American Bar Association. They are America's number one enemy. Place the situation back into the hands of those who united the couple in the first place, then let them settle it.

Martin, 54, Pennsylvania production worker

Anybody who says he's retained the same lawyer as the wife, or vice-versa, because "they really agree on most terms," must have rocks in his head! Or saying you really don't need a lawyer also means you don't have all your marbles. It is imperative that you find a lawyer with whom you're comfortable personally, because you are going to be "living" with him for a long time. One who doesn't intimidate you and one with whom you can be as candid as possible. In this situation, a good lawyer is golden.

Roland, 48, Connecticut engineer

Don't defend yourself to people's speculations about the reasons for the divorce. And after you've survived the divorce, try not to be bitter and resentful. Look ahead, not back.

Jean, 45, Illinois secretary

Don't let anyone assume responsibility for your decisions. Decide everything in the light of self-welfare and don't feel guilty. Be happy with yourself.

Mary, 26, California student

Learn to "talk" and cooperate with your former spouse, as it makes all types of communications easier.

Wendie, 33, New York (no occupation given)

Drop relatively unimportant issues before they grow out of proportion. Try harder to see the other's side. Try to discuss situations civilly and come to terms before seeking legal advice.

Linda, 34, California legal secretary

People out to get a divorce ought to have counseling, even if they don't want it. The lawyers are eager to take the cases, and if you aren't "sure" they do all they can to convince you to get a divorce so they can get their money. People ought to try to save marriages.

Marylou, 25, Rhode Island (no occupation given)

Get around people of the opposite sex to whom you are attracted as immediately as possible. Let them help you. Get with others!

Sandra, 32, Missouri professor

Attempt to resolve the settlement conditions yourselves before hiring an attorney. Failing that, get only one attorney but check him out thoroughly before retaining him. Many men fail to realize that they have to prove their complaints.

Ted, 35, Nebraska divorce counselor

Keep busy and involved; keep an optimistic outlook for the future. After divorce, most people say they'd never go back to their spouse and are much happier.

Diane, 32, California homemaker

Get counseling at intervals during marriage to avoid frictions while they're still small.

Jacob, 52, Colorado exec

First, choose a lawyer carefully. Everything is so cut and dried and many lawyers don't seem to care. Second, it would help much if husband and wife could iron out their agreement ahead of time.

Margaret, 55, New York (no occupation given)

My advice is to wives still married: don't make your husband your whole life—if and when he leaves, you have to rebuild your whole self, as I did. Let your emotions cool for a period of separation before the divorce, so you can work out as much as possible yourselves. Lawyers only inflame the situation and you find yourself arguing about what you thought was already settled.

Barbara, 28, New York bank teller

Don't trust your lawyer as far as you can throw him. He's a specialist in screwing you for a profit.

Nick, 37, Virginia electrician

I wouldn't have said this even five years ago, but I wonder now—if it really isn't a pretty good deal: "trial marriage," "contractual marriage," just "living together," there is really no other way to get to know someone and discover if the value systems, life-styles, interest in sex, attitude towards children, etc., are as compatible as they must be in a marital relationship. Our present system of courtship and marriage may have been valid in a less sophisticated social structure, but between women's lib and a de-emphasis on the so-called "old values," our existing system is just not doing the job anymore. As far as the specifics you mentioned are concerned, I think once the decision to part is made, it is absolutely essential for both people to really act in their Adult roles, especially if there are children involved. This business of trying to "get back" at your ex—through playing footsy with the children's visitation (late pick-up and/or arrival, etc.), making nasty phone calls, not depositing child-support checks, "bad-mouthing" your ex around town (if you happen to live in the same town), and the list is endless, is strictly for the birds.

Lee, (male) 37, Iowa city employee

Keep busy through a job or volunteer work, help others and don't indulge in self-pity. Join groups like Parents Without Partners to help you realize that you aren't different after all.

Joan, 48, Kansas medical receptionist

I'd advise anyone getting a divorce to fully understand the law. I was frightened and hostile. I went out to dinner with a man before the divorce was final and was threatened with losing my children—I didn't know it wasn't possible at the time. It is an emotional experience no matter how (equitable) it is.

Terese, 40, Michigan secretary

If both parents really want to be in their children's lives after the divorce, try not to take revenge on each other through the children.

Jan, 35, California medical secretary

First of all I would try to ascertain all the facts in a particular case. Once I know that there is definitely a need for divorce, I would then ask one simple question, which I would want the same answer to then, and a month from then. "Are you sure —absolutely sure—that you want to go through with this?" If there is even the slightest doubt in their mind, and they cannot ascertain that they are walking out of that door for the last time as a married person, then there can be no help for that person. To these people I would say, and have said to one friend I know, "Come back and see me when you have definitely made up your mind. I'll be only too glad to help you then." Given a couple who both love their children, are quite qualified as good parents, and definitely need and want a divorce, I would first advise them to think of their children above all else. I would then advise them of their rights (sometimes only supposed rights) and then tell them to attempt to work something out with their spouse regarding free and liberal visiting rights, and possibly a half-and-half custody agreement where the mother would have custody for a period of six to nine months, and then the father would take custody for the duration of the time. Custody has caused an extreme amount of friction and hostility between the parties in question both inside and outside of the courts, and has indeed caused many a divorced couple to come out of the courtroom hating each other more than they did before commencement of a divorce action—to say nothing of what it has done to thousands of poor innocent children. If a woman were to come to me for help, unless of course there were extenuating circumstances, I would remind her that if a woman is asking for a divorce, she is once again placing herself in society as a self-sufficient, self-supporting woman, and had DAMNED WELL better get that through her pretty little head before she starts praying the court for unreasonable amounts of alimony. This too, has caused much high friction and hatred between divorced people. But, of course, it is one thing to convince the parties involved in this (if you can) and it is quite another thing to convince an attorney or judge. Any other points I could make would, I think, depend on all of the circumstances and situations involved.

Alice, 29, Minnesota factory worker

Do it quickly. The moment you recognize, or give me the symptoms that your marriage is at an end, get with it and get it over with. If there is another man or woman, don't hesitate and take a chance of losing him/her. There are few, very few that each of us can live with and if we do not find that one or two we are doomed to a life of loneliness. So, don't mess around. Get that divorce! It won't hurt the children. It is much worse for them to live a life of constant bickering than to be with just one or the other parent and in quiet and harmony. Try for an early and equitable property settlement, be rational, make it so that each is hurt the least amount. For the man, remember that the things you leave with your wife will be willed to that set of children, so be generous, that is the reason you collect things in the first place. Don't look back. The moment the decision is made, get with it and go the whole route and right away. Recognize the signs of dissolution, the infidelity, the loss of interest, the hating to see the spouse and the fear of the constant nagging and the misery that goes with it and the moment these are present, act!

R., 45, North Dakota M.D.

What are your thoughts on alternatives to divorce?

There can be no alternative to divorce, because that implies an alternative to marriage. And once you decide there's an alternative to marriage, you get the religious cuckoos on your back, and in this country, that's a very strong lobby.

Stan, 40, Pennsylvania pilot

Mandatory divorce insurance.

Beverly, 45, New York teacher

I've never considered alternatives, because I've never sanctioned "arrangements" or "open marriages" and that type of "outlet . . . "

Emily, 33, New York R.N.

I believe people can be very happy together . . . without being legally tied. I don't like the communal idea, because I think the children suffer, but I have seen people who have been together a number of years happily, and I have been (living with a man) happily for more than a year myself.

Peggy, 24, California cashier

Perhaps the two parties ought to stay married and just live apart.

John, 45, California artist

Even in North Dakota, with a very provincial culture, there appears to be viable substitutes for marriage forming which eliminate the financial and legal difficulties of divorce. At a dinner party the other night, I was with a group of professional people—attorneys, physicians, etc.—and out of 12 couples at the table who were living together, only three were married; and I doubt I could have found that situation five years ago in North Dakota.

David, 33, North Dakota corporate pres.

New laws are making divorce easier—divorce is a legal necessity to make a clean break.

Sheila, 38, California housewife

I think separation is the only alternative, but a better one than I had for three years. The deserting spouse should not be allowed access to the home and "at will" visitation rights. He should miss the children.

Barbara, 45, New Jersey researcher

Getting professional guidance for the whole family, and learning how to make a marriage work.

Elaine, 53, New York housewife

I think if it were as costly and difficult to get married as it is to get divorced, people would be more serious about the long-range implications of marriage.

Aileen, 43, Illinois teacher

Marriage contracts, or some similar arrangement, perhaps a trial marriage period to see whether the relationship is mature and lasting. When trouble occurs, try a complete temporary separation, maybe long vacations separately. Don't rush into divorce—think carefully and try counselors.

Barbara, 26, California sales rep.

Make children less of a burden on the parents.

Carol, 36, Illinois secretary

Mandatory counseling before marriage; personality testing for compatibility so that people might see some problem areas.

Bill, 30, California teacher

Make it harder to get married. Or make divorces easier, depending on the number of children and their ages, and the ability of the wife to work. I think women should be expected to contribute to their own financial support and not be a drain on their ex-husbands. He shouldn't have to pay for her to just sit around.

Karen, 31, California journalist

For my generation there is very little to think about on alternatives to divorce. There are men who leave wives after 20 years or more of marriage to remarry. This is brutal today, when a woman has been primarily a housewife. I believe this type of man should be held responsible for temporary alimony and tuition to a school where the wife can learn to make a living. For young people, I feel the premarital counseling should be a must before marriage, particularly when both are under 25. A renewable marriage license might also help, provided there were no children at the time it became subject to renewal. (I have found) that formerly marrieds who go together for any period of time usually enter into a sexual relationship. Some may consider this immoral, but I feel that it is apt to prolong a relationship where the man may agree to marriage hastily without it. Some women still use sex as a weapon to get a wedding ring. Sexual problems can be solved before marriage—discovered. An affair can give a couple more time to get to know each other better. Arguments can bring out differences and the people involved can learn to solve them. If only one of the parties wants marriage, it sometimes takes time for the other to get to feel the same way. This is far better than promiscuous sex for either.

Gloria, 46, Kentucky bookkeeper

I don't think there are any alternatives, until they repair the imbalance in the law and give equal rights as far as custody and child support goes. A woman can just get up and walk out anytime she wants, but if a man tries it he can land in jail. The only alternative I can think of is to try to live together in harmony until both parties feel they can make it on their own. The actual divorce isn't all that important unless one person is being stubborn.

Bob, 35, California sportsman

It seems ridiculous to spend more money getting divorced than you do to get married!

C. (male), 31, Illinois personnel mgr.

I don't have any thoughts on the subject, except that there should be a way for people who don't have the money for a divorce and aren't educated enough to do their own, to be able to have it done free. Maybe something like a "divorce clinic," run by volunteers who have been through it all.

Camille, 28, California corporate mgr.

Contracts? Open marriage? Each individual case is so different . . . .

Pat, 34, California writer

Don't get married.

David, 25, California student

The L.T.A. (Living Together Arrangement), if it's convenient because some feel less restricted.

Ann, 37, California homemaker

Of course, a married couple can split up on their own, as long as some financial agreement can be reached and stuck to. They could even go on living under the same roof, married in name only.

Ron, 36, California teacher

The only alternative is a more serious approach to marriage in the first place. What you're really asking is, what are the alternatives to marriage? And the answer to that question requires some realistic re-thinking of social and religious mores. The alternative, of course, is simply to live together, practice appropriate birth control, and whenever one gets sick of the other, to split. The only reason for getting married, should be to have children—it's corny, but we're seeing that it's the sensible and, ultimately, the most moral approach.

Don, 34, Illinois insurance agent

I still believe in the institution of marriage, but it holds absolutely no appeal to me, for I value my personal independence more. Unfortunately, too many of my friends still believe it's a "man's world" and that "the world travels in pairs." What alternatives are there? I think five-year contracts would alleviate the pain of parting after 25 years, force people to be more honest through the

years, and keep them sincerely asking themselves if the relationship should endure. Children become a problem; possibly more
nursery homes so mothers could work would be an answer. But I
think a renewable contract would force men to think of their
wives in other ways than as chattels. Unfortunately, it seems so
ingrained, even enlightened men have a difficult time really accepting a wife's individuality, and if a wife kept her maiden name
after marriage it might be good for her, but it would be hard for
him. As long as a man feels he is "head of the house" it follows
like the night and the day that he'll think the "head of the house"
has the right to make important decisions (unilaterally) and do
things without too much explanation for, after all, hasn't he ex-
changed his freedom, and doesn't this mean a great sacrifice?

Doris, 47, California journalist

Get counseling before marriage.

—anonymous

Premarital contracts to cover an equal division of
property . . . . our present community property laws rip men off
and aren't equitable. Because a lawyer is the only one who wins
in a divorce action, divorce should be handled much the same
way that small claims are handled in our courts, without the
presence of an attorney.

Barbara, 37, California teacher

Rather than an alternative to divorce, how about an alternative to
marriage?

Linda, 31, California (no occupation given)

Mandatory counseling might help people face the truth about
their shortcomings and failures in the marriage, with the hope of
correcting the problem.

Ron, 29, California (no occupation given)

I think a pre-divorce agreement before getting married would
sober some youngsters!

Sam, 40, New York barber

I still feel marriage is good and the real solution. Loose arrangements (which are really non-commitments) don't make sense. The

financial disasters which result in many cases are really bad for all concerned. However, the courts seem to be more sympathetic these days to the man's total position. I do feel a man must remain responsible for his children, which often is not the case. The courts should get tough on "skip-out" fathers.

Tom, 46, California advertising exec

Alternatives would depend on the reason for the divorce and the children involved. If one spouse is involved with another person, I see no alternatives possible. If it's mutual incompatibility, then some kind of separation within the house might be possible if arrangements were made to formalize relations and minimize contact.

Robert, 24, California tech.

There are some alternatives already being tried:

a. living together arrangements—before wedding vows, may give more young people a chance to know a person outside of marriage before entering into a lifetime contract.

b. financial agreements—pre-nuptial contracts or agreements (that may be revised during marriage) in case of separation. This is important in second marriages when children of both are involved.

c. clear agreements between parties in the marriage as to what they want out of life together.

d. separation—decided in court for a specific time and revised by court action later if one party still seeks a divorce.

Janet, 57, California housewife

An alternative is just to live together, and if plans are made to become legally married, then a marriage contract should be drawn up to protect each party should a divorce result.

Marsha, 24, California postal worker

I realize that we all have our faults and I believe that when a divorce becomes inevitable we should have laws which do not always make one of the parties the "guilty" one. Also, when there aren't any children involved a couple should be able to just fill out a form stating that they have agreed to a settlement of their assets and debts and requesting a divorce decree. They shouldn't have to go through all the present procedures required.

Charles, 37, North Dakota engineer

The alternative is not to be afraid to wait for the right person. Premarital conferences are so important!

> Marilyn, 38, California school administrator

The whole divorce structure is unrealistic—the laws need changing, not marriage.

> Don, 44, New York restaurateur

There are no legal alternatives as long as you have money or property.

> Larry, 42, New York film producer

Maintain a separate residence and see your spouse only in the presence of a third party!

> Galen, 37, California teacher

Don't formally marry. You can have intimate relationships without legal ties.

> Patricia, 30, California teacher

Alternatives to divorce—are you kidding? It's against the law to live together, it's hell to stay with a rotten marriage, being a bachelor isn't all that Playboy makes it out to be, and living in a hippie commune is just a shortcut to the hospital. The only alternative I can figure out is to learn to live with a bad thing, and try to make the best of it without getting in each other's way.

> Mike, 39, Illinois real estate salesman

One alternative is doing away with our Victorian ideas about marriage. I'm a strong advocate of classes being taught in schools, covering virtually every aspect of marriage.

> Nancy, 33, Maryland teacher

I had a dissolution of marriage, in which we worked it all out ahead of time. Then we retained a common lawyer for consummating the deal, which I think is a good alternative to the common hassle. I have probably gone out with 40 different women since I was fourteen. Most of these I have known intimately. Of this group, I don't suppose 10 actually knew what they were doing sexually. Thinking this, I don't wonder at the large number of divorces. Very few women know anything about their body functions, as to the needs of their partners. You and I know that when we're applying for a specific job, we know whether we can handle it or at least we have a general idea of our capabilities. I've known women to go from one man to another feeling frustrated sexually, thinking it was their partner's fault. They just did what came natural to them, with no thoughts as to how they were performing, or why they weren't able to have a climax. I have found that you have to be tuned to your partner's needs in order to make them happy. But, if you ask them, they can't actually tell you. I also feel, upon examination, that there are many women who have problems of a surgical nature instead of psychological. These are some of the things I would like to see (understood better) when thinking about marriage.

Charles, 32, Iowa assembler

Couples should try to get a legal separation for a year, or even two, and during this time have equal custody and equal counseling.

Sharon, 31, California bookkeeper

To me there is no honest alternative to divorce. The only honest alternatives would be through improved divorce laws that would dissolve the marriage within a short period of time and that would make property settlements within the same period. Uniform support and custody laws.

Francis, 54, Wisconsin salesman

No-fault divorce laws should be passed in every state. Incompatibility comes close. If you can't live together, there is no marriage. It's time the courts reflected life as it is. I have no objection to trial marriages, as long as no children are involved. You can't legislate morality. No one really knows what it is like to live together until you actually live together. We have testing grounds for everything else, why not for marriage? What else affects a person's life more deeply? But this view will be very unpopular. All high school students should have sex education classes that include complete and detailed birth control information. They should also have marriage courses that are realistic. Girls have been having to get married since Adam and Eve. Knowledge will not make them any more or any less promiscuous, but it can save them from a tragic mistake. I do not feel abortion is the cure-all. Sensible birth control begins at conception, not after pregnancy has already occurred. Marriage should not occur because of moral or social pressure, or because of the acceptance of an unwanted responsibility.

Kathleen, 31, Michigan secretary

Marriage contracts specifying who is responsible for what, etc. Trial marriages, also—for a stipulated period of time before children are permitted. Marriage insurance, to ease the very real financial burdens of divorce.

Jim, 40, California salesman

Required proof of having had some counseling before a marriage license can be issued. Trial marriage, or other temporary arrangements in which birth control is used but the couple can really get to know each other in everyday, "nitty-gritty" situations. That should be encouraged, not frowned upon.

Elizabeth, 32, Tennessee C.P.A.

There is no solution once the dollar enters the picture. Just pray for a good lawyer. You may get lucky and find one.

Jerry, 44, New York sales mgr.

I'd encourage the couple to enter into a trial marriage for a set period of time, say one year, and then they would have to "divorce" or get married. If they wanted out, they could do so with no hatred or ragged edges. If they wanted to stay married, because they didn't want to part with each other, why they would have a damned good basis on which to make such a decision.

Steve, 38, Ohio truck driver

The only alternative to divorce is not to get married. Writing a "divorce contract" when a marriage is "good" would be helpful.

Elsa, 31, New York secretary

If two people are married and they just can't make a go of it, I don't see any alternative but divorce. However, I think compulsory counseling prior to the divorce might be a good idea. Admittedly, you can lead a horse to water but you can't make him drink. Possibly some financial reward for the partner who does get counseling, at the expense of the partner who doesn't . . . . Then too, if two people aren't married, and don't anticipate children, then living together can make a lot of sense.

Howard, 46, California engineer

Alternatives to divorce. The obvious way to circumvent the legal and financial barriers to divorce is not to get married until you have to do so. The only reason I can see for getting married is to provide some legal protection for children—and I'm not sure that there isn't some way around that. But until children are present or on the way, there is nothing that one can't get without a marriage contract that you can get with it. I have accordingly proposed to my daughter that when the mood takes her, she live with her chosen partner, at least until children arrive. By that time it is possible—but doubtful—that public opinion will have changed so that even then marriage may not be necessary. There is value in being together without that legal document. The marriage certificate is a crutch. It says, in effect, that the other partner cannot get away without certain consequences. It is, in fact, a club. But it also means that neither partner need really make any great effort to keep things together, as they will stay together anyway until things get so intolerable that the effort to break that contract must be made. But if there is no such contract, then each party knows that the other is free to go at any time. Under such circumstances, both will work at the partnership, to make it work. It should be a much better partnership than the one cemented by law. I know of quite a few people who live together happily without marriage; my married friends are for the most part not happy.

J., 43, Delaware marketing man

If I couldn't live with a person, there would never be any other choice for me but divorce. I would need my freedom.

Margaret, 37, Texas secretary

Take the profit out of divorce for everybody—lawyers, wives, etc., so that nobody wins money. That's a must. Eliminate litigation entirely and submit to investigation. Submit to the findings of a qualified panel.

Bill, 50, New York stockbroker

An alternative would be to seize every opportunity to make a good thing better during the happy times. For example, anyone reading your book who thinks he's really got a happy marriage going, should sit down with his wife and go through a "mock" divorce. Try a property settlement, who gets what kids, if at all, whether to sell the house or divide all property as equally as possible, all of it. The object of the game would be for each partner to "win," that is, come out on top financially. Then sit back and think about how much you've got going for yourselves, and for God's sake, appreciate it!

> Paul, 37, California cab driver

I'm not sure what you mean, to say nothing of not being sure what I think.

> John, 32, California tech.

Don't marry unless you can take the divorce that might come up. Require stricter marriage laws and higher fees. Let some have a temporary marriage or a trial marriage for compatibility.

> Jim, 50, Arizona retired U.S.A.F. navigator

Perhaps a trial marriage or a common law one. Primarily, premarriage counseling for both parties. Also, low interest long-term financial assistance.

> Tony, 57, New York (no occupation given)

In Massachusetts we need a law which allows divorce on the grounds of "irrevocable personality conflicts," as in other states.

> Margery, 42, Massachusetts R.N.

Maybe we can find a way to match people psychologically or some other way. In nature it is definitely the female who chooses the mate. Males can respond to almost any female, but females are definitely selective; I don't care what today's promiscuous literature says! Only during the boy-crazy stage of adolescence does she respond (indiscriminately) to anything in pants (as we said in my day—today girls are in pants, too). Masters and Johnson are so wrong. Theirs is the male's viewpoint because Virginia is so in love she thinks everything he does is right (universal female response). Wait until Masters and Johnson are divorced, and then we'll hear a different story.

> Gwen, 59, New York housewife

Guaranteed income to families abandoned without means, and with no waiting period to humiliate persons who must beg to exist until the new job or other means of support comes along.

> Elizabeth, "over 30," Nevada (no occupation given)

I can see no alternative to divorce—either a couple tries to maintain their marriage or they split and seek new marriages. I have known people who left their mates and moved in with lovers without benefit of legal action, but they do not appear to be any more content than I am. I do feel that once two people have reached a financial agreement to care for the children, they should be able to file for an immediate divorce with a minimum of legal interference. After all, the two of them arranged their marriage in the first place without legal counsel, why should it be so involved to dissolve it?

Harriet, 44, Maryland secretary

I personally think contract marriage is the ultimate answer. Women now have more freedom, they can support themselves, they no longer feel they have to stay in an unhappy marriage.

Frank, 33, California warehouseman

Don't divorce. Just permanently separate and live with someone instead of getting married again.

L., 35, California housewife

A marriage contract, renewal every one or two years. The word "divorce" was never in my vocabulary, so I never even considered what would happen if the marriage dissolved. You have to be more realistic than that.

Jack, 36, California hotel exec

Maybe the people getting a divorce should be reviewed by a professional board of examiners, so that optimum objectivity can be maintained. Whatever they decide, would be the terms of separation, settlements, etc., and then the lawyers and shrinks and counselors will not have screwed things up by trying to rip off each party for as much as they could.

Tim, 28, California writer

I'll never marry again. After my children are grown, I will live with a man possibly, as one would in marriage, but I'd never make it legal again. Marriage has a way of taking the giving away; suddenly expectations are placed on both parties and giving is impossible when it is demanded or expected.

Penny, 34, Texas travel agent

Eliminate lawyers as they now play their role in a divorce and you will have eliminated one of the problems which make seeking an alternative desirable. They should have an official appointed who will act as an arbitrator and be paid by the state.

Daniel, 45, New Jersey industrial mgr.

You don't need one. Divorce is so easy now . . . .

Elaine, 33, California homemaker

Better, more realistic and comprehensive preparation for marriage. Changing our laws and our society to make divorce and divorced people more acceptable.

Cheryl, 33, New Jersey teacher

Something like the 3-year renewal marriage contract would enable people to part with fewer complications, and to know that if they are still living together it is because they want to. There should be a form of legally recognized cohabitation which people could enter into without submitting to blanket and often discriminatory laws (such as the woman having to take the man's name, requiring the pooling of money and assets in community property states, obligation of man to support the woman, etc.). Support payments for children should be withheld and forwarded through the social security system, to make sure the children receive it.

Emily, 38, Maryland librarian

I believe every couple should be obligated to take out and pay for divorce insurance. While I get only $30 a week for an 18-year-old boy and a 14-year-old girl, some men are made to pay an exorbitant amount.

—anonymous female, 49

Make marriage a time-limited legal contract which would have to be periodically renewed or it would become automatically null and void.

W. (male), 47, Delaware (no occupation given)

I fully believe that, if it's possible, a young couple should live together for a while to get to know each other before marriage. I feel the marriage license is very expensive to tear up and it isn't so binding that it insures anything! If a man is inclined to take care of his family, he will do it, married or not. How many divorced men do not make their child support payments? So what good was the license? By living together you would get to see the bad points of a person that don't appear when you are only dating!

Harriet, 46, Illinois (no occupation given)

I believe one should be 30 years old before being able to marry. Seems this makes for a better bond. Values change more, I believe, between the ages of 20 and 30.

Verletta, 50, Illinois factory worker

The only way to circumvent current legal and financial barriers would be to live common law, or to improve the legal situation, which I see as terribly punishing.

Sylvia, 36, Connecticut secretary

More realistic pictures of the aftermath of divorce and understanding the effect on children should be given to all who contemplate divorce.

Olive, 52, Pennsylvania bookkeeper

Some people are fulfilled just living together. For myself I would not feel secure in that arrangement because I feel the male could walk away too easily. If you love me enough to live with me, you'll have to marry me, too.

Jeanne, 33, Connecticut rental agent

Inexpensive and well-publicized clinics for help in all problems; better trained ministers and priests in our churches for those persons afraid of clinics.

Margaret, 53, Kansas librarian

Avoidance of marriage is the best alternative. Also, it would be advisable to secure better laws and the proper interpretation of them.

Richard, 43, Minnesota divorce counselor

My second husband and I did try living separately in the same house, but that blew hot and cold. We couldn't stay far enough away from each other, which complicated the platonic attitude. The bed was an easy answer to any schism in our relationship.

Otherwise, the divorce law of California seems to be working—that there is no guilty party, that counseling replaces the coldness of the courtroom, and that the money is for actual costs.

Joyce, 40, New York college professor

No-fault divorce. And get the lawyers out of the deal; they only make it worse.

Russ, 65, Pennsylvania retired builder

No alternatives, maybe, but they should try to determine the difference between cases and evaluate each on its own facets.

Mildred, 54, Ohio (no occupation given)

I'm not too much interested in alternatives to divorce as I am in alternatives to the results of divorce. Maybe to alternatives to marriage, too. Divorce, to my mind, is a desirable course, when indicated—it's a "clean break" and (can be) therapeutic. Do you prefer divorce Italian-style, or Catholic-style, where you're left dangling forever? I'd like to see fathers who are fully equipped emotionally break the conventions and start contesting child custody cases. I'd like to see judges get themselves up to date and start acting with more sensitivity. I'd like to see alimony scaled down in proportion to the wife's income.

Roland, 48, Connecticut engineer

Divorce lawyers create the problems—they have to create and maintain barriers to justify their profession. There must be another way.

Jean, 45, Illinois bookkeeper

If the courts established a principle which assigned one attorney to both parties in a divorce action, there would be some objectivity brought into the otherwise costly and emotionally destructive negotiation process. No-fault divorce and clear criteria for divorce actions. Often clear issues are complicated by erosive mores and religious prohibitions.

T., 44, Pennsylvania minister

The whole legal game stinks! We need temporary contracts that can be broken by mutual consent.

Mary, 26, California student

Vanish. Just take the dough you've been saving, decide whether to kidnap your kids or let her have them, and just drop off the face of the earth. If you do it right—and thousands of us do—they'll never find you.

George, 34, New York architect (not former name or occupation)

I don't see any alternatives.

Linda, 34, California secretary

I think every couple should have a legal separation for a certain length of time, plus counseling, before any divorce even comes to court. As for financial, I really don't know any alternatives to that.

Marylou, 25, Rhode Island (no occupation given)

Since I don't presently believe in marriage at all except where it involves financial advantage for me, and absolute sexual freedom, I think everyone should be single.

Sandra, 32, Missouri professor

An alternative to divorce is not marrying in the first place. Divorce just seems to be a punitive alternative to the bitterness, jealousy and revenge that becomes part of a breakup.

Diane, 32, California homemaker

Marriage contracts. Also, social services offering job training for middle-aged wives.

Jacob, 52, Colorado psychologist

There is some talk about writing up some kind of divorce insurance. This would help financially and legally.

Margaret, 55, New York (no occupation given)

I believe sensible adults should try to avoid drastic alternatives, especially when children are concerned. However, sometimes divorce is the only solution.

Sandi, 23, New York lab tech.

There has to be some kind of do-it-yourself inexpensive divorce. It could take, say, two years, so it couldn't be just impulsive. So that even uncontested ones don't turn into a battle.

Barbara, 28, New York bank teller

There is an analogy to this question in the proposition that for all the physical and emotional agonies involved in an abortion, don't get pregnant in the first place. The best way to avoid a divorce is not to avoid getting married, but rather to make it more difficult to get married. All you have to do now is "pass" a blood test and pay $5 (depending on state) for your license, then get your friendly neighborhood minister or J.P. to pronounce the magic words. Let's make premarital counseling a requirement and either through the church or state (or both) have courses in, then oral and written exams on, human biology (for all of my excellent academic background prior to marriage, I did not learn until three or four months after our wedding that the clitoris is not located inside the cervix! Equally tragic, my wife didn't either!); interpersonal relationships (how to "fight creatively" and perhaps some Transactional Analysis); money management (no, dear, we can't buy all our furniture the first year on what I'm making); and child psychology (good parents don't just happen). And unless you pass those tests with good scores, you don't get married! And what of those who don't?

Well, in spite of all the pretty poetry about companionship and "building a life together," I pretty much believe that most young men (and probably a lot of "dirty old men," too) marry as much for sex as for any other reason. And perhaps women do, too, though I think with them—at least when I was in my early 20's—it was "social pressure," "the thing to do," more than anything else. In light of this, let's be honest enough to admit that some people are just not temperamentally or psychologically fit to be married, much less become parents, but simultaneously, also admit that they—both men and women—do have sexual needs. Then the next obvious question is: "But you're saying let's legalize prostitution." Well, of course, "prostitute" as a word has so many negative overtones that we would not dare use it. But I would suggest that those women—yes, and I'm sure there are male whores, too—do indeed serve a useful social and biological function, and I think it is high time we stopped giving them the low rung on the social totem pole, along with dope peddlers and child-beaters. Let's give them a new name—"biological support person?"—an appropriate social status ("A little lower than the angels?"), organize them into self-protective group, so they could have the usual fringes, plus decent salary and retirement, and let them help to lower the divorce rate!

Lee, 37, Iowa city employee

Sure there's an alternative. But only one: live in misery for the rest of your life.

Ann, 38, Massachusetts waitress

Make them separate for one year, and have counseling together. Then not get married for one year after the divorce.

Welden, 40, Ohio (no occupation given)

I think of people as being people, not men and women. I have many men friends whom I would not think of marrying. I like living alone; I would just suggest that people live alone and have a constructive job and many friends. I was so miserable being married (twice), I just don't believe that marriage is for everyone, and the last ten years alone have been the happiest of my life. I have no intention of remarrying, and sometimes I don't date a man because I think he wants to get married and I feel I'm wasting his time.

Marilyn, 49, New York (self-employed)

(Author's Note: Scores of female interviewees over forty, when Marilyn's attitude was mentioned, indicated they would pay practically any amount for her address book!)

Live together and don't get married in the first place. But this isn't an (alternative) for those who want to commit themselves in a definite way.

Terese, 40, Michigan secretary

Don't get married in the first place—just live together.

Donald, 39, Ohio physicist

I don't know about an alternative to divorce . . . freedom or commitment, those are the only choices, really. Separation is like living in limbo . . . I think I'd rather just live with a man. I wish divorce laws could be made more human. There's enough pain in deciding on divorce without the anguish of fighting it out in court to get a piece of paper that says your marriage has ended. I don't mean divorce should be easy . . . but certain people have tried everything and there's no chance to save it, and then they want to just call it quits. When they say, "For God's sake, let's get it over with," there should be some way to do just that—get it over with!

Dawn, 23, Maryland mother

There are no alternatives to divorce as long as there are marriages and there is no better state for the country than that of marriage, nor for the children. The common-law wife, the trial marriage, the living together in love that doesn't have to be bound by a "piece of paper" is a lot of rot. Marriage does not have to be contracted for love. It can be done for convenience, for property, and these are all right, having the option of a mistress.

R., 45, North Dakota M.D.

What the numbers tell you

We've heard the story of the statistician who drowned in a river whose average depth was only three feet. Statistics themselves can be flagrantly misleading (as the government calculates and expresses the annual cost of living index increases), but they can even be utterly meaningless (one out of three have insomnia, yet no one in this crowded room has; one out of ten is homosexual, yet none of my four dozen friends is, etc.).

Nevertheless, some statistical analyses of our survey of divorced persons may be significant to many of you for various reasons. Other statistics here are significant to the ongoing study and evaluation of the divorce phenomenon in America today, especially since we believe this survey is the most comprehensive sampling of divorced persons ever undertaken.

Many questions weren't asked which might have been, and some questions were asked which turned out to be irrelevant or else were beyond the scope of our inquiry. We've been told during lectures, question-and-answer periods, and interview sessions that this expert or that says the first—or the third, or the seventh—year of marriage is the critical one. We've replied, "Maybe so, but that was not only beyond the scope of our survey, but also is not borne out by those in the survey who volunteered related information." We've also been told that so-and-so had a wonderfully amicable divorce with no difficulties whatsoever, and we have replied, "That's wonderful, but we have tried to uncover serious *problems* in the divorce process, and one can't do that in a case history in which there's been *no* problem."

More important, we may be accused of only presenting information from people who are bitter, or who are particularly strident in their opinions, or who've an axe to grind. To them we explain that *any* survey—whether a political poll or a television rating system—*must* rely on people willing to reply to a question. One can't get much information from the reticent.

A few valid generalizations did emerge from the survey. It's a fact that the odds of a marriage ending in divorce are *significantly greater when those marrying are in their teens, or even under twenty-five.* The danger is that the people become rather different after ten years of marriage. The young man and woman have, at marriage, practically no experience, no trial-and-error background on which to base enormously important social, financial and professional decisions. The married person's "value" in a marriage, i.e., his status in relation to his spouse, is precisely the same as the business executive's "value" to his company. As a young mail clerk, a man or woman may not "mean" much to the firm, and the firm may not "mean" much to the clerk. It is a growth time, a time of learning. But later, the clerk turned vice president is far more valuable to his firm, and in most cases his firm is far more valuable to him.

Though we didn't calculate the average age of those surveyed (we tried not to equate age with "maturity"), we did find that a majority of divorces occur after ten years of marriage. (This, too, may bear out the young-marriages-tend to-end-in-divorce theory.) Fully 52.9% of survey respondents had been married more than ten years at the time of their divorce, while 31.3% said they'd been married more than five years. Thirteen percent had been married from two to five years, and only 8% were divorced before their second anniversary. (21% were married more than once.) Yes, there are exceptions. Charles and Annie Hutzell of Boonsboro, Md. celebrated their 75th wedding anniversary on August 24, 1974. Charles and Annie tied the knot in 1899, when they were teenagers—he 19 and she 17.

Sex

The survey wound up surprisingly close to being even as far as sex mix is concerned. At the outset, we expected more response from men, because we guessed that since men have traditionally been the biggest complainers about the inequities of alimony and child support judgments, they would be the first to sound off. But 58% of the respondents were female while 42% were male, and not all were happy with their accidental status.

Age

The survey included ages 16 to 86, but the characteristic bell curve distribution prevailed in the end. The 16's were statistically negligible, as was the 86 and only a few respondents were in their 70's. There were 12.2% between 21 and 30; 58.8% between 30 and 45; and 31% were 45 and over. A few women refused to give their age; no man did.

Education

The majority of respondents had "some" college—67.3%. Only a high school education was indicated by 24.1%. The balance either didn't indicate their educational level or never got to high school at all.

Age when married

This represents one of the most statistically important figures to support the generalization mentioned earlier. The age-when-married of the majority of those surveyed was between 21 and 30 (58.3%). A whopping 31.7% were under 21 when they were married, and only 10% were over 30. This bears out the idea once again, that a young marriage tends to run into trouble faster. Our findings indicate that men tend to ignore the early signs of deterioration in a marriage, even refuse to acknowledge the trouble, *while women tend to try virtually everything to "save" it.* Eventually the wife becomes mature or "fed up" enough to initiate action. There are instances where the husband-wife role in this generalization is reversed, but very few.

As we've seen in the responses to Question #2, and will again see in the statistical review to that question, there seems to be something in the psychological makeup of a man that hinders him from perceiving a turn for the worse in his marriage. It's for the psychologists to analyze, but we may theorize that a man relates the failure of a marriage more to his role *as a man*—to his masculinity, if you will—than a woman does to her "femininity." When a woman goes to a counselor for help, or to a minister, or to psychotherapy of some kind, the most prevalent response of the husband is on the order of "It's *your* fault, not mine, so *you* go get help." Or, "If *you* think the marriage isn't working, then *you* do something about it." Another variation: "We've been to two sessions already (or three, or one, or six), and this guy isn't doing anything for me (or doesn't understand *our* situation, or doesn't make sense, or costs too much), so *you* keep going if you want."

In like manner, it seems—also theoretically—that a woman will forgive adultery on her husband's part and try to patch up the relationship through one means or another, but a man cannot handle adultery on his wife's part. There seems to be an awful lot of sexual insecurity on the part of men involved in the ultimate *reasons* for a marriage not working. (Fact: 25.3% preferred not to have had a divorce in the first place, and *most of them were women.* This 25.3%—and many more, although their opinion was inferred rather than blatantly stated—thought their marriages could have been saved with a little more effort. And *most* of those persons blamed their lawyers or the court process for *causing* the divorce, i.e., not permitting a more strenuous effort at reconciliation!)

Number of children

Nine percent of the group had no children. One child at the time of divorce represented 14%, and 36.4% had two children. Three children: 20.7%. Four, 8% and five, 7%. More than five were the lowest percentage.

Occupation

On the premise that a person's occupation has little to do with the real reasons for his divorce (the high rate among doctors, lawyers and the totally uneducated notwithstanding), we categorized the occupational status of the surveyed group only as professional (doctor, lawyer, architect, etc.); creative (artists, writers); white-collar (teachers, secretaries, bookkeepers); blue-collar (truck drivers, factory workers, waitresses). We also assigned a special category for homemaker and student. Of those surveyed, 20.3% were professional; five percent, creative; 29.2%, white-collar; 12.2%, blue-collar; 15.6%, homemaker or student; "no occupation given," 17.7%. Our original premise proved correct: occupation seems to run the gamut from the highest paid professional to the lowest income worker when it comes to analyzing the breakup of marital relationships.

Now we come to the questions which were the major considerations in our survey. While the actual number of questions asked in a large portion of the interviews exceeded the seven itemized in the written questionnaire, the first six questions are the most significant.

Reasons for divorce

Throw away your time-worn figures on the reasons for divorce. Money and financial woes are manifestations, not reasons. Frigidity or poor sex doesn't have much to do with the underlying reason either. Nor does alcohol or drugs or religion or that time-battered scapegoat of all time, the mother-in-law. *A staggering 81.7% of all divorced people will admit that they got married too soon,* i.e. will list either "immaturity when married" or "incompatibility" when asked to do some honest soul-searching and pinpoint a reason why their marriage didn't work. (We defined "immaturity" earlier as an inexperienced age, rather than a chronologically early time in life.) When questioned as to what, exactly, "incompatibility" meant, respondents explained in terms of "growing apart" as a result of "maturing" at different rates because of the mutually naive age when married. For example, after ten years of marriage, a man of 29 may be interested primarily in job, bowling and fixing up his car, while his wife may have gone from the proverbial shrinking violet to a politically active, bra-burning activist who lectures on Camus in her spare time. It seems that people tend to get married too soon, or at least used to, considering the "years married" figures. And "too soon" simply means *before you've decided who you want to be* during your marriage.

Conclusion: *Use the so-called new morality to your advantage when considering marriage or when evaluating a present one.* Plan not to experience any *new* decision-making confrontations after the marriage, including confrontations involving sex, money, personal freedoms (Can't I go to the movies alone without you becoming suspicious?), life-style preferences, attitude toward family responsibilities, etc. Remember that the marriage that's "all together" when it starts may fall apart completely the first time an in-law dies and a funeral is expected to be attended.

The way the question fared in the survey was: immaturity when married, 49.5% (practically one-half right there!); incompatibility, 32.2%; adultery, 24% (but what *caused* it?); financial, 14.4%; alcohol, drugs, etc., 7%; *poor choice of partner*, 7% (to be added to "immaturity," or "incompatibility?"); mental, psychological problems, 6%; frigidity (impotence), 5%; and other (desertion, abuse of children, in-laws, etc.) the balance. (N.B. The reason these figures do not add up to 100% is that multiple reasons were listed or quoted during each interview. We have assigned priority values to each according to the order of prevalence.)

Did you try to "Save . . . . ?"

Of everyone contacted and interviewed, fully two-thirds—67% even—tried to "save" the marriage by going to some outside source, whether professional counseling or ministers or family doctors or even to a good friend or sympathetic relative. Men and women, 67%. It's important to realize here that most divorcing people seem to want to recoup, to "save" the relationship they once had. The male-female breakdown is the men represent 26.6%, the women 40.2%. While we can conclude that twice as many women as men want to "save" their marriage (regardless of the reason for the problems in the first place), the overwhelming majority of everyone surveyed indicated that marriage is worth saving, even if it's a bad marriage. Apparently it's easier to live out one's life—even to salvage some semblance of having a good time of it—while married, than it is while living as a single, divorced person.

The methods of trying to "save"—or do something about—a failing marriage broke down as follows: 53.8% counseling; 13.9% psychotherapy; 6.7% religious counseling; 21.6% doctor's advice, trial separation, etc.; and 25.5% no professional or otherwise authoritative advice whatsoever. Once again, these figures do not add up to 100% because most interviewees listed more than one "method" and we gave weights to their replies according to the priorities they listed.

The conclusion we draw here—and not necessarily from the statistics themselves, but from the general overview of having spoken with more than 1,000 of the divorced themselves—is that counseling, whether divorce counseling or marriage counseling, most often occurs after it has become too late for counseling to do any good. More couples should see a qualified counselor as a matter of routine, say once every two years, rather than wait until they "know there is a problem." By and large, the divorced people who would have their druthers not only would have preferred to stay married but also would have acted sooner to seek outside help. (One of the problems here seems to be the tendency to see oneself as the intellectual superior of a potential "helper," hence a "challenge," and "threat," or whatever—again, to the psychologists to analyze more deeply.)

It should be noted before we leave it, however, that 74.5% of the divorced persons interviewed tried some form of outside counseling, and a vast majority of those (probably another three-quarters) thought it was worthless. This raises the question: is counseling a gigantic rip-off of distressed persons, or do marriage (or divorce) counselors exist who genuinely try to help the persons involved in the anguish of the divorce decision? *The divorced themselves turn thumbs down on marriage—or divorce—counselors as a viable method of solving the dilemma of whether to divorce or "save" a marriage.*

Unexpected trauma?

The most important contribution this book can make to you, the reader—married or separated—is to wave the flag of caution. Look before you leap. Divorce in all its ugly, shadowy spectre for the uninitiated, is even more ugly, more shadowy and more trauma-ridden after you've been through it. Listen to the advice of others, and realize that *your case is not unique.* Virtually everyone surveyed expressed some form of surprise after the divorce proceedings had commenced, whether it be simply the shock of seeing and hearing the man you slept with for ten years state that you had been frigid, or finding out the lawyer you hired is charging you $3,500 instead of the paltry $1,250 he had quoted originally. If you decide to get a divorce, get ready for lies, deceit, emotional grief, seeing your children cry out for you while a bailiff restrains them, having your own father defame your character, seeing with your own eyes the attorney for the plaintiff consult with a nodding, smiling judge just prior to a staggering decision against you, etc. There was no limit to the surprises the surveyed related to our disbelieving ears. One man found his son, assigned by the court to the mother because she was "more beneficial" to his welfare, with a "damaged penis, requiring corrective surgery because the wife's homosexual brother had been declared one of the child's guardians by the court." The child was seven-years-old.

The outcome? A surprisingly large 45.3% found their poor financial situation *after* divorce totally unexpected and equally totally unsettling. *Divorce is more expensive than you think,* seems to be the axiom. *You will be poorer than you think after the divorce,* is a universal truth.

An unexpected *social* trauma was experienced by 25.4% of

the survey. These persons expressed their troubles in the context of the immediate circle of friends. For example, wives generally indicated that they were ostracized from circles of friends, either because they immediately became "threats" to their married friends or because they "didn't fit" into dinner parties or other "fifth wheel" situations.

Deep personal difficulties were experienced by almost half of the subjects. In this category we lumped introspective guilt feelings, psychological problems associated with sex, etc. There were 18.2% of those surveyed who indicated they experienced no trauma whatsoever, and 9.2% indicated things got so much better they actually bordered on euphoria.

The message here seems to be that virtually regardless of how one prepares for the split, there will be some unexpected situations arising which may throw off your mental or emotional balance. An empty bed becomes not only the absence of a spouse to cuddle, but an empty house! A man who believes he will become the playboy of the Western world suddenly finds himself throwing back the last ounce of a distasteful drink at some bar at two in the morning and going home to a bed strewn with dirty underwear and probably a mateless sock. The symbolism is almost disgusting. Let's just end by stating that an overwhelming 75% of those interviewed experienced *some kind of unexpected trauma,* regardless of counseling, advice or preparation prior to the actual divorce proceedings.

Do anything differently?

While we have already pointed out that 25.3% would have preferred not getting divorced in the first place, a significant amount of divorced people in America today have had great difficulty either with the legal profession or with the courts themselves. No less than 15.6% related what they would do differently to legal/lawyer related subjects, and probably an equal amount thought the biggest mistake they had made was retaining a lawyer in the first place. Finances were the subject of 14.8%—those who thought they could have done something about their financial outcome *before* entering into the divorce proceedings (hoarding, assigning property away, purposely degrading one's earning capacity to avoid a burdensome alimony payment, etc.).

And timing had a lot to do with more than 20% of the respondents. Those who would have divorced their spouses sooner numbered 16.9%; those who would have waited a bit longer, 3.8%. "Try harder to save" as a specific category listed 12.2%, and those who said they would have done nothing whatsoever differently were only 6.3%.

Violent solutions were advocated by 1.2% (murder, beatings), and 2% opted for not having married in the first place.

Investigations?

Most people who have been divorced—31.7% specifically—think something should be done about the inequities in the legal/judicial proceedings. When we added "laws"—22.4%—and "child custody decisions"—10.5%—a total of 64.7% *of all di-vorced people surveyed think there is something drastically wrong with the legal system in the country.* Again, most of these had borne bad experiences with divorce attorneys.

Financial subjects were indicated by 20.3% of those who would like to see Federal investigations initiated, and desertion and consideration of the role of children in the ultimate divorce outcome were indicated by 12.7%.

It is perhaps the point of this whole book that the final statistic, while seemingly inconsequential, is most poignant: 19.5% wanted to make marriage harder to enter in the first place. This was an unsolicited response which cropped up spontaneously throughout many interviews; 5.5% want to see *why* we get married analyzed further.

So, it seems, do the other 94.5% of America's divorced.

INDEX